# What Is Literature?

# What Is Literature?

*Edited with an Introduction by*

PAUL HERNADI

INDIANA UNIVERSITY PRESS
*Bloomington & London*

Manufactured in the United States of America

**Library of Congress Cataloging in Publication Data**
Main entry under title:

What is literature?

Includes bibliographical references.
1. Literature—Philosophy—Addresses, essays,
lectures. I. Hernadi, Paul, 1936-
PN45.W46 1978   801'.9   77-23640
ISBN 0-253-36505-8   1 2 3 4 5 82 81 80 79 78

# Contents

Preface                                                          ix

Introduction                                                     xi
*Paul Hernadi*


## 1. DEFINITIONS: THEORY AND HISTORY

On the Possibility of Saying What Literature Is                  3
*F. E. Sparshott*

What Is Literature?                                             16
*René Wellek*

What Isn't Literature?                                          24
*E. D. Hirsch, Jr.*

Why Theorize about Literature?                                  35
*Edward Davenport*


## 2. CANON-FORMATION: FORCES AND PROCEDURES

"Literature": A Many-Sided Process                             49
*George McFadden*

A Procedural Definition of Literature                          62
*Charles Altieri*

v

Prolegomena Grammatologica:
Literature as the Disembodiment of Speech          79
*Elias L. Rivers*

The Social Definition of Literature          89
*Richard Ohmann*

Literary Works Express Propositions          102
*Robert J. Matthews*


3.   LITERATURE: ACTS, EFFECTS, ARTIFACTS

The Literary Work: Its Structure, Unity, and
Distinction from Forms of Non-Literary Expression          115
*Joseph Strelka*

The Mirror as Metaphor for Literature          127
*James I. Wimsatt*

Native Readers of Fiction: A Speech-Act and
Genre-Rule Approach to Defining Literature          141
*Robert L. Brown, Jr., and*
*Martin Steinmann, Jr.*

Aesthetic Intentions and Fictive Illocutions          161
*Monroe C. Beardsley*

Literature as Illusion, as Metaphor, as Vision          178
*Murray Krieger*

"All Discourse Aspires to the Analytic Proposition"          190
*Michael McCanles*

Literature as Transaction                         206
*Norman N. Holland*

"Literature": Disjunction and Redundancy          219
*Morse Peckham*

Toward a Semiotics of Literature                  231
*Robert Scholes*


Index                                             251

# Preface

This book has grown out of the 1975 meeting of the Modern Language Association of America. As chairman-elect of the discussion group "General Topics I: Literary Theory and Poetics," I had chosen "What Is Literature?", a frightfully general topic, for the San Francisco meeting. When inquiries began to reach me I could not but realize that the seventy-five minutes allotted to the group would fall far short of accommodating all the attractive papers that were being proposed or could and should have been solicited for the occasion. I thus decided to use the four papers actually read at the meeting as the nucleus around which to organize the present collection of essays by selecting from the proposed papers and soliciting others. As is the nature of such projects, complete editorial wish-fulfillment has not been granted by the entire group of men and women approached, mainly because printer's deadlines needed to be met, and, understandably, not everybody has a concise answer to the question, "What Is Literature?", just about ready for the typewriter. But the eighteen essays collected here surely represent a sufficient variety of contemporary approaches to prompt readers who do have an answer, however tentative, and readers who are troubled by not being able to give or endorse one, to explore worthwhile alternatives in the light of each other.

The University of Iowa has supported the project by generous assignment of funds for research assistance, secretarial help, and duplication. I am particularly grateful to Florence Pierce for expert typing and to Alan Axelrod, Janet McNaughton, and Charles Schuster for reading proofs and preparing the index.

P.H.

# Introduction

## *Paul Hernadi*

Contemporary literary studies reflect a great variety of conflicting opinions about the very nature of their subject matter. As the reader of the ensuing essays will soon discover, disagreement is widespread even concerning the *kind* of answer demanded or admitted by that deceptively simple question, "What Is Literature?" Persuasive arguments can be advanced for taking either avenue at several major crossroads. Let me hint at some of them:

(1) Shall we try to define literature as "things said" or as "things made" by means of language? The paradigm of spoken utterance prompts us to see literature, whether we encounter it in spoken or written form, in the context of verbal communication, while the paradigm of written text enables us to invoke the context of artistic creation and elaboration.

(2) Shall we frame our concept of literature in neutral or in approval terms? Only a descriptive definition would logically permit value judgments like "bad literature," but an honorific definition of literature as necessarily "good" would more easily justify statements of the kind, "Now that just isn't literature."

(3) Shall we aim our definition at literary works or at a literary quality assumed to inform some or all discourses to varying degree? A definition of the former type would facilitate practical decisions: what books to buy, how to shelve them, why include them in a particular reading list, and so forth. Yet our always partial statements about complete works in conversations, classroom discussions, or critical papers seem to call for a definition of the latter type.

(4) Shall we search for literature or the quality of literariness in actual texts and utterances or in verbally triggered mental acts? Both in literary and in other kinds of experience, objective and subjective components interact to the point of making the very distinction between objective and subjective highly controversial. Yet, surely, at least two types of arguments about this matter deserve careful hearing. According to the first, there is always more in the beholder's eye than just the eye of the beholder; after all, that "more" has motivated him to look in one direction rather than in another. According to the second, different acts of both ocular and mental vision will necessarily focus on selected aspects of the external cause of any experience. All things considered, "objective" concepts of *literature* or *literariness*, however defined, must thus compete with "subjective" concepts of the kind of reading and listening that responds to texts and utterances in a *literary way,* however defined.

(5) Shall we attempt to specify necessary and sufficient conditions which every work, quality, or response must meet if it is to be considered literary? An attractive alternative would be to say that works, qualities, or responses are literary only by virtue of what Wittgenstein called family resemblance[1]; we could thereby avoid embarrassment upon noticing that two particular members of the "family" happen to have no single specific trait in common. For the moment I leave it to the reader to ponder the respective advantages of a firmer but more rigid and a looser but more flexible approach to saying what literature is. But I will

suggest something of a compromise in this respect as in some others toward the end of the present Introduction.

To our five major sets of alternatives several further puzzlers might be added. One is the elusive identity of "works" of oral literature including ancient sagas, perennial folktales, and perhaps even contemporary jokes. Another is the problem of a text's multiple or changing functions epitomized by the familiar phrase "the Bible as literature." A third—and my final—example is the literary or non-literary nature of performed drama and its second cousins: the opera, the cinema, the radio play, and perhaps even such non-verbal arts of story-telling as ballet and pantomime. In view of such a thicket of fundamental dilemmas it is hardly surprising that some contributors to this volume sound quite confident when they question the question, "What Is Literature?", and rather more tentative when they proceed to give their various answers to it. But, after more or less hesitation, each responds to a question that quite a few professional lovers of literature always wanted to but never quite dared to ask, or else did ask and failed to answer to their complete satisfaction.

Now a collection of responses to such a basic yet troublesome question should rather comprise a large variety of succinct statements than a handful of elaborate and, in all likelihood, still not exhaustive disquisitions. But the view that there is a five-page and a five-volume version of almost any argument presupposes the skillful author's and the sympathetic reader's understanding of a given format's strengths and weaknesses. Since severe limitations of space had to be imposed on the kindly consenting contributors, the reader will on occasion wish for more thorough development of a particular line of inquiry. The book as a whole, however, is designed to compensate him in at least two ways: through frequent references to fuller treatment of related themes by the same critic or others, and through easy access to complementary or rival views just a few pages

away from almost any opinion expressed between the covers of
the present volume.

The three sections of the book deal with different, albeit
closely related, aspects of the basic concern at hand. The essays
of Section One engage in one or both of two endeavors: the
theoretical exploration of the meaning and purpose of asking the
question, "What Is Literature?", and the placement of contemporary answers to that question in a historical context. Having
surveyed some philosophical implications of "the possibility of
saying what literature is," Francis Sparshott concludes that most
attempts to define literature are likely to come from people wish-
ing to justify the use of literature for some educational purpose.
Much of René Wellek's historical survey of the definitions implied by the varied meanings of the word *literature* and its cognates bears out that conclusion, as does E. D. Hirsch's argument
against the aesthetic concept of literature—a concept endorsed
by Wellek—as the basic criterion for what should be taught and
how by members of literature departments. Educational concerns, both in the collegiate and in the broader cultural sense of
maintaining a sharable tradition of insights, motivate Edward
Davenport's plea for definitory theories; he sees them as
possibly fallacious but certainly necessary means of articulating
and, as a frequent result, modifying or abandoning implicit assumptions that underlie not only judgments of taste but also the
gathering of relevant data.

The next two sections in turn focus on one or the other radius
in the classifier's version of the hermeneutic circle: How do I
know what literature is before I know on what particular instances to base my general definition, yet how do I know on
what instances I should base my definition before I have defined
literature? A comparable dilemma is, of course, implicit in all
conceptual thinking. It is by pulling harder on one or the other
horn of the dilemma that the essays in Section Two and Section
Three, respectively, stress the processes and the principles of

the formation of a literary canon—processes and principles, that is, of establishing what may count as evidence in discussions about literature. Ingarden's concept of the "life" of literary works in their manifold "concretizations" by individual readers[2] allows George McFadden to divide any text's potentially life-sustaining audience into three groups with markedly different types of preferences: other writers, professional scholars and critics, and the general reading public. Each of those groups is capable of keeping its own "canon" of texts alive perhaps because, as Charles Altieri argues, our sense of what literature is ultimately "depends on applying procedures we learn from exposure to canonical texts." Elias Rivers and Richard Ohmann call attention to the role of vastly different instruments of cultural prestige and hegemony in the formation of literary canons when they discuss, respectively, the impact of written language in Antiquity and the Middle Ages and the influence of the *New York Times Book Review*, the *New York Review of Books*, and a very few other periodical publications in contemporary America. Robert Matthews in turn attempts to account for the part played by criticism at large not only in canonizing particular works but also in making each what it is in its "art-institutional context."

The essays assembled in Section Three discuss literature in terms of acts, effects, and/or artifacts. Joseph Strelka argues that the poetic and fictional qualities of literature call for its study as verbal art. In the tradition of crediting art with the disclosure of concrete universals, James I. Wimsatt revives a time-honored metaphor as he insists that great works do not simply "mirror" reality but allow us to see what the mirrored reality in truth signifies. In a joint attempt to define fictionality on the basis of speech-act conventions, Robert L. Brown and Martin Steinmann take their philosophical cues from J. L. Austin and John Searle.[3] Monroe C. Beardsley also draws on speech-act theory when he argues that the writer of fiction signals his aesthetic intention (and thus produces literature) by conspicuously *pretending* to perform illocutionary actions which, if performed in earnest, would go into the making of historiography, philosophy, and other kinds of discursive prose. Bridging the gap between aesthetic and convention-oriented theories, Murray Krieger insists that a literary work is "both a constructed emblem that contains the world and a deconstructed breath of air that does not begin to describe it." Krieger's further characterization of literature as "sustained seeing without any assurances of the existence of the seen" is paralleled by Michael McCanles when he argues that fictive discourse (unlike aggressively "imperialistic" non-fiction) creates a generous "discursive space wherein potentially competing novels, poems, and plays may dwell without calling into question the competing statements of still other fictional works." Just as McCanles adds that readers are free to honor or ignore a text's claim of being fictive or non-fictive in this sense of the words, Norman Holland recognizes that we need not follow a literary work's promptings to "transact literarily," that is, to respond to the perceived speech acts of the text within the private sphere of our evolving identity rather than in the public realm of intersubjective action. Morse Peckham shares Holland's view that literature, properly perceived, does not call for immediate (re)actions. But noting that the use of language makes human behavior both indeterminable and determinable, Peckham is more concerned with the semiotic effect of literary discourse on an entire society than with the psychological effect of individual works on individual readers. From a likewise semiotic point of view, Robert Scholes amplifies and modifies Jakobson's aesthetic concept of literariness as resulting from the predominance of the "poetic" function of language in a particular text over other functions operative in every speech event.[4] Scholes argues that not only the verbal MESSAGE but each of the other five factors of communication distinguished by Jakobson as the ADDRESSER, the ADDRESSEE, the referential CONTEXT, the physical and psychological CONTACT, and the linguistic CODE operates as a complicated, "duplicitous" constituent of literary discourse; he further suggests (and here we return to Sparshott's linking of definitions of literature to educational goals) that the training acquired through the study of subtly complex literary structures can enhance both our understanding of and participation in human communication at large.

The fact that all contributors speak principally as "consumers" rather than "producers" of literature may explain why so much more attention is devoted in the following pages to how works work than to how they have been wrought. Eighteen poets, novelists, or playwrights would have told a vastly different story or, more likely, eighteen vastly different stories. I have resisted the temptation to include a handful of such self-analyses because I feared the consequences of clearly arbitrary sampling. A small selection of statements by the more indigenous or the more translatable foreign critics would likewise have given the American reader a distorted view of the critical scene abroad. It is all the more fortunate that most contributors, although principally active in North America, show awareness of the international horizon of literary theory; quite a few even refer to specific recent developments in Europe without claiming, or allowing the volume to appear to claim, the status of a comprehensive survey.

Given the conflicting plurality of contemporary notions about literature in any one country, some essays will at first seem especially pertinent to some readers and quite wrongheaded to others. Perusal of the entire volume will, I hope, lead to a careful review of such initial attitudes.[5] Repeated consideration of all included papers has certainly influenced my own views to be outlined in the following paragraphs.

I see literature as a matter neither of purely objective fact nor of purely subjective consciousness. Just as our minds "half create" the written marks and uttered sounds that we conceive ourselves as having perceived in the world, our minds "half create" the meanings and propositions that we conceive ourselves as having received from other minds.[6] For most purposes, of course, the preceding formulation is far too cautious to be accurately descriptive of significant human praxis. Our usual attitude toward any postulated object of both sensory perception and hermeneutic interpretation clearly relies on profound disregard for possible doubt concerning the independence of the object's existence and characteristics from our consciousness.[7] Thus what we perceive and interpret as a written text or spoken utterance can safely be regarded as it is normally regarded: a "thing said," that is, a sequence of words through which a writer or speaker, using a particular system of verbal signs, conveys some information to readers or listeners. But a verbal sequence is not only a "thing said." It is also a "thing made," and as such it can be potentially beneficial and/or pleasurable to its user. Theoretical awareness that all texts and utterances are both things said and things made[8] can help us to understand why people discern some contemplated verbal constructs as more "literary" than others.

As a "thing said," every text or utterance potentially communicates and represents at the same time. Strictly speaking, communication takes place between the writer or speaker and the reader or listener while representation "connects" a verbal sequence with what it conceptually signifies and perceptually evokes. But the actual contexts of communication and representation are much larger. On the one hand, writers and speakers as well as readers and listeners confront the world as their *source of motivation* and their *field of action;* on the other, every instance of employed language and all information conveyed through the use of a language system partake in the world as a *reservoir of signs* and as *representable by signs.*[9] Now a text or utterance seems to me non-literary to the extent that it invites and rewards the more or less *independent exploration of one or some of its fundamental relationships to the world:* its effective cause in the writer's or speaker's private and public motivation, its final cause in the reader's or listener's decisions and actions, its material cause in the components and combinatory rules of a language system, and its formal cause in the components and correlations within the worldview implied by its informational content.[10] Conversely, a text or utterance is literary to the extent that it invites and rewards the *integrated exploration of its constitutive principles as interacting factors within the "thing said"*: an implied writer's or speaker's appeal to an implied reader or listener through the evocation of a coherent world by means of a well-designed sequence of words. According to such a definition, no text or utterance is completely literary or non-literary, but the proper response to a predominantly literary text or utterance involves the partial suspension of two kinds of concern: one is the ethical concern with the *correspondence* between the actual writer's or speaker's intention and the likely impact of his text or utterance on actual readers or listeners, and the other is the cognitive concern with the *correspondence* between the information conveyed by a contemplated sequence of words and particular details of our own view of the representable world. What motivates and can on occasion justify such suspension of significant ethical and cognitive concerns? Only values perceived in the contemplated text or utterance under its aspect of a verbal object—a "thing made" for our benefit and/or pleasure.

Beyond doubt, benefit and pleasure often accompany the "use" of predominantly non-literary verbal objects also, and not all benefit and pleasure accompanying the use of predominantly literary verbal objects is literary. Thus we must proceed from the influential Horatian adumbration of those potentially literary values as the poet's alternative or combinable goals[11] to this realization: the beneficial and the pleasing, the useful and the sweet are necessary but not sufficient conditions of literature as such. Now, Horace's advice to combine *prodesse* and *delectare* or *utile* and *dulce* was offered to facilitate simultaneous success with both the older and the younger members of the poet's audience. But the same advice strongly suggests how literature as art can simultaneously rather than selectively appeal to the agelessly young and old—the more vigorous and the more mature potential—in the human psyche. The "young" wants to be entertained through thrill and gratification, while the "old" wants to be committed within cosmic (natural or supernatural) and social contexts. It seems to me that the most representative "things made" by artists, including the authors of literary works, will help to achieve a delicate balance between the self-assertive need for pleasurable entertainment and the self-transcending need for beneficial commitment in each of us.[12] In contrast, many texts and utterances place their habitual consumers in far less poised—although, for the short run, hardly less life-sustaining—force fields where a single pull in one of the following directions prevails: self-transcendence either through cosmic or social commitment or else self-assertion either through gratifying or thrilling entertainment. This is conspicuously the case with verbal sequences directly propagandizing a particular attitude or course of action or else procuring vicarious experience of what the television censor's simplified vocabulary terms sex and violence. But the relative predominance of one such pull may characterize parts or wholes even of typical works of verbal art. If the four *mythoi* or fundamental story patterns distinguished by Northrop Frye as Tragedy, Comedy, Romance, and Satire could exist in pure form, they would very nearly represent two pairs of directions in which literature points beyond the undistinguished but potentially tragicomic or satiromantic way of the world: Tragedy and Comedy, respectively, offer us the thrill and gratification of self-sufficience; Romance and Satire, the cosmic and social horizons of self-transcendence.[13]

A theory of literature as verbal art mediating between different types of entertainment and commitment would not need to rely on the Kantian definition of the beautiful as that which is neither true, nor good, nor useful, nor simply pleasant, and yet rewards contemplation by the aesthetic pleasure of *interesseloses Wohlgefallen*. [14] With certain reservations it could more readily endorse the position stated by the leading Prague structuralist, Jan Mukařovský: "the influence of aesthetic value is not that it swallows up and represses all remaining values, but that it releases every one of them from direct contact with a corresponding life value." [15] My own view is that no clear-cut distinction between aesthetic and non-aesthetic values is justified along these lines. Especially when "released" by the centripetal literariness of "things said" from the centrifugal "direct contact" with corresponding life values, the presumably non-aesthetic values of a literary work turn out to be promoting the dynamic equilibrium of such quasi-aesthetic attitudes as the (tragic) endurance of the painfully finite, the (comic) indulgence in the desirably varied, the (satirical) indignation over the curably incongruous, and the (romantic) admiration for the awe-inspiringly sublime aspects of the human condition.

To sum up: even if literature is to some extent in the eye of the beholder or in a special way of beholding, it makes sense to explore just what is seen through that mode of vision and to base a concept of literature on verbal constructs that especially invite and reward a literary response. As "things said" or vehicles of communication and representation, such constructs tend to balance as much expressive intensity, persuasive power, verbal design, and informational coherence as can mutually enhance each other. As "things made" or occasions for entertainment and commitment, such constructs are geared to promote the humanizing mediation between the extremes of self-sufficiency and self-transcendence: the coarser varieties of thrill or gratification on the one hand, the more radical versions of cosmic or social disparagement of individual life on the other. While this sketch of a literary theory postulates different kinds

and degrees of family resemblance among texts and utterances
that are only tangentially literary, it also tries to delineate what
all fundamentally literary works have in common as perhaps the
most puzzling "things said and made" by human beings.

# NOTES

1. Ludwig Wittgenstein, *Philosophical Investigations* I, 66f, trans. G. E.
M. Anscombe (Oxford, 1953), 32. For applications of the concept "fam-
ily resemblance" to literature, see Charles L. Stevenson, "On 'What Is a
Poem?'," *Philosophical Review* 66 (1957), 329-362 and Colin A. Lyas, "The
Semantic Definition of Literature," *Journal of Philosophy* 66 (1969), 81-95.

2. Roman Ingarden, *Das literarische Kunstwerk* (1931), 3rd rev. ed.
(Tübingen, 1965), 353-380 and *Vom Erkennen des literarischen Kunstwerks*
(Tübingen, 1968), passim. McFadden's references are to the English
translations of these works.

3. See esp. J. L. Austin, *How to Do Things with Words* (Cambridge,
Mass., 1962) and John R. Searle, *Speech Acts* (Cambridge, England,
1969).

4. Roman Jakobson, "Closing Statement: Linguistics and Poetics,"
*Style in Language*, ed. Thomas A. Sebeok (New York, 1960), 350-377.

5. Even if a reader should believe that "the very expansive, adven-
turous character of art, its ever-present changes and novel creations,
makes it logically impossible to ensure any set of defining properties,"
he is quite likely to consider at least some general theories of art and of
literature helpful "as serious and argued-for recommendations to con-
centrate on certain criteria of excellence." Cf. Morris Weitz, "The Role
of Theory in Aesthetics," *Journal of Aesthetics and Art Criticism* 15 (1956),
27-35.

6. The repeated phrase in quotation marks echoes Wordsworth's not
so distant poetic parallel to Kant's *Kritik der reinen Vernunft (Critique of
Pure Reason)* in "Lines Composed a few Miles above Tintern Abbey,"
lines 105-111.

7. Whoever wants to analyze, criticize, or remove our customary
disregard for such doubt as an instance, say, of socially or psycholog-
ically conditioned repression is involved in a curious circularity. He

cannot help but turn that disregard into an object of attention and postulate *its* existence and characteristics with obvious disregard for doubt. This holds even for Jürgen Habermas' thought-provoking tripartition of rational inquiry into empirical-analytic *Naturwissenschaften*, historical-hermeneutic *Geisteswissenschaften*, and the "critically oriented sciences" motivated by emancipatory interests (as in Marx, Nietzsche, or Freud). Cf. *Knowledge and Human Interests,* trans. Jeremy S. Shapiro (Boston, 1971), esp. pp. 301-317.

8. For cogent remarks on the affinities of literature with saying and making as well as doing, see William K. Wimsatt's "Epilogue," esp. pp. 752-755, in his and Cleanth Brooks' *Literary Criticism: A Short History* (New York, 1957).

9. For a more detailed discussion of how texts and utterances simultaneously operate along the rhetorical axis of communication and the mimetic axis of representation, see my "Literary Theory: A Compass for Critics," *Critical Inquiry* 3 (1976), 369-386.

10. My application of the four Aristotelian "causes" to literature is in part indebted to O. B. Hardison's extensive commentary, esp. p. 96, appended to Leon Golden's translation of *Aristotle's Poetics* (Englewood Cliffs, N. J., 1968).

11. Cf. Horace's "Epistle to the Pisos" on the art of poetry, lines 336-346.

12. Besides Horace, I. A. Richards, *The Principles of Literary Criticism* (London, 1924) and Arthur Koestler, *Insight and Outlook* (New York, 1949) have contributed conceptual ingredients to the above statement.

13. For Frye's most detailed discussion of the four *mythoi,* see his *Anatomy of Criticism* (Princeton, 1957), 158-239. A fuller account of my view outlined in the last three sentences will be found in "Tragicomedy: Complex Mood or Mixed Genre?" (forthcoming).

14. Cf. esp. the first book of Immanuel Kant's *Kritik der Urteilskraft (Critique of Judgment).*

15. Jan Mukařovský, *Aesthetic Function, Norm and Value as Social Facts,* trans. Mark E. Suino (Ann Arbor, Mich., 1970), p. 89. Cf. also p. 88 with the following overstatement made, perhaps, in the heat of polemical self-defense against the charge of formalism: "The work of art appears, in the final analysis, as an actual collection of extra-aesthetic values and nothing else." In the same paragraph, Mukařovský asserts that the "aesthetic value (. . .) binds the work into a unity."

# What Is Literature?

# 1

## Definitions:
## Theory and History

# On the Possibility of
# Saying What Literature Is

## F. E. Sparshott

Theories are mostly about problems: a theory is an attempt to explain something, and an explanation is called for when a problem has arisen. Most problems have to do with events—one wants to know how or why something has taken place, or has failed to take place.

But sometimes there are problems about things, as for instance about the stripes on tigers. Why do tigers have stripes? Their having them is not an event exactly; rather, the stripiness is a problematic aspect of tigers, and the existence of the stripes is a problem about the stripes. One can then produce a theory about tigers, suggesting an answer to the problem about their stripiness, which would also be a theory about tiger-stripes, suggesting a solution to the problem about how or why there come to be such things.

But what would a theory of tigers be? It could hardly be a single theory offering an answer to all possible problems about tigers, because such problems might be indefinitely various and mutually connected in no other way than that they somehow had to do with tigers. Perhaps one might say that the natural way to give a specific meaning to the phrase "theory of tigers" would be to restrict it to answers to the question, "What is a tiger?" But what is the *problem* here? Tigers are not inherently problematic entities, such that their nature poses one and only one evident question. There may be all sorts of different problems about *what tigers are;* and if we were told that someone had come up with a new theory about what tigers are, we would not have the least idea of what to expect. "I didn't know there was a problem," we might say; or, perhaps more likely, "He must be some kind of nut."

In what circumstances does it make sense to have a theory about what something is? Only, I suspect, if the thing itself is postulated for a specific theoretical reason; or if the application to the thing of the word that the theory uses is itself enough to indicate a specific theoretical concern. And in the former case one would be likely to speak of *the* theory of the thing, not *a* theory of it: the field of Mr. Pickwick's expertise was the theory of tittlebats, not a theory of tittlebats. It is in the latter case alone, where the word used for a thing might connote a theoretical concern but not a specific theoretical content, that people are likely to put forward theories of so-and-so that amount to explaining what so-and-so really is.

Do the foregoing considerations suggest that there could be a theory of literature explaining what literature is? Literature is not one of those things whose very existence is postulated to satisfy a theoretical demand. It is there already, before theorizing begins. Whatever literature exactly is, or should be said to be, it exists: it comprises some or all of the sorts of things we read and hear, and we know roughly what sorts. If we say that literature is all and only that spoken and written discourse that we attend to not for any practical purpose but for its own sake, not everyone will agree with us but no one will dispute that what we have said serves to single out some at least of what people are talking about when they use the word "literature."[1]

Is it then the case that "literature" is a word which, when

applied to songs, stories and such, has strong but vague theoretical implications of a sort that lead one to wonder how best to describe or delimit those items to which it properly applies? It seems likely, at first. Why else should we apply so portentous a polysyllable to things for which simple names with unproblematic meanings—book, song, story, poem—are at hand? But what sort of theoretical concern would it be? "Literature" is not a word, as "poetry" is, that has a long and honorable history of debate behind it. Reference to the *Oxford English Dictionary* is disheartening: the history of the word is brief and inglorious. Its only relevant use, to mean literary production of aesthetic value, is a product of the late nineteenth century. Shall we then say that the only real problem is why the term *literature* was ever coined; or why anyone should suppose that there could be a theory of it; or why anyone should think that there was a problem about what literature was? Such scepticism would be too hasty. The definition culled from the dictionary suffices to give the question, "What is literature?" a clear, threefold meaning: it calls for a general explanation of what aesthetic value is, for a specification of what aesthetic value in literature is, and for a reasoned account of whether *literature* is a term used to segregate works having such value from works having none or a term applicable to all works insofar as they possess a kind of value in which all discourse has some share, however unequal the shares may be. If qualms remain, it is because the notion of "aesthetic value," a phrase peculiar to the jargon of our own befuddled and pretentious pedantry, may have no clear content. It may be just a fancy way of pointing to the fact that some books are worth reading and others are not. And it may be that the aspects of books that make them worth reading are as various as books themselves are, or as people are.

Let it be agreed that literary discourse is discourse to which we attend for the sake of qualities we look to find in it, for the sake of what it is in itself, and not for the sake of what it tells us

about or stimulates us to, and in general not for the sake of some
other thing that is the true object of our interest; discourse,
moreover, that we do not merely esteem but think well of ourselves for esteeming. What manner of discourse might this be?
Some sort of explanation is certainly called for. But the question
seems at first sight too elusive and slippery for us to pin down.
In such cases, a traditional strategy is to ask what the origin of
literature is. What is sought under this rubric is not a historical
account of how it began, which would be a confusing story even
if we could tell it, but an explanation of how it begins, though it
is customary and agreeable to enshrine the explanation in a fable
about beginnings. The strategy of the explanation, a perennial
favorite in political theory, is as follows: each of our major institutions in fact serves a multiplicity of purposes, but must be
supposed to exist for the sake of one fundamental purpose that
accounts for its distinctive features. To explain what this one
purpose is, we imagine ourselves lacking the institution, and
ask ourselves why we would have to reinvent it—or something
very like it—and what form our invention would have to take.
Every human institution and mode of behavior, among which
literature is surely to be counted, is what it is in virtue of the way
it fits into the tissue of human purposes; therefore, to discover
what it most truly is, we think it away and imagine what purposes its absence would deprive of any fulfillment.

To explain the origin of literature and thus tell what literature
is, two rival myths have achieved currency. Of these, one places
the origin of literature before the rise of everyday speech, the
other after.

According to the former myth, a favorite in one form or another of eighteenth-century romanticism, pre-linguistic man
begins to become human and hence capable of culture when he
discovers that he can evolve gestures, including those complex
gestures that are dances and chants, that will express both what
he feels is essential to some recurring phenomenon and his own

attitude to it. What recurs and is thus symbolized is not an object, as Aristotle had thought, but a significance. The gesture in effect creates what it symbolizes, by fixing its character and identity; but the gesture can be repeated, and by that repetition imparts a definite meaning to an experience that itself becomes at the same time significantly repeatable. In time, the corpus of repeatable gestures becomes what we know as language, but each of us retains the capacity to originate gestural utterances and thus create new meanings, and this capacity survives as what we call art. On this showing, a literary work would be one in which language, though using old words in established ways, functions as a unified verbal gesture, occasion of an experience that can be repeated only by repeating the work verbatim, because the work as a whole in its original unity defines an experience. Literary utterance thus has a triple value, as source of merely useful and uncreative utterance, as occasion of experiences that are especially genuine and authentic, and as that use of language which expresses directly the creative activity of mind.

The alternative account of the origin of literature takes a less exalted view of humanity. Human beings, it says, are like rats; ceaselessly, restlessly, they explore their environment. Being very brainy rats, much of their exploration is done inside their heads. When needs are satisfied and utilitarian language is well developed, human beings have leisure to explore the limits of the linguistic world that cages their thoughts and to test the limits of their language-making prowess. Literature is nothing other than this practice of saying things for the sake of seeing how one can say what. Every domain of practical endeavor thus begets its exploratory counterpart: building engenders architecture, language generates literature.[2]

The two myths about how literature begins or began can hardly be reconciled. Literature cannot be both the necessary precondition of language and its inevitable outcome. The credentials of the two rival accounts of what literature is, originative utterance and elaborated utterance, seem equally good. That being so, we have no grounds for choosing between them, and to say what literature is would be to make a decision that it would be irrational to make. Literary utterance on either showing is marked by its departing from the quotidian use of language and by its opacity—its being itself an object of attention and not a mere vehicle of meaning. But beyond that we cannot justifiably go.

The split between the two views of what literature is cannot be resolved in principle, but in present practice it is illusory. Here and now, when all writers and readers are sophisticated in the use of language, we cannot revert to our prelinguistic origins. The only way back to absolute originality must lie forward, through a creativity that transcends artifice. It is an old story: the contrast we draw is the same that R. G. Collingwood drew between art, which is expressive and creative, and mere craftsmanship, which is manipulative and reproductive.[3] Collingwood's discussion sank into absurdity whenever he applied this beautifully clear distinction to practical realities. Creation without artifice is empty, artifice without creation is blind. A large part of literary theory is, or could and should be, a drafting of the terms of a treaty that shall reconcile them.

One provision of the treaty of reconciliation might run as follows. Though the virtue of art as art may be beauty, the virtue of discourse as discourse is truth. The virtues of kinds of discourse are kinds of truth. Literature must then number among its virtues a kind of truth. But what kind? If literary discourse has its value in itself, its truth cannot lie in conformity to any fact or reality separable from itself. It can only be, as it is often said to be, some form of fidelity: truth-to, not truth-about. Insofar as literary utterance is creative linguistic gesture, it must be faithful to the experience it fixes and articulates; insofar as it is artifice, there is nothing for it to be faithful to except the idea of the work to be done, an idea that takes no final shape until it is realized in the work itself. And these two fidelities may be made out to be the same: the linguistic artifact cannot be unified otherwise than as an experience, and the original experience cannot be otherwise articulated than as a linguistic artifact. In neither case is there anything for the work to be faithful to, other than itself. But the demand that it be true to itself is strict.

The requirement of fidelity in literature is then that the work be just the work it is because that is what it has to be: in other words, that it have the status of a text. The demand is that nothing in the work be changed, not because there is a specifiable requirement to which it must strictly conform but just because there is none. We cannot tell in advance what in the work may not prove crucial to some aspect of its value yet to be revealed.[4]

If textuality is a hallmark of literature, one might entertain with favor a thesis, advanced by certain linguists, that a literary utterance may be defined as one of which it is required that it be preserved without verbal change. An individual who demands this of any work treats it as literature; if a society demands it, the demand brings the work within the scope of the society's literature; and if the work itself is such that the demand imposes itself (should such a thing be possible), then that work is literature whatever anyone may think.

The foregoing thesis, however attractive, cannot stand as a definition of literature in the sense that concerns us. The demand that a work be preserved without verbal change may be a necessary condition of literary status, but is not a sufficient condition. Legal and sacred texts are no less inviolable. They are inviolable because they are required, for different reasons, to be authoritative. If law is to do its work, we must know what the law is. But we cannot know what the lawmaker meant by his law, or how the courts will construe it. All we can know for certain is what the law says. The letter of the law is the fixed point around which the life of the law turns: what the law is is what is meant by the words of the law and no other words. Sacred texts, on the other hand, are inviolable because their status as sacred requires that their authority and that of their putative author be higher than that conceded to any interpreter. The author's thoughts are inscrutable, except just insofar as he has authorized these very words: whatever the saving message may be, we are assured that it is a message that can be conveyed in these words and not in other words.

If literary texts are held inviolable, it is not because anyone needs them as an authority; it is because the focus of our interest is the text itself and not the range of its meanings. But what interests us is the meaningful utterance, not merely the sounding structure: the verbal artifact as embodying and subtending an indeterminate hierarchy of meanings, a world in which the reader may dwell and on any part or level of which he may fasten his attention.[5] To function as a world of meaning, its determinate structure must allow indefinite variety; and to this end its ambiguities, whether intended or unintended, are essential, as are the possibilities, as yet unachieved, that may be opened up through shifts of meaning in the language or in the lives of readers. It is above all the preservation of these ambiguities and possibilities that requires the inviolability of the literary text.[6]

The idea of a text, which has crept into our discussion with such an innocent and conciliatory look, threatens, once admitted, to subvert any attempt to provide a unified account of what literature is. Etymologically, literature has to do with letters, that is, with the written as opposed to the spoken word. What is written down acquires the status of a thing, an object that can be scrutinized, refined and altered. But the spoken word flies over the hedge of teeth and is gone. It is no object to be shaped, but a transaction in the conversation of mankind. We live in our speaking, we work on our writing. Even the idea of a word seems to belong to written rather than spoken language; and so, in consequence, do the ideas of verbal repetition and textual integrity. An oral poet may recite the same poem many times, but will not use the same words: the idea of such identity has not occurred to him. He simply relives the same passage of verbal life. If literature is the art of letters, then we must consider an alternative account of what literature is: it is discourse bearing the distinguishing marks of written as opposed to spoken language.

The bifurcation of the idea of literature that now confronts us is comparable to that between original and elaborated utterance, which we confronted and overcame. Perhaps this one will not be bridged so easily. On one side we have literature as carefully shaped utterance, utterance that can be attended to because it is trapped in writing and its whole character thereby changed; on the other side we have literature as utterance that is inviolable because its value lies in itself with the totality of its possible qualities and meanings. The latter is not swallowed up in the former, because the oral poet, though he lacks the notion of verbal identity, prizes identity no less than the writer does. He simply uses different criteria of identity. He works at his songs and elaborates them, but as a player improves his game rather than as a jeweler works on a setting.

How might we overcome the duality that threatens us? We might do so by insisting that the literature that concerns us is inviolable utterance, but that many critics and teachers, just because they operate within an educational system based on literacy, contaminate that notion of literature with quite irrelevant ideas and standards which they import from the alternative idea of literature as utterance that celebrates its writtenness. Or we might do so by saying that for us in our literate world the inviolability of literature can be realized only in modes indelibly marked, if not intrinsically shaped, by the characteristics of the written word as such. And here one might seek a parallel in the way in which music has been changed by the invention of staff notation: every detail of the practice of music has changed profoundly, yet the art of music remains essentially what it always was.[7]

And yet the idea of literature as the written word is not so easily dismissed or defused. Writing remains unnatural as speaking is natural, and the formality and artificiality of the written word are such that every text, and *a fortiori* every text written for publication, is an elaborated artifact. All professional writers face essentially the same problems in the appalling labor of constructing a book. Distinctions between the literary and the non-literary in terms of fidelity or other high-flown aesthetic requirements are elusive if not chimerical. Professional writers tend to feel that academic critics go in for that sort of thing because they know nothing about writing, and know nothing about writing because they are not serious about it.

We have considered four notions of what literature is: originative discourse, elaborated discourse, inviolable discourse, and written discourse. How are these four related? There are at least four possibilities. First, it might be that we have thus identified four "literary making" factors, and that a piece of discourse tends to be regarded (or is properly regarded) as literary in so far as it is marked by one or more of them. Second, it might be that a work of literature is identified as such insofar as it seems to be the same sort of thing as something else that is indubitably literature, and that our four notions are clumsily pretentious ways of capturing a few of these indefinitely various and subtle analogies. Third, it might be that some theorist of Hegelian stamina and effrontery could combine all four notions into a unified account of the literary absolute as it achieves itself in history. Or it might, finally, be that the term "literature" is radically equivocal. And of these four possibilities the last seems most probable. Different sorts of distinctions among utterances are needed for different purposes in different contexts, and the word *literature* is used quite unsystematically to make a lot of these distinctions. To say in general terms what literature is would be to suggest, quite absurdly, that some of these distinctions were important and others negligible, regardless of context and purpose. A unified account of literature would be not only useless but harmful in tending to blind us to what we might often need to see.

The conclusion of the last paragraph cannot stand. It fails to explain why there are theories about the nature of literature. Human folly is no explanation: a fool is not someone who lacks good reasons for what he does, but someone who ignores better reasons for leaving it undone. And after all we do know why there are theories of literature. It is because literature must be taught, and there must be a rationale for teaching it. All that needs to be explained is why there should be a problem: why the practice of teaching literature should have grown up in advance of its rationale. And the explanation of that is simple and familiar.

Songs and tales are taught, in the first instance, to young children, to teach them to read and to indoctrinate them in the ways of thinking and feeling proper to their community. What remains to be explained is why such things should be taught to older children and young adults, already indoctrinated and able to read. The answer is that at one time our civilization, having little else to be proud of, prided itself on its ancestry, so that the songs and tales to be learned were in obsolete languages that had first to be learned with much time and labor. But in the course of time we became prouder of our own attainments, and substituted vernacular writings for those in learned languages. It was just at the time when departments of national literature began to be established in institutions of higher learning that the term *literature* began to be used in the sort of sense that has concerned us. Thus, songs and tales in the vernacular came to be studied at a level originally judged appropriate only because of the unfamiliarity of the language employed. But now, what was there to teach? On the face of it, the object of study was what persons of culture would be expected to read anyway. Literary theory was required in order to make literature *difficult enough*. The question, "What is literature?" simply means, "What shall we choose for our students to read? How shall we justify our choice? What can we find to say about it, and how are our procedures to be justified?" The theory of literature is a rationale for curriculum selection and pedagogical procedure, and in the first instance that is all it is. The subject might then be left to those who find themselves saddled with this implausible educational assignment. The rest of us may watch with amused sympathy. Except, of course, that it might be discovered that there really is something to teach, much as Fleming discovered penicillin on a dirty plate.[8]

## NOTES

1. The statement in the text is not beyond dispute. A theorist might decide to reserve the name of *literature* for some kind of discourse so exotic that no specimen of it could be certainly identified until the theorist or his fans concocted some. But such shenanigans take place on the lunatic fringe of literary theory, and, except insofar as literary theory may be all lunatic fringe, need not concern us.

2. One can envisage a variety of exploratory modes whereby the rat runs the maze of his language. He may exploit the rules of his language to articulate thoughts no one has thought; he may elaborate, modify, or supplement the rules themselves; he may seek new modes of meaning by violating the rules; or he may simply elaborate the verbal surface. There are familiar literary arts that take just these forms. But it could also be that literary discourse is any discourse insofar as it is attended to for its own sake, without further specification of what the properties might be that reward attention.

3. R. G. Collingwood, *Principles of Art* (Oxford: Clarendon Press, 1938).

4. This way of looking at the matter is borrowed from Nelson Goodman, *Languages of Art* (Indianapolis: Bobbs-Merrill, 1968).

5. The idea of a hierarchy of meanings is developed by Roman Ingarden, *The Literary Work of Art* (Evanston: Northwestern University Press, 1973).

6. The situation is complicated by the fact that some literary works exist in various versions, supplemented by incomplete drafts. Each may be treated as a separate work, but need not be. In extreme cases, it is as though an indeterminate system of texts, pre-texts and variants took on the status of inviolable text. These complexities can be handled, practically and theoretically, in a number of different ways. The substitution of such a system for a text changes nothing in principle: all that happens is that the kinds and number of ambiguities are augmented in this way or that.

7. The effects of introducing notation into an art are illuminatingly discussed by Goodman in *Languages of Art* (see n.4 supra).

8. An elaborated version of the argument of this paper may be found in the author's "On the Possibility of a General Theory of Literature," *Centrum* 3.1 (Spring 1975), 5-22. The general problem of defining terms like 'literature' is discussed in his "On Saying What Philosophy Is," *Philosophy in Context* 4 (1975), 17-27.

# What Is Literature?

## René Wellek

I shall discuss the question raised by the title of this book in historical terms. "What is literature?" I shall assume, asks for an answer to what has been or is now called literature. Very simply, one can distinguish today between meanings which gradually narrow down the most general and obvious meaning, justified also etymologically, the view that "literature" is anything in print. *Littera* means letter, and *litteratura* in Latin was a translation of the Greek word *grammatikē*, the knowledge of reading and writing, as Quintilian tells us in his *Institutiones*.[1] This widest use is obvious today when we speak of literature about a pharmaceutical product or about campaign literature. In many modern theories or prescriptions of what literary scholarship should be about, there is often the assumption that anything in print is its province. Edwin Greenlaw's *The Province of Literary History* (1931) argues that nothing in print can be excluded from literary study: with him, literary history is identified with the history of civilization, for which, of course, pictorial or other material records, unearthed by archeologists, also serve as legitimate documentation.

But historically literature has been used to define writings of

some significance, to books of whatever subject which made an
impact. Some criterion of quality or value (intellectual, moral,
aesthetic, political, national) is implied. This is the conception
which prevailed for centuries since antiquity under two names:
*litterae* and its derivatives in the modern languages: letters and
*litteratura*. I have made a special study of this history which
proves the continuity of these terms over many centuries and
am therefore surprised when I am told, e.g., by Roland Barthes,
that "literature" is a recent term, a creation of the nineteenth
century, or by Maurice Blanchot, that it is a "mot tardif, mot
sans honneur."[2] In Cicero, one of the most influential and
widely-read writers of all times, we find the terms *Graecae litterae, historia litteris nostris*, and *studium litterarum*. The term *litteratura* is used by him in the sense of erudition, literary culture,
when he speaks of Caesar having *litteratura* in a list of qualities
which includes "good sense, memory, reflection, and dili-
gence."[3] We have to go to Tertullian and Cassian in the second
century A.D. to find the term used for a body of writing. They
contrast secular pagan writing, *litteratura*, with *scriptura*, the Bible, the sacred Writ.[4] *Litterae* in antiquity is used exactly as many
of us use it today: it refers to the corpus of Greek literature, to
the history and study of literature, etc. In practice, it was, as
Aulus Gellius tells us, identical with *humanitas*, or *paideia*.[5]

In the Middle Ages the two terms seem to have disappeared:
*litteratus* is used in the sense of literate. In the trivium, poetry is
of course recognized as an art assigned to grammar and rhetoric.
But with the Renaissance the term *litterae* reappears, mostly
combined with the adjective *humanae* to set it off from sacred
theological writings, or *bonae* as a term of praise. You find it all
over Erasmus, Rabelais, Du Bellay, Montaigne and others; and
Dryden still speaks of "good letters."[6] In the seventeenth century the term "belles lettres" emerged. In 1666 Charles Perrault
proposed to Colbert, the minister of finance of Louis XIV, an
Academy with a section of *belles lettres* which was to include

grammar, eloquence, and poetry.[7] The term was felt to be identical with *lettres humaines*, as e.g. the *Dictionnaire de Trévoux* (1704) shows.[8] It had nothing of the faintly derisive implication with which we speak today of "belletristic." The French term spread quickly to England. It was used by Thomas Rymer in 1692.[9] Hugh Blair became the first Professor of Rhetoric and Belles Lettres at the University of Edinburgh in 1762.

By that time the term "literature" had emerged in the sense, at first, of literary culture, erudition, or simply knowledge of the classical languages. In the 1721 edition of the *Dictionnaire de Trévoux*, *littérature* is defined as "doctrine, connaissance profonde des lettres," and in the great *Encyclopedia* an article, signed D J, i.e., le chevalier Jaucourt, defines Littérature as "terme général qui désigne l'érudition, la connaissance des Belles Lettres." It is used in the same way in English, when in 1691 John Selden, the antiquary, was called "a person of infinite literature"[10] or when Boswell, almost a century later, referred to Giuseppe Baretti as "an Italian of considerable literature."[11] This use of the word survived into the nineteenth century. John Petherham wrote a *Sketch of the Progress and Present State of Anglo-Saxon Literature in England* (1840), in which "literature" must mean the study or the knowledge of literature. Incidentally, in the term "comparative literature," the older usage was revived. It means the comparative study of literature and is not as Lane Cooper complained "a bogus term which makes neither sense nor syntax."[12]

Apparently very early in the eighteenth century (to judge from the recent research of Claude Crispin in *Aux origines de l'histoire littéraire*, 1973), the term was used for a body of writing, though it is sometimes difficult to draw a sharp distinction between the concurrent use of "literary culture, erudition." Here is the title of a book by le Père Cl.F. Menestrier: *Bibliothèque curieuse et instructive des divers auteurs anciens et modernes de littérature et des arts* (1704). It clearly refers to a body of writing in François

Granet's little-known *Réflexions sur les ouvrages de littérature* in
1737. Voltaire in *Le Siècle de Louis XIV* speaks in 1750 of "les
genres de littérature" cultivated in Italy.[13] The Abbé Sabatier de
Castres published *Les Siècles de littérature française* in 1772, the
very year in which Girolamo Tiraboschi began his monumental,
many-volumed *Storia della letteratura italiana*. In Germany the
new use was completely established even earlier. Lessing's
*Briefe die neueste Litteratur betreffend* (1759ff.) applies clearly to a
body of writing, and so does Herder's *Über die neuere deutsche
Litteratur* (1767).

In English the same process took place. The Oxford Dictionary
is mistaken by at least 60 years when it quotes the first example
for "body of writing" from 1822. In 1761 George Colman the
elder thought that "Shakespeare and Milton seem to stand
alone, like first-rate authors, amid the general wreck of old English literature."[14] In 1767 Adam Ferguson included a chapter
"Of the History of Literature" in his *Essay on the History of Civil
Society*. In 1774 Dr. Johnson, in a letter, wished that "what is
undeservedly forgotten of our antiquated literature might be
revived"[15] and John Berkenhout in 1777 subtitled his *Biographia
Literaria, A Biographical History of Literature*, in which he proposed to give a "concise view of the rise and progress of literature." Examples from the late 18th century could be easily
multiplied. Still, the first book in English called *A History of
English Language and Literature* by Robert Chambers dates from
as late as 1836.

In all of these cases literature is used very inclusively. It refers
to all kinds of writing, including those of erudite nature, history,
theology, philosophy, and even natural science. Only very
slowly was the term narrowed down to what we today call
"imaginative literature": the poem, the tale, the play in particular. This is a process intimately connected with the rise of aesthetics, of the whole system of arts which in older times was not
clearly set off from the sciences on the one side and crafts on the

other. The traditional linkage of the arts and sciences was, I
believe, first clearly dissolved in Charles Perrault's *Parallèle des
Anciens et des Modernes* (1688-97) where the *beaux arts* are contrasted with the *sciences,* though the *Dictionnaire de Trévoux* in
1721 has still the term "Lettres" defined as: "se dit aussi des
Sciences." In the polemics between the conservatives and the
*philosophes* the term "littérature" emerges in the new narrow
meaning of fictional literature, to set the humanities off against
the new geometrical spirit, the new rationalism. Jean-Georges
Le Franc de Pompignan in *L'Essai sur l'état présent de la république
des lettres* in 1743, uses "littérature" as a synonym of *belles lettres*
and narrows it expressly to the "epic poem, the tragedy, the
comedy, the ode, the fable, history and eloquence."[16] Another
early conscious declaration of this new use I found in the Preface
to Carlo Denina's *Discorso sopra le vicende della letteratura* (1760), a
widely-read book which was soon translated into French and
English. Denina professes "not to speak of the progress of the
sciences and arts, which are not properly a part of literature." He
will speak of works of learning only when they belong to "good
taste, to eloquence, that is to say, to literature."[17] That literature
was used in this new aesthetic sense at that time may be illus-
trated by Aurelio de Giorgi-Bertòla's *Idea della bella letteratura
alemanna* (1784), which is an expansion of an older *Idea della
poesia alemanna* (1779). The change of title was made necessary
by the inclusion of a new chapter about the German novel, in
particular the *Sorrows of Young Werther.*

To speak sweepingly one can say, summarizing, that in antiquity and in the Renaissance, literature or letters were understood to include all writing of quality with any pretense to
permanence. The view that there is an art of literature, which
includes both poetry and prose insofar as it is imaginative fiction, and excludes information or even rhetorical persuasion,
didactic argumentation or historical narration, emerged only
slowly in the eighteenth century. The discussion of taste, the
rise of the virtuoso, the invention of the term aesthetic by

Baumgarten in 1735—all this and much more led to Kant's *Critique of Judgment* (1790), the treatise which gave clear formulas for distinguishing between the beautiful, the good, the true, and the useful. The slow rise in the prestige of the novel, long frowned upon as frivolous, collaborated in establishing a concept of literature parallel to the plastic arts and to music which is still with us today.

I leave it to others to discuss the further question of how one can define the boundaries of fictionality, of the narrow concept of literature as imaginative fiction against the wider use as significant writing. Shall one exclude Montaigne, Pascal, Burke, Gibbon, Berkeley, etc., from literature because they do not even pretend to write fiction? And if we, sensibly, include them in this concept (for how can we imagine a history of English literature in the eighteenth century without Gibbon, Berkeley, and Burke?), we must still confront the problem of the peculiar nature of imaginative literature; of the play, the poem, and the tale. There will be inevitably borderline cases where it is difficult to distinguish between fiction and reportage: think of Defoe's *Memoirs of a Cavalier* or even his *Journal of the Plague Year* or between philosophy and myth-making as in Plato. But these cases have to be adjudicated individually: they do not refute the basic distinction between literature as an art, as fiction, as making, between Homer, Dante, Shakespeare, and Goethe, and the great philosophers and historians who, after all, make a claim to literal truth. The recent attempts such as that of Roland Barthes propagating the term *écriture* in order to eradicate this distinction or that of Hayden White in his *Metahistory* (1973) to assimilate historiography to fiction seem to me mistaken. In the case of Barthes and the French structuralists and their adherents in this country, they seem to be strategies to elevate criticism to the same status as creative writing, to defend a criticism which has become personal, fictional, and even completely arbitrary, proclaiming misunderstanding, misreading, misprision as positive virtues. But this is another topic.

## NOTES

1. Liber 2, Chapter 1, Section 4.

2. Roland Barthes, *Essais critiques* (Paris, 1964), p. 125. "Depuis que la 'Littérature' existe (c'est-à-dire si l'on juge d'après la date du mot, depuis fort peu de temps), on peut dire c'est la fonction de l'écrivain que de la combattre." Maurice Blanchot, *Le Livre à venir* (Paris, 1959), p. 242. "Littérature—mot tardif, mot sans honneur."

3. M. Tulli Ciceronis in M. Antonium, *Oratio Phillipica Secunda.* "Fuit in illo ingenium, ratio, memoria, litteratura [in some texts: litterae], cura, cogitatio, diligentia." Loeb Library edition of the *Phillipics*, trans. Walter C. A. Ker (London, 1926), pp. 178-79.

4. *De Spectaculis*, 17, 6. "Si doctrinam saecularis litteraturae ut stultitiae apud deum deputatum, aspernamur."

5. *Noctes Atticae*, 13, 7. "Sed 'humanitatem' appellaverunt id propemodum, quod Graeci *paideían* vocant nos 'eruditionem institutionemque in bonas artis' dicimus." Quoted in article "Humanitas" (by J. Heinemann) in Pauly's *Enzyklopädie der classischen Altertumswissenschaft*, Supplementband 5 (Stuttgart, 1931), column 285.

6. "Good letters" in Dedication to the *Aeneis* (1697) in *Essays*, ed. W. P. Ker (Oxford, 1908), 3, 240.

7. Charles Perrault, *Lettres*, ed. P. Clément (Paris, 1868), 5, 512f.

8. "On appelle des lettres humaines ou les belles lettres, la grammaire, l'éloquence, la poésie."

9. *A Short View of Tragedy* (1692) in *The Critical Works*, ed. C. A. Zimansky (New Haven, 1956), p. 83.

10. From NED quoting J. Edwards, *Author, Old and New Testament*, p. 239.

11. Boswell, *Life of Samuel Johnson*, ed. G. B. Hill, rev. L. F. Powell, 6 vol. (Oxford, 1934), 1, 302.

12. *Experiments in Education* (Ithaca, N.Y., 1942), p. 75.

13. Ed. René Groos, 2 vol. (Paris, 1947), 2, 145.

14. *Critical Reflections on the Old English Dramatick Writers. Extracted from a Prefatory Discourse to the New Edition of Massinger's Works* (London, 1761).

15. Letter to the Rev. Dr. Horne, April 30, 1774, in *Catalogue of the Johnsonian Collection of R.B. Adams* (Buffalo, 1921), no pagination.

16. P. 189: "le poème épique, la Tragèdie, la Comédie, l'Ode, la Fable, l'Histoire, l'Eloquence."

17. (Turin, 1760), p. 6: "Non parleremo . . . dei progressi della scienze e delle arti, che propriamente non sono parte di letteratura . . . al buon gusto, ed all eloquenza, vale dire alla letteratura." Denina's book appeared in French translation in Paris in 1776, and in English translation at Glasgow in 1771 and 1784. The connection with Glasgow is due to the fact that Denina knew Lady Elizabeth Mackenzie, the daughter of the Duke of Argyle, when her husband was the British Minister in Turin.

# BIBLIOGRAPHY

I know of no history of the term. Some helpful quotations, besides those in dictionaries, are in

Eduard Wölfflin, "Litteratura," *Archiv für lateinische Lexikographie und Grammatik*, 5 (1885), 49-55

Robert Escarpit, "La Définition du terme 'Littérature,'" *Actes du IIIe Congrès de l'Association Internationale de Littérature Comparée* (The Hague, 1962), pp. 77-82

————, "Littérature," in *Dictionnaire international des termes littéraires* (The Hague, 1973), Fascicle L, 47-53

Claude Crispin, *Aux origines de l'histoire littéraire* (Grenoble, 1973).

Of my related writings:

"The Name and Nature of Comparative Literature," in *Comparatists at Work*, ed. Stephen G. Nichols and Richard B. Vowles (Waltham, Mass., 1968), pp. 3-27. Reprinted in *Discriminations* (New Haven, 1970), pp. 1-36.

"The Attack on Literature," in *Expression, Communication and Experience in Literature and Language. Proceedings of the XIIth Congress of the International Federation of Modern Languages and Literatures*, ed. Ronald G. Popperwell (London, 1973), pp. 1-16. A version without notes appeared in *The American Scholar*.

"Literature and Its Cognates," in *Dictionary of the History of Ideas*, ed. Philip P. Wiener (New York, 1973), 3, 81-89.

# What Isn't Literature?

## *E. D. Hirsch, Jr.*

My title seems to imply a skepticism almost total about the validity of any boundary lines marking off literature from non-literature. Therefore, let me state immediately that such an extreme position, arguing the absence of any distinction between literature and non-literature would be false, demonstrably false, by the following demonstration: I can gather a group of educated persons and set before them a series of texts paired off in groups of two. I can then ask them to write down on each text either the letter L or the letter N, standing for "literature" and "non-literature," I can choose the examples with care to exclude borderline cases, and then look confidently at the results of the experiment. After some trial and error, I can easily devise a list which always produces uniform and unanimous judgments from all educated persons. Armed with these absolutely consistent results, I can state with assurance that among educated speakers of English there is a genuine and demonstrable distinction between literature and non-literature. Though I have never heard of this experiment being performed, and have not troubled to perform it myself, I believe we could all agree that it probably could be performed successfully. If, for instance, the pairs of examples always consisted of poems by Keats, technical reports from *Science* magazine, and sonnets of Shakespeare, the results would be reassuring.

On the other hand, I am equally sure that I could devise an experiment which would produce results that were anything but unanimous and reassuring. I could include letters by Matthew Arnold, and Jane Austen, histories by Macaulay, Hume and Eugene Genovese, biographies by Boswell and Mary Moorman, political speeches by Burke and Harold Macmillan, legal opinions by Cardozo and Warren Burger, scientific works by Darwin and Heisenberg, and a number of examples of still more doubtful classification by writers who have not yet entered the canon. In this experiment, we can be sure that the results will be extremely varied in a number of respects. We would have to report that our usage panel assigned L to the letters of Jane Austen by a vote of 70 per cent to 30 per cent, but that they withheld the classification from the letters of Jane Carlyle by a majority of 60 to 40. And we would find a further inconsistency in the pattern of voting. Some respondents, who side with the majority in one case, will side with the minority in another. We can predict these results also with some confidence, and perhaps someday an experimenter will decide to confirm this exceedingly obvious prediction. But even with these results before us, we need not suppose that the one experiment somehow negates the other, or calls into doubt the existence of such a thing as literature. No one doubts the reality of chairs, and yet nobody knows where chairs fade off into sofas and ottomans on one side and stools on the other; any similar experiments conducted with chairs would be likely to yield similar results.

So, my aim is not to suggest that the class literature doesn't exist as an understandable and real entity, any less than does the class chair. Moreover, I don't want to suggest that the great variety of borderline cases is an intellectual embarrassment for serious literary study and criticism. The word *science* suffers the

same difficulties; so does the word *art*. So, of course, does
the word made famous by Wittgenstein, the word *game*. One of
the great insights to be gained from reading Wittgenstein is a
realization that language and thought require us to use
classifications which slip and slide into domains of indispensable vagueness. We get into trouble only when we assume that
the classification really *has* a boundary line or means the same
thing in different uses. The only embarrassment to be suffered
from the amorphousness of words is the attempt to pretend that
they are not amorphous. Literary theory gets into trouble only
when it pretends that the word *literature* can be satisfactorily
defined, and then tries to erect generalizations on such a delu-
sive definition. My skepticism, then, is not aimed at the existence of the class, literature, but at the attempt to falsely constrict
its existence through definition. This paper might be considered
a defense of literature against literary theory.

I think, though, that justice demands a sympathetic understanding of the dilemma of literary theory and the reasons it
should wish to make definitions of *literature*. First of all, literary
theorists share with the rest of us a tendency to assume that a
word which we all understand *must* have a definable meaning.
We know what literature is; let us therefore make that knowledge precise by distinguishing those traits which make a work
literature from those which do not. Now, what I tried to show in
my two imaginary experiments is that we know what literature
is only vaguely, so that any attempt to remove that vagueness in
a definition actually falsifies our knowledge of the word, rather
than clarifies it. To define is to mark off boundaries distinguishing what is literature from what is not, but our knowledge of
literature has no such defining boundaries; there are many cases
about which we are not sure—important cases, not just periph-
eral ones. What the theorist should understand is that his
definitions do not create literature, but can only attempt to
clarify and make explicit what is already implicit in our use of

the word. The theorist who defines literature is in a position exactly analogous to the linguistic theorist who formulates a grammar. All sophisticated linguists know that their job is to formulate explicit rules for what is implicitly known by every native speaker. The native speaker is the court of last resort; he can never be wrong; only the grammarian can be. If the rules of the grammar do not coincide with or precisely describe the √ usage of native speakers, then the grammar is defective. So it is with definitions of literature; if they deviate in the least from the usage of educated men, it is the definition that is wrong, and not common usage. The literary theorist is like the grammarian in that he describes and clarifies a reality, but does not create the reality he describes.

It may be that the defining theorist retains an uneasy feeling that his work is not just descriptive, but prescriptive, that he has the job of telling us what we *ought* to conceive literature to be. There are a number of reasons he should wish to take this upon himself, and certainly with theorists like Coleridge, who had a sense of cultural mission, such a reformulation of our concept of literature is at once noble and valid. I shall be dealing with such normative aims a little further along in this paper. But we should be clear that present-day literary theorists of the academy have not for the most part taken on the prophet's robe. Their aim is to follow in the footsteps of Aristotle, and describe that which *is*, to do it better than anyone has before, and then to give a solid intellectual foundation to the great enterprise or industry which is the academic study of literature. The subject exists; the field exists; let us be clear about the essential nature of our subject. Then we will know how to proceed in our work, what problems to tackle, and what methods are particularly appropriate to the subject as we have defined it. The hopes are worthy, and the history of criticism continues to be strewn with the wrecks of these hopes. I concede that even unsuccessful descriptive definitions can be helpfully illuminating, of course. But the hope of success is a false hope, and can be proved to be a false hope. Like many other boys, I tried for years, off and on, to find a method for trisecting an angle with ruler and compass alone. Like the tribe of literary theorists who still attempt to define literature, I refused to give up the challenge, and spent many amusing but fruitless hours devising ever more sophisticated methods with ruler and compass. I was only willing to stop when a precocious mathematical freshman at college explained to me that I was trying to solve a problem having three un-knowns by using only two equations; hence the attempt really was logically fruitless and impossible. I wonder whether such merely logical proofs will ever stop people from trying to trisect angles or define literature.

The reason I want to defend literature against the definitions of literary theory is not just a purely logical and disinterested reason, though that has its own delight and interest. I want to expose the futility of such definitions because they have done and continue to do a certain amount of harm. Besides being misleading, they always confine and constrict the subject in a way that makes the teaching and study of literature more nar-row and one-sided than is good for ourselves, our students and our culture. In particular, the aesthetic orientation of the usual definitions has tended to aestheticize our choice of texts-to-be-studied and our way of teaching those texts. If literature were just a sub-species of the category *art* and if *art* were something that is only properly understood and appreciated under aes-thetic principles, then our literary and cultural lives would be much impoverished. For we have not yet escaped from the fact that the only really successful delineation of the aesthetic mode of perception has been achieved by Kant and his successors. And the hallmark of this aesthetic mode is the disinterested contemplation of beauty. This high calling is in no way to be scorned or underestimated, and I wish to avoid even the hint of doing so. Nonetheless, definitions of literature in our time have tended to be oriented to the aesthetic as a guiding assumption of the definition. And to regard literature as primarily and essentially aesthetic is not only a mistake; it is also a very unfortunate narrowing of our responses to literature, and our perceptions of its breadth and possibilities.

Let me therefore return to the reasons for the results of our two experiments. We were able to achieve complete and unanimous agreement about what literature is, in the first experiment, because we chose texts which belong to literature by virtue of fulfilling a number of quite different canonical traits. And the non-literary texts of the experiment were so chosen that they, too, could be excluded from literature on *every* implicit ground that underlies our normal use of the word. In the second experiment, however, the results were uncertain because the works chosen exhibited some traits which qualified them and other traits which might normally disqualify them. The predictability of our experimental results resided in the variability of the criteria that we use in classifying a text as literature. To explain this point, which we all implicitly know in any case, I will present a few examples of these sometimes conflicting criteria.

The most obvious (and presently the central) criterion we use is that of genre: poems, stories, plays. Now even if these fictional works, which earlier theorists called imitations, were the only works which we happened to call literature, we would find ourselves beset by problems of definition and classification; for the genres themselves merge into hybrid forms which cause just as many problems as the great big genre which we call literature. Take the example of poems, which we now think of as any text in verse, or perhaps as any text exhibiting uneven line lengths on the printed page. But even this tolerant, modern conception, about as broad as any native speaker is likely to conceive in using the word, leads to uncertainty of classification, as may be shown in several instances where prose has been converted into poetry by the simple expedient of transcribing the prose in irregular line lengths. In addition, the question, "Is this text poetry?", suffers still further difficulties and complications when the normative criterion of poetry, also part of our vague conception, is brought to bear. No long poem can be all poetry, asserted Coleridge, and many educated persons refuse to accept as "true" or "genuine" poems certain texts which fail to meet their qualitative standards. The texts are excluded from the class called *poems* as rejects that do not meet the approval of a quality controller. They lack some trait which must be superadded to the mere trait of line-length or form. So powerful is this normative and conceptual principle of classification that some ancients, who stressed imitation or fictionality as the important defining trait of poetry, did not conceive of lyric poems as belonging among the recognized genres.

Let me quickly enumerate some further confusions in the very center of our sense of literature, before moving ahead to the positive conclusion which I intend to draw. My first example is literature by association, on the pattern of guilt by association. Milton is one of our great poets; his work stands at the center of the canon. Because he is a canonical writer, some of his texts, like *Areopagitica* and *The Doctrine and Discipline of Divorce* are included within literature by a large number of persons. Wordsworth is a canonical poet; into literature, therefore, goes his travel book on the Lake Country, along with Dr. Johnson's *Tour of the Hebrides*, under the following principle: literature is anything written by a great literary figure. Another principle is that any text in any genre may be included in literature if it exhibits some excellence of form or style. Nearly everyone would include the Platonic dialogues because they are imitations. On the other hand, are there good reasons for excluding Aristotle's work? Perhaps, but if we exclude his *Poetics*, why should we not exclude Wordsworth's *Prefaces*? And if we include the *Poetics* of Aristotle, on what grounds do we exclude his *Metaphysics*, a far more interesting, imaginative and nontechnical work. Shelley, as we all know, wished to include even some legislative statutes of parliaments under poetry because they

created order and harmony out of disorder. Modern usage has
not accepted Shelley's comprehensive principle altogether, but
we have introduced our own versions of his expansive literary
imperialism. We accept Nietzsche and Kierkegaard of course,
but also Tacitus and Darwin. I recently asserted that Darwin was
a much more interesting figure in 19th century literature than
was Walter Pater, and I mentioned explicitly *The Origin of Species*. This was challenged in subsequent discussion by the late
W. K. Wimsatt, who said I should have chosen *The Voyage of the
Beagle*, which had more right to be called a literary work. A
correspondent wrote me that I was just being eccentric, and that
I knew perfectly well that *The Origin of Species* was not a literary
work. Yet so various are the criteria by which we actually make
such judgments, that I was able to direct him to four expert
authorities who had preceded me in print in considering *The
Origin of Species* to be literature.

Need I call your attention to the fact that a great many persons
consider the Bible to be great literature? But I do not think we
would find unanimity in the criteria on which this judgment is
based. Some would stress the stylistic magnificence of the
Authorized Version. In a large literature course, when I first
started teaching, the Bible was conceived to be literature largely
because of its poems and stories. But the criterion which many
people use in deciding to call the Bible literature is very similar
to the Coleridgean principle of bringing the whole soul of man
into activity, and this is a principle which has for me a great
appeal. Reading the Bible brings the whole soul of man into
activity. And this principle can be extended or attenuated to
include everything that De Quincey called "The Literature of
Power." But it cannot be overstressed that this principle of
engaging a reader on more than one level of his being—not just
the intellectual or just the emotional, but both—is not and cannot be a truly objective principle of classification. It is in its very
essence subjective because the perlocutionary effects of a text

are highly variable effects, differently engaging the hearts and minds of various readers. I cannot remember ever reading a book that more engaged my rapt soul than the small volume by Niels Bohr on the relation of atomic structure to the periodic table! Order out of chaos—high poetry in Shelley's sense. For me, that was and is a work of literature, one which altogether obliterates any clear division between the literature of knowledge and the literature of power.

Is it any wonder that no single definition of literature has embraced the whole continuum of uses to which educated persons put the word? Every attempt to make such a definition, without exception, has ended up being a stipulative definition, that is to say, a definition which stipulates how the word literature *ought* to be used, but entirely fails to define how it actually is used by great numbers of educated native speakers. John Ellis recently tried to turn the trick, in an otherwise sensible book called the *Theory of Literary Criticism,* by distinguishing between trait-definitions and use-definitions, the latter being the right way out of the muddle and confusion which surround the word *literature.* That was a sophisticated and intelligent tactic. The only defect in its performance was that his use-definition did not in fact embrace all the uses to which we put the word *literature.* Ellis was forced into the position that uses which fail to correspond to his use-definition are just wrong uses. So we were given yet another stipulative definition of literature: that is, a definition which tries to legislate, but does not actually describe the way competent persons actually use the word.

Now for my positive conclusions. First of all, I have argued that while the word literature embraces an enormous variety, and implies an unsteady, changeable system of criteria, the word is nonetheless meaningful and not entirely arbitrary. While some might include Darwin and Niels Bohr, nobody would include the article "Visual Disturbances after Prolonged Perceptual Isolation" by Heron, Doane, and Scott. The word *literature* has a very great range, but does not embrace all that is written down. Secondly, I believe that the enormous range of the word, embracing as it does both descriptive (that is, generic) criteria, as well as normative criteria, is not at all an accident. The widespread use of the word arose late in the Victorian period in order to fill an important cultural need, and particularly an educational need. Humanistic instruction at the schools and universities had always included a very wide range of texts that were considered important or valuable on a variety of grounds. This remained true so long as the classics formed the basis of humane education in Europe and America. When one read the classics, one read Tacitus and Pliny as well as Vergil and Homer. Nobody then argued whether or not *De Rerum Naturae* by Lucretius was truly literature or truly a poem. To read it was part of a classical education. So, I think it was no accident that, when classical education became displaced by mass education in the local, national languages, that was also the time when the word *literature* in its more or less modern uses began to occur more and more frequently. A word was needed to embrace in the national language the great variety of canonical texts that were required to replace the classical canon. It was the Victorian scholar and educator Edward Dowden who warned against a limitation of the word *literature* to stand only for belletristic writing, to the exclusion of philosophical and other valuable texts.

In recent years, we modern educators have not heeded Dowden's advice. In our eagerness to show that literature was a subject and a substance *sui generis*, with its own special and appropriate methods, we lost sight of the larger educational goals that helped foster the currency of the word itself. We decided to give the word a predominantly aesthetic flavor, and to subsume literature under art. In order to narrow the word in this way, we were hurled into endless attempts to define literature to suit its special claims as a form of art rather than as a canon of texts worthy to be taught, read, and preserved in a culture. My interest in showing that these attempts at definition have resulted in merely stipulative definitions has also had an educational motivation, and I have tried to suggest that the narrowness of a predominantly aesthetic definition can lead, and sometimes has led, to a narrowness of educational goals. In the heyday of the literary study of literature, which meant the aesthetic study of literature, I was once scolded by a class of sophomores for having assigned them Mill's *Essay on Liberty*. Of course, they were right in a sense. It was, contractually, a literary course, and what I was giving them to read did not correspond with what they had been taught to accept as literature. But in a more traditional and still current sense of literature and humane education, they were absolutely wrong. Let me, then, end with my own stipulative definition of literature. Literature includes any text worthy to be taught to students by teachers of literature, when these texts are not being taught to students in other departments of a school or university. That is a stipulative definition for which I claim mainly this virtue: it encourages us to think out our responsibilities in humanistic education, and make curricular choices on the basis of those responsibilities. That seems to me a better and immensely more interesting foundation for the teaching of literature than one derived from a stipulative definition of literature as art.

# Why Theorize about Literature?

## *Edward Davenport*

We need a theory of what literature is only when we have some problem with our own intuitive or commonsense notion of literature. Thus most people are never moved to inquire what literature is: they have a rough notion which suffices. Without a specific problem with our present notion of literature we are not only not moved to ask for a better theory, but if by some chance we were so moved, we would have a difficult time answering the question; for in order to recognize a superior theory of what literature is, we need to know what is wrong or problematic about the notion we already have. The kind of answer we want depends upon the kind of problem we want to solve. How do problems with a commonsense notion of literature arise?

It is possible for a student to read enthusiastically and widely in college, and even in graduate school, without feeling constrained to alter his intuitive or commonsense notion of literature inherited from childhood. If the student is not in the habit of comparing his rough theory closely with his experience of reading he may never notice any conflicts, and this without being a superficial reader. Northrop Frye goes so far as to say that "a critic may have a precise and candid taste and yet be largely innocent of theory."[1] Quite possibly the young critic believes that literature is now one thing, now another—for example, imitation in some cases and expression in others. The need to inquire further into theory arises only when the young critic meets with some troubling contradiction or intriguing conflict. This conflict may occur when he notices that some of his favorite writers, such as Dickens and James, or Lawrence and Joyce, not only have different styles, but also different theories of literature, and that they sharply criticize one another for their misconceptions about writing. At this point the critic may take up the problem of deciding which writer has the better answer to the question, "What is literature?" It is not necessary to suppose that either writer is wholly in the wrong, or that literature is too narrow to contain such controversial spirits, in order to be interested in this question of who has the better theory of literature. And it is usually in some such way as this, with the discovery that our literary tradition contains not only different theories but also conflicting theories of literature, that the student of literature comes to question his commonsense notion, and to seek a better general theory of literature.

The problem I am going to consider in this paper is one which has occurred to many students of literature during the past half century, and goes to the heart of any attempt to determine the truth or falsity of the conflicting theories in our literary tradition. The problem is this: do we need a general theory of literature? Do we need a theory which will tell us why some writing is literature, and some not, or why some writing is great literature, while other writing is second rate? These two functions of literary theory are independent but both are needed to answer the most interesting questions about literature. Is it even possible, in principle, to discover a theory which will explain what literature is?

The problem has been set for us by the discoveries of other disciplines, which early in the twentieth century began to challenge our theories of art. From anthropology, for instance, we began to hear of "cultural relativity," which suggested that the literary standards by which we judged not only current works, but all literature, regardless of time or place, could at best be only relative standards—standards accurate only for our own time, place, and cultural or even individual values. According to the new anthropological perspective, the art of different ages and cultures is based on different premises, and valued for different reasons. The lesson for literary study seemed to be that it was unhistorical, provincial, and grossly unfair to suppose that a single literary theory could account for all that we call literature. At the same time that we were learning from anthropology, certain philosophers were telling us about the imprecision and possible subjectivity of language: it turned out that it was not so easy for any two people to understand the same thing from the same word—especially a word like "beauty." The problem of the imprecision of language became such a pressing one for modern writers that T. S. Eliot, in his *Four Quartets*, suggested that language was not capable of carrying the weight of truth, nor the human mind of receiving it, except in flashes of mystic insight.

Because of these difficulties it has in our time become problematic whether evaluation and general theory of literature are really fruitful; it has been the conclusion of many that if an evaluative theory of literature could not be objective—that is, if we were bound to incorporate cultural and personal bias into our judgments—then evaluation was pointless if not actually dangerous.

For many the solution to this problem was to conclude that the true task of the student of literature was to avoid general questions, and to engage in appreciation, classification, and observation. This solution does imply a general literary theory of its own, or rather three possible theories: relativism, subjectivism, and agnosticism as to literary value. Relativism holds that there are no value distinctions in literature—that anything may be called good literature. Subjectivism holds that all theories of literary value are subjective—literary evaluation is a purely personal matter. Agnosticism, the theory I shall give the most attention in this paper, holds that there may be real distinctions in literary value, but that our subjective value systems will prevent us from knowing anything about the real values. The agnostic theory holds that any attempt to be objective must fail, and may also produce bitter controversy.

All these answers may seem to solve the problem of the shakiness of our theories of literature: they seem to be tolerant of literature from all cultures and value systems; they seem to encourage the widest variety of new literature; and they seem even to remove a quality of rancor from scholarship by pointing out that we are free to call one work good without calling its neighbor mediocre.

Yet the relativist view achieves all this by denying that literature is a subject of study at all; the relativist view is probably irrefutable, as it consistently denies that there is anything to discuss.

The subjectivist view is open to the same objection; if our notions about literature are irretrievably subjective, then there is really no ground for discussion, and no point to inquiry.

The agnostic theory of literature is more serviceable. We can say we don't know *why* a mediocre piece of writing is bad—in objective terms—or even whether it is bad, for certain, but we may nevertheless operate upon our intuitions, in the hope that at least some readers will share them with us. The agnostic theory allows that there are probably differences in the quality of literature, but insists that it is a waste of time to articulate general literary theories since these must remain forever subjective. Thus our theory of literature is for the agnostic largely a matter of taste; and taste, for agnostics, is a faculty which may be developed by reading, but which cannot be developed via general theory, and cannot be articulated theoretically. The agnostic avoids theoretical debate as rancorous and fruitless, and so will not want to give a comprehensive answer to the question "What is literature?"

It will be the purpose of the remainder of this paper to examine and criticize the agnostic theory of literature, and to suggest an alternative theory which will allow for the interest and usefulness of general literary theory, while also providing some help with the difficulty of achieving objective criticism.

In order to provide a concrete example for this discussion, I must digress for a moment, however, to introduce a piece of literature.

About one thousand years ago, in Japan, a novelist, the Lady Murasaki, wrote a long novel called *The Tale of Genji.* This novel begins as a rather fanciful tale of an amorous prince, and ends, some eleven hundred pages later, as a kind of feminist novel of education; it begins by showing the love life of medieval Japan through the eyes of men, and ends by showing it through the eyes of women. Almost exactly in the middle of this novel comes an interlude when the main characters take refuge from the summer heat by reading old Japanese romances. They become fascinated with these stories and with the power of fiction over their minds, and they begin to discuss the question "What is literature?" Prince Genji offers his own answer in the following words from part III, chapter vii:

> I have a theory of my own about what this art of the novel is, and how it came into being. To begin with, it does not simply consist in the author's telling a story about the adventures of some other person. On the contrary, it happens because the storyteller's own experience of men and things, whether for good or ill—not only what he has passed through himself, but even events which he has only witnessed or been told of—has moved him to an emotion so passionate that he can no longer keep it shut up in his heart. Again and again something in his own life or in that around him will seem to the writer so important that he cannot bear to let it pass into oblivion. There must never come a time, he feels, when men do not know about it. That is my view of how this art arose.[2]

Murasaki has given here a very powerful answer to our question, "What is literature?". Literature is a record of moving events. We can see that both the classical theory of Aristotle that epic as well as tragic poetry is imitation of a noble action, and the romantic theory of Wordsworth that poetry is the spontaneous overflow of powerful feelings, bear some likeness to this theory of Murasaki's. We can also see that Murasaki's theory, like the classic and the romantic theory, may have limitations as a general theory of literature. For instance, the theory was formulated for the medieval Japanese romance, so that it is fair to ask whether it applies equally well to, say, the modern American novel. Also, what Murasaki finds a moving event may be determined by her culture or personality to an extent which makes it difficult for many modern readers to appreciate her novel.

Yet despite these possible limitations, the passage stirs in us the conviction that Murasaki is speaking about literature—all literature—including literature as we know it. Genji's speculation demonstrates vividly the problem which literary theory comes to solve. The problem is to explain the power which literature has over our minds, to determine whether this is for good or ill, and to recognize when and why literature meets our highest standards.

The fascination of the question, "What is literature?", has led many writers besides Murasaki to bold attempts at answers. The agnostic theory of literature, however, tells us that none of these attempts is really an answer about literature as a whole—that it cannot be, because Aristotle, for instance, was ignorant of the literature of the past two millenia. It is even said that Aristotle was not trying to give an answer to the question, "What is literature?", but was only giving a description of the particular drama of his own time; according to this argument Aristotle had nothing to say about what makes literature great or second rate, but only explained how to tell when a play diverged from the norms of his time.

The agnostic theory of literature thus makes two assumptions about any theory of literature, whether Aristotle's or Murasaki's. First the theory cannot be comprehensive, since the morrow may always bring a new work of literature which does not fit the theory. Second, the attempt at comprehensive theory, given that it is impossible, is not only fruitless but destructive of the enterprise of literary study, and probably even destructive of literature itself, since theories will tend to serve as public prohibitions against certain kinds of experiments. This is why the agnostic critic would consider it undesirable, or at least problematic, to attempt to give a comprehensive answer to the question "What is literature?" From the agnostic point of view, it would be better to work at a purely descriptive and classificatory theory of existing kinds of literature—a descriptive theory which is non-evaluative.

The agnostic position I describe is an ideal type, and perhaps it exists nowhere in its absolute form. Yet it is so much in the spirit of our time that it affects the thinking even of people quite interested in literary theory.

For instance, Northrop Frye bases his rejection of evaluative literary theory on the grounds I have mentioned: such theory has always failed.

Distrust of evaluative literary theory leads him to reject all evaluative comparisons. He says, "On the ethical level we can see that every increase of appreciation has been right, and every decrease wrong: that criticism has no business to react against things, but should show a steady advance toward undiscriminating catholicity."[3] *yet, but nothing apart from theory because*

Frye does not reject value distinctions in literature, but merely the articulation of them. He explains that our knowledge of superior literary value results from a direct experience which can never be put into words.[4] Nevertheless he does believe that *but* critics can develop something called "good taste" which has an *—s don approach* inductive basis, and which may make the reader more sensitive to the recognition of literary value.

I suggest that taste, if it exists, is just a theory unexpressed, and that whether it is wrong or right, it is not something which reliably emerges from the data, but is rather a necessity prior to observation: theories are tools which any observer must use even to gather data, and of course to make sense of them. If we wish to improve literary theory we need to articulate the direct experience or intuition which leads us to recognize literary value.

There are two objections which the agnostic theory makes against the articulation of general theories of literature. First of all, according to agnostic theory, any general theory is bound to be wrong, just as Aristotle and Murasaki would be wrong if their theories were taken as comprehensive answers to the question, "What is literature?" Secondly, according to agnostic theory, a general theory of literature is likely to inhibit the free development of literary study, and of completely new forms of literature, by establishing public norms.

Taking the second objection first, let me point out that there need be no connection between formulating a general theory and attempting to enforce one. Let us suppose for the sake of argument that both Murasaki and Aristotle meant their theories to be comprehensive. It is possible that people who have taken either theory to be correct in all points have been inhibited from many kinds of experiment—though I am skeptical of there being any serious check of literature or criticism for this reason. For people who take Murasaki and Aristotle to be good theoreticians, however, without supposing them infallible, their definitions of the nature and limits of poetry might be very useful. Suppose that when a writer heard Aristotle say, "A work of literature must have a beginning, a middle, and an end," he interpreted Aristotle to mean that without these things the writer was unlikely to write an intelligible and satisfactory work. (Even if Aristotle was more dogmatic than this, one can use his theory without his dogmatism.) Then, if the writer has any inclination to dispense with the beginning, middle or end, he will be aware, because of Aristotle, of an important problem—namely that if he neglects these elements he may have to compensate in some way for whatever clarity and excellence they would contribute. Thus the artist can learn from the theory what things are likely to be problematic in private experimentation. It is possible for a writer to ignore all such problems, and simply to write as he is impelled or inclined to, but in fact successful experimental work is usually that which innovates by solving problems in the tradition.

If the comprehensive theories of literature in our tradition provide no total or certain answers, they at least point out problems that arise from the conflict of theory with theory, or of theory with experience. These problems are often of the greatest interest to later writers and critics: consider the interest among realist and romantic writers in the nineteenth century in the conflict over the theory that literature is mimesis.

Thus the existence of comprehensive theories of literature can be a stimulus rather than a hindrance to experimentation. An era without theory may even be stagnant creatively, for lack of understanding of the tradition in respect to which experiments are made.

It should be noted here that the use of the word "tradition" is itself called into doubt by the theory of cultural relativism, for if cultures are islands of value-systems, then the idea of a connected literary tradition would seem to be mistaken. Nevertheless, literary tradition may take into itself as much of the distant and of the past as it wishes, giving a new valuation to old works, and in this way creating a continuous tradition. It may be objected that this is unhistorical—that T. S. Eliot's Donne is not the Elizabethan Donne; nevertheless, Eliot's Donne is a real figure upon the literary landscape, because of the power and clarity with which he has been drawn. As Eliot and Borges have both argued, the meaning of the past can be altered, in a real sense, by the events of the present, as when Homer's epics are read in the context of Vergil's and Dante's epics, which were written to some extent in emulation of Homer. While it is valuable to try to imagine how Homer sounded before Vergil and Dante (and others) wrote, it is equally valuable to us now to recognize Homer as part of a new tradition, a tradition without walls, which comprehends the whole of literature.

The claim that theories of literature are useless because they are doomed to be found inadequate can be answered in the same way as the claim that these theories must prove obstructive. Just as a theory need not be dangerous because it is incomplete, so a theory need not be useless because it is incomplete. It may be useful even if quite untrue. A theory which is probably false, such as that all great literature deals with love, is useful, if only in bringing to light the large proportion of literature which does fit this description, and the smaller portion which does not. This false theory might well lead to some true or at least more complete theories about the relation of literature and love.

An uncertain theory also has its uses, since if we have the assumption that all theories are likely to be proven wrong eventually, a good theory provides us with the challenge of finding out how it is wrong, and this problem may be a stimulus to new literature as well as to new criticism. Thus the theory that a work of literature must have a beginning, a middle, and an end was tested by Laurence Sterne, in *Tristram Shandy*, and found to be dispensable. Yet even this exception succeeds only by inventing new methods of shaping continual digression into a coherent narrative—i.e., by solving a problem suggested by Aristotle's theory.

There is yet another claim against a general theory of literature which deserves attention, and this is that our theories are bound to be subjective, and that evaluation is therefore only the grounds for endless disputation. On this point I will refer to a recent paper by the philosopher of social science I. C. Jarvie

called "The Objectivity of Criticism of the Arts."[5] Jarvie makes
two points in that paper which bear on the problem at hand.
First he makes a distinction between response to literature, and
evaluation. According to Jarvie there is likely to be a greater
variety of response to a given work than there is variety of
evaluation. Thus I may dislike Milton and really enjoy Raymond
Chandler—that is a response which may distinguish me from a
colleague who enjoys Milton and can't read Chandler. Nevertheless, says Jarvie, my colleague and I are more likely to agree
on our evaluation than on our response to these works; in other
words, we are likely to agree that Milton is first-rate literature,
and Chandler only second-rate. The evidence that evaluation is
more likely to be consistent than is response is an indication to
Jarvie that evaluation may rise above mere subjectivity. Nevertheless he reminds us that there is no guarantee that any given
evaluative statement is objectively true; here we come to Jarvie's
second contribution to this discussion. He says that even though
there is more agreement on evaluation than on response, there
is still a great deal of controversy and no access to clearly objective statements. Nevertheless, to Jarvie this controversy is not
evidence of the worthless subjectivity of all evaluation; on the
contrary, controversy is often evidence of an attempt at objectivity. Jarvie says controversy is the best method of providing a
check on subjective judgment. We have a tradition of literary
criticism in which our individual attempts to judge objectively
are reinforced by the criticisms of others, when they find our
judgments either wrong or subjectively limited. Objectivity is
possible only within such a tradition, Jarvie argues, never in
individual statements, but in the process of articulation and
criticism. It is the tradition itself, with its continuous challenging
and improving of theories, which is the most objective instrument of literary judgment we have.

Adequate controversy, however, depends upon articulation
of the theories in use. If we accept the agnostic position that

articulation is useless, and that development of an inarticulate taste is the best course for literary study, then we avoid the very controversies in which reside our hope of objective judgment.

Let me conclude by saying that we do want comprehensive answers to the question "What is literature?" We want answers which tell us more than the general theories we already have. We need not treat Murasaki's or Aristotle's or our own theories as merely descriptive, and we need not be afraid to use our theories to evaluate literature, or even to make suggestions or predictions about the literature of tomorrow. As long as we continue to foster a critical tradition, wherein none of our theories is permitted to stand unchallenged, the uncertainty and even falseness of our theories, should they be discovered, do not make them worthless. Our knowledge of what literature is must remain conjectural, but such conjectural knowledge can be useful, and can be improved, by further attempts to formulate general theory.

## NOTES

1. Northrop Frye, *The Well-Tempered Critic* (Bloomington: Indiana University Press, 1963), p. 113.

2. Lady Murasaki, *The Tale of Genji* translated by Arthur Waley (New York: The Modern Library, Random House, 1960), p. 501.

3. Northrop Frye, *Anatomy of Criticism: Four Essays* (Princeton: Princeton University Press, 1957), p. 25.

4. *Anatomy of Criticism*, p. 27.

5. "The Objectivity of Criticism of the Arts", *Ratio*, 9 (June, 1967): 67-83.

# 2

## Canon-Formation:
## Forces and Procedures

# "Literature": A Many-Sided Process

## *George McFadden*

I begin with Roman Ingarden's definition of the literary work. (Not the literary work *of art*, please note, because I hope to be able to discuss the question "What is literature?" without asking for agreement on what, exactly, literary artistry is.) Here is the gist of it: the literary work is a purely intentional formation. Its source of being is twofold, in the creative acts of consciousness of its author, and in the text where it has its physical foundation. By virtue of its strata of sounds and meanings, the work is intersubjectively accessible, and can also be reproduced. Thereby it becomes an intersubjective intentional object, related to a community of readers. But the literary work stands apart from all experiences of consciousness, whether of its author or of any of its readers.[1] Its mode of being is incomplete and schematic because its structure requires filling out by the community of readers to whom it relates.

To this notion I must make a very important addition not from Ingarden: that there is a special class (some call it "privileged") of works called literature, which have a special relation to the community of readers. I think we can say that literature is a body of works—a canon—selected because it helps a community to define itself.

At this point we could introduce the question of art and ask, to what extent must a literary work be a work of art in order to enter the canon of literature? But this seems to me a useless approach. It is much more productive to inquire into the different ways in which works of varying artistic value do relate to the readers within a community, who in their turn, anyway, will possess varying abilities to respond aesthetically, or "fill out" a literary work of art of whatever quality. One could distinguish many different groups of readers by reference to the two criteria of communal self-definition and response to aesthetic value,[2] but it is enough here to name only three: the "reading public," the members of the educational institution, and the publishing institution (including, especially, writers).

Ingarden's description of the reading public is typical of an attitude that now, I think, seems old-fashioned and unsophisticated.[3] It is also, may I add, very unlike Ingarden's normal openness. The "preponderant majority of readers," he says, care nothing about a faithful reading. They care only about "their own experience" and their pleasure. He calls them "consumers" and says they are "of interest only to the psychology or sociology of the mass consumption of art" (*Cog.*, 172). Ingarden goes on to attack reading that is merely "a way of having emotional contact with the objects portrayed in the work of art"—for example, "in a novel one is pleasantly moved by the vicissitudes of the 'hero,' one is erotically excited, one becomes ardently interested in the realization of certain social, ethical, or religious ideals, etc.; but all this has nothing in common with the original aesthetic emotion and the values revealed in the aesthetic experience" (*Cog.*, 213).

Despite Ingarden, I think many of us would admit that "all this" has a lot in common with our own early experience of literature, even though as aesthetic response it may have been dubious. All of us, however, might be willing to admit that Ingarden gives an accurate description of the reading habits of many students, at least when they enter our classes.

Still, we can see how genuine a thing literature is (though perhaps not entirely a good thing) because of the change it induces in the reading response of this public, normally consumers. When they read a "classic" they are willing to make some effort beyond mere consumption. But at first it will in all likelihood be an effort of understanding, answering the question "Why do they tell us this book is Literature?" rather than a free activity of realizing aesthetic values. This might prompt us to say, cynically, that literature is an institution wherein art and aesthetic value, if they exist at all, exist to be exploited. Perhaps "expended," in the generous Nietzschean sense, would be a better term.

This view of literature and its functioning in society is based on ideas characteristic of Husserl's phenomenology. The most basic is that, along with the signifiers and the signifieds, communication requires acts of meaning-bestowal. So, in addition to the signs of the work itself and their potential, someone must carry out a particular fulfillment of that potential—a reading or concretization. The second Husserlian idea concerns the schematic nature of the work. No work is complete; in fact, its concretizations always go beyond it in one way or another. Therefore the work always seems more full than it is, because even a faithful reading adds elements which the work does not determine, although it allows them.

Thus seen, the work itself, in its schematic formation, will be different from any and every concretization, but not in the sense of a Platonic idea, since the readings are necessary to fill in and to make the work meaningful or valid, or even available, in an aesthetic sense. This openness of a work's schematic structure is crucial to a definition of literature which emphasizes process.

The objections to attempts at defining literature as a privileged

category are based on either linguistic or general grounds. If
there is no separately-valid literary language apart from ordinary language, one may argue there cannot be a specially-
defined class of "literary" works. This linguistic objection does
not affect my case, for I am not taking a stand on the identifia-
bility of special "literary" language. On the other hand, the
general argument attacks literature because the establishment of
a privileged canon is repugnant in itself; it presumes elitism,
ethnocentrism, and surrender to the institutional machine. My
contention nonetheless is that the most radical anti-literature
spokesmen always rely on a canon, and indeed their own works
form a most distinguished canon. A more practical observation
is that the educational institution, while it may be stultified by a
worship of sacred cows and idols of the tribe, is crippled without
some effective canon. What is needed is an open view of the
works and a dialectic view of the composition of the canon and
of its continual change. The formalists go some way in this
direction when they define literature as the performance of
creative defamiliarization upon an existing canon or repertory of
language. But we require a broader basis than literariness alone
to arrive at a valid concept of literature.

The position of Roland Barthes on this matter is instructive,
but I think it is open to question. Recognizing that the process
has a necessary social side, Barthes posits the "Institution of
Literature" where I suggest the Educational Institution. Barthes
leaves his "institution" up in the air, however, by confining it to
the conventional expectations of readers in general. His conception of *écriture* and of the *scriptible* emancipates "writers" from
such conventional expectations, thereby excluding them from
his Institution of Literature. What socially recognizable agency
then remains to establish the conventional expectations of
readers of books? Only 1) the media in general, 2) the printing
and publishing industry, and 3) the Educational Institution. I
think it is plain—in fact, it is the mark of recognition that what

we are talking about is indeed literature—that only the last, the Educational Institution, provides the indoctrination and the vast majority of the individual judgments involved in setting up and reinforcing literary expectations today. The activity of transforming what Barthes calls "writable" but "unreadable" books into "readable" works is one that can ordinarily occur, in our society, only in the educational institution—which, for all its shortcomings, is still open enough to include such organizations as the Ecole pratique des Hautes Etudes.[4]

Alvin Kernan and E. D. Hirsch have pointed out the sudden and surprisingly recent provenance of "Literature" as a single word tending to supplant such older phrases as "belles-lettres," "polite literature," or the original term "poetry."[5] Literature, used in the current primary sense, entered the European languages in the mid-nineteenth century. Matthew Arnold, though he often used the old term "poetry," really had literature in mind as a human mode of activity focussed in a canon of works that included, besides much that was not poetry, much that was neither belles-lettres nor even literary in the restricted sense of "fine writing." Arnold, like Renan and many others, aimed to institutionalize literature to fill gaps left by the decay of organized religion and the class ethos. It is hard to deny this connection, or to contend that any institution other than literature has stepped forward since Arnold's time. Science, of course, has had important spokesmen, but their important utterances took the form of literature. What we call the media, however great their influence may be, largely reflect in a more or less displaced way the canon of literature. Unless we insist upon defining literature in a historical and social vacuum, therefore, we must not over-emphasize literariness or exclude instrumental as opposed to purely aesthetic writing.[6]

A theory that enables us to distinguish between the literary works and their exploitation in the canon of literature saves us from the odious necessity of positing the literary value of a work

in social esteem or mere popularity. It permits the individual
work an enduring ontic status, regardless of the frequency or
quality of its readings at any given time. But this ontic status, as
I have already said, must not be taken as a mystic essence.
Ingarden makes a careful distinction between the total of merely
individual readings and what he calls a "reconstruction," that is,
a description arrived at by a professional consensus in close
touch with the work, setting forth what is schematically there in
the text to stimulate or to inhibit possible concretizations. A
work will have meant different things to different ages, and
scholars will be able to study this process of change in the status
of a work so as to make comparisons and thus clarify, first, what
really belongs to the work itself, and secondly what distinguishes its concretizations in a particular period. For all his
concentration on the literary work, Ingarden recognized the
necessity of bringing it back into "concrete spiritual and cultural
life"[7] especially because most works contain gaps that need to
be filled in by references to life, and all have potentialities that
need to be made actual by living readers, since their concretizations must always be the form in which the work is apprehended.

I think that we would agree that the term *literature* cannot be
defined in an ultimate sense without reference to "concrete
spiritual and cultural life" in a given community. Some works
achieve a fleeting exemplariness of this life which gives them a
short-lived membership in the canon, despite weak literary
value. Others, though their aesthetic features are not dominant,
nevertheless have a "founding" rather than a merely illustrative
value. A work like Montaigne's *Essais* cannot be "relegated," as
Wellek suggested,[8] to some domain other than literature; not
only was it important to the writing of Shakespeare's plays, but
it still continues to have an active founding influence on contemporary writing.

Literature cannot be defined without some recognition of

literary value inherent in the works. Yet we must acknowledge that the ability to perceive literary value does vary greatly, both in historical time and among readers in any particular epoch; in fact it varies from day to day in the experience of any reader, as Raymond Williams reminds us.[9] Accepting Ingarden's terms, I should argue that a definition of literature ought to include especially those works which are actually living in the sense that some readers are currently making concretizations of them. But the class is always open to deletion and addition. Finally, the definition should take into account that there are at least three (probably more) categories of readers, and that any work is likely to be out of phase, during some part of its life process, with readers in one or more of these groups.

First there is the "reading public." Its normal tendency is to read as consumers, that is, to impose its fantasies or expectations upon a work without full and accurate response to what the work determines or allows. Second are the academic scholars or critics, professionally aware of the existence of innumerable works, but as a group displaying marked shifts of concentrated interest. This sub-community does most to establish the canon of works because of its influence on the reading public through the educational institution. At the same time, the academics antagonize the third group, the writers, because works perceived as living by the academics are dead to the writers, and works enthusiastically concretized by the writers are not yet adequately read by the academics (though, strangely, they sometimes succeed with the reading public). The term *literature*, I suggest, ought to include every work which is "alive" by being in phase with one or more of these groups of readers.

This manner of definition may seem to be too indulgent, or lacking in standards; I would reply that it is merely cautious and realistic. Segments of the consumption-oriented public have occasionally anticipated by many years the interest and favorable judgment of the academic scholar and critic, even in the case of

whole sub-genres of works. And there is, I think, an unavoidable dialectic in which writers will always be striving to transcend and overcome whatever limits the academics may have
defined for literary activity. The definition of literature, therefore, must account for a rather complex combination of processes, each of which proceeds with a rhythm of its own and at a
somewhat different rate from the others. On one side we have
the different groups of readers, who by their concretizations
give actuality to some works, and not to others; on the other side
we have the works, which have fuller or shallower reserves of
potential value, as well as varied staying power with the different reading groups.

I should say, then, that literature is a canon which consists of
those works in language by which a community defines itself
through the course of its history. It includes works primarily
artistic and also those whose aesthetic qualities are only secon-
dary. The self-defining activity of the community is conducted
in the light of the works, as its members have come to read them
(or concretize them). The readings of canonic works change
throughout the course of their establishment in the canon. Also,
works drop out and others are added. The defining and founding of literature thus incurs a kind of consumption, in the form
of over-exposure or over-familiarization, not so much of the
work itself as of those specific concretizations which the community has preferred and become habituated to. Each work has
a life within the canon, depending on how successfully its
readings endure this exposure.

I'd like now to trace the rise and fall of the literary work in the
course of its life, to explain how a work may have a continuing
mode of existence and a value, and yet not be found in the ranks
of literature; and conversely how once-living works of literature
may in actuality come to lack value and become mere dead-
wood. When an audience listens to a formulaic epic, watches a
play, or reads a book, each of its members makes an imaginative

concretization of the work. By virtue of these concretizations, certain works will be co-opted into the canon and count as litera- ture, to be used consciously or unconsciously as a means of self-definition. As the object of a manifold of more or less effec- tive readings over the years, each canonic work develops in one direction or another. It takes on stylistic features, at first only allowed by its structure, but later perceived to inhere in it along with certain other works of the same period. When a crisis of changing style comes along, the work "weathers" it somehow, or else it atrophies and (except, of course, for academic special- ists) ceases to live. The life of a work in its concretizations is thus marked by phases of perfection and enrichment, of consolida- tion and impoverishment, and of eventual atrophy and decay. The language in which it is written may at length lose its power of manifesting literary qualities, until such time as readers can be trained to decipher or translate it so as to restore this power. This most extreme form of change—rebirth—shows that a work, unless stillborn to begin with, does possess a continuing iden- tity.

Through its concretizations the work maintains relationships with generations of readers and writers, who relate it to their concretizations of other works and to their culture and life in general. We can see the work as a sort of force field with its patterns of flow prepared, organized, and directed, but only schematically; this open field still needs to be energized, so to speak, and closed as a circuit by being activated in the reader's imaginative experience. Until then it is "hardly possible," as Ingarden comments, "to foresee how a given specific concreti- zation may be formed" (LW, p. 339). Readings will differ from reader to reader, and even more perhaps from one epoch to another. (Here, by the way, we have a means of distinguishing literary works of art from scientific works or mere records. Works of art are written to sustain a wide range of completions and determinations by the reader. Scientific works employ means intended to narrow down this range as much as possible.)

Thus it may happen that in the course of change a living work may be so transformed, in a single accepted concretization, as to lose its proper identity. It is alive, but no longer itself. Against such "absolutizing" of one reading, Ingarden protested that there should be "in different eras, concretizations of one and the same work that could adequately, or at least in a manner allowed by the work, express its unique features and still differ variously and radically among themselves" (LW, 348). Likewise, we should acknowledge that the "canonization" of a work as a masterpiece of a determinate kind, and its insertion into a "great tradition" as if into a museum, or into a curriculum as one of the workhorses of multi-purpose education, is an invitation to atrophy. This is the "moment" when anti-literature makes its appearance. In their original attacks, Rimbaud and Verlaine had this ossifying and exploitative use of the canon in mind. Artaud and many others, also, had in mind the imprisoning effect of such atrophied but consecrated readings, which remove all freeplay, all rawness, and dictate the tone and content of a pre-cooked response.

We may say, then, that a work may die of over-exposure as well as from neglect. Also, once a divergent reading has reached the point of obscuring it, a work might well go through a long period of falsification, during which it would disappear from currency and be replaced by a counterfeit. A major task of criticism is to unmask such falsifications and to restore the work to its proper appearance. The opposite possibility is that something genuinely new or individual might be introduced in a work. It would call for entirely new acts of self-definition by the community. Set against an order of words already established, and in a society disinclined to re-define itself, it would seem a mere irrelevancy. As Barthes says, it would be "writable" but not "readable." To discover its novel functioning in both the literary and the social context would then be the express concern of criticism.

The special dialectic of literature and anti-literature has been going on just about as long as the concept of literature has existed. The peculiar obnoxiousness of literature, so far as attackers like Verlaine, Apollinaire, and Artaud—or Pound, Williams, and Kenneth Patchen—are concerned, was in part its failure to establish the kind of founding works these writers required, and in part its co-option in support of a secular-liberal ideal of a uniformly rationalized society. The works canonized as literature, concretized in self-serving patterns by an elite, became the objects of attack by writers who were performing in a more radical way the task of social self-definition through imaginative works. Instead of reinforcing accepted patterns, these writers were separating the living from the dead. While life-giving, this dialectical exchange is itself exploitative of all the literary works involved in it. As with movie stars and politicians, any public image attached to a literary work is likely to be a false one. It is the responsibility of the academic critic to save the aesthetic claims of works both old and new from the consequences of their ethical or ideological notoriety. But at the same time, as Hirsch suggests, we should not treat literature as a sanctuary of privilege, where the technically effective is magically fused with the morally good.[10]

In spite of all such obscuration, a work nevertheless exists as one focus of a particular system of changes developing as a typical and uniform whole (to use Ingarden's language).[11] This process of growth, culmination, and decay is characteristic of all life. And, while a literary work does not live in a literal sense, the analogy is strong enough to support the working definition I have offered.

Still, the continuance of a process of change in the concretizations of a work need not mean ever-growing falsification nor inevitable decay. Progressive change along one line of readings may still develop new insights allowed by the work, even after centuries of intense inquiry. A more general truth, however, is, as Ingarden says, "the known fact that every epoch in the over-all development of human culture has its own particular type of understanding, its own aesthetic and nonaesthetic values, its specific predispositions to precisely one and not other modes of apprehending the world in general and works of art in particular" (LW, 348). Such epochal changes have the good effect of preventing exhaustion and dead-ending of many lines of inquiry into literature by diverting us to new and productive approaches. Meanwhile, it is a function of criticism and literary history to retain whatever can be kept valid, though it was achieved along lines that have become outdated. Period studies afford us the training we need to reactivate the successful concretizations achieved in the past, and they should help us to mediate between purely historical readings and ones more in tune with the present epoch. In this way a praxis of criticism develops in an active community of scholars and critics, or better still, in an interacting exchange between this academic group, professional writers, and the reading public. Our field of interaction will still be literature, though it will include many a moment of anti-literature in its process.

## NOTES

1. Roman Ingarden, *The Cognition of the Literary Work of Art* (English translation by Ruth Ann Crowley and Kenneth R. Olson of *Vom Erkennen des literarischen Kunstwerks* [Evanston, Ill., 1973]). Cited as *Cog.* (First published in 1937.)

2. Thomas Roberts, "The Network of Literary Identification," *New Literary History*, 5(1973), 67-90.

3. I prefer the more sympathetic (and, I think, historically accurate) account of Raymond Williams, "The Growth of the Reading Public," in

*The Long Revolution* (New York, 1966), pp. 156-72.

4. See *S/Z* (Paris, 1970), p. 10.

5. E. D. Hirsch, Jr. rejects the dominant present usage, that "Literature comprises any linguistic work, written or oral, which has significant aesthetic qualities," because it gives privileged status to the
aesthetic approach (p. 50). He prefers a return to a definition of Literature that "covers everything worth preserving in written form" (p. 53).
See "Some Aims of Criticism" in *Literary Theory and Structure: Essays in
Honor of William K. Wimsatt* (New Haven, 1973), pp. 41-62, and Alvin B.
Kernan, "The Idea of Literature," *NLH*, 5(1973), 31-40.

6. Kernan (p. 34) points to much recent criticism as functioning to
impute "literariness" by rather un-literary associations in an "aesthetic
of justification" depending on psychology, mythology, and form.

7. Roman Ingarden, *The Literary Work of Art.* English translation by
George Grabowicz of *Das literarische Kunstwerk* (Evanston, Ill., 1973).
Cited here as *LW*.

8. *Theory of Literature* (New York, 1956), p. 26.

9. See Williams, p. 172.

10. Hirsch, p. 62n.

11. For many of the ideas presented in this paper, see Ingarden's *The
Literary Work of Art,* pp. 343-55, dealing with "The 'life' of a literary
work in its concretizations, and its transformations as a result of
changes in the latter" (first published in 1931).

# A Procedural Definition of Literature

## *Charles Altieri*

It is obvious that we do not need to define literature, for the fact that we have yet to agree on a definition does not prevent us from enjoying literary works and discussing them intelligently. Moreover, as Morris Weitz points out, definitions can do as much harm as good since they both call attention to features of literary works that may not be noticed and tend to narrow our concerns to those particular features which the theorist considers important.[1] An adequate definition is worth seeking nonetheless if it can show the limits of particular methodologies and keep us alive to the variety of experiences literary texts can produce.

There are two basic observations which can open the way for a new way of defining literature—not in the terms of necessary and sufficient conditions which are required for analytic definitions but in terms of the actual procedures that we follow when we take a text as a literary one.[2] First we must recognize that something's being literature is not a natural fact about an object like its being of a certain extension, weight and color. For if that were true, we could not explain a phenomenon unique to literature among the humanities, that certain texts which originally had as their primary purpose a non-literary function came to be taken as essentially literary works in the course of time. A given text may become material for a historian, but it does not become a work of history the way the Bible, *The Decline and Fall of the Roman Empire*, or *The Laws of Ecclesiastical Polity* became works of literature.

Second, we must notice that we frequently take literary works in ways not intended by the author, even if we know his intentions from signs embedded in the text. Many contemporary poets, like Allen Ginsberg, seek to break through the idea of persona and present their work as the author's direct personal speech addressing an audience. Yet we take such poems less as personal speech than as performance, to be understood and assessed in terms of the intellectual, moral, and emotional qualities they exhibit in response to what we take as a dramatic situation. And we immediately generalize the situation: the poem becomes not simply a man speaking to others but an image of how one can respond to a situation that is typical of an age, a general human problem, and a particular style of thinking and feeling. In a similar way surrealist writers desire to break down all conventions to present the immediacy of experience before language structures it, yet we take surrealist texts primarily as images of a way to organize experience under the influence of certain beliefs and attitudes. We can summarize this second observation by noting that literary attempts to deny the conventions of literature may slightly change the way we read, but we eventually transform these dreams of transforming consciousness into alternative structures of experience to be treated with the same aesthetic attitude and roughly the same procedures we employ in reading what they attack.

Now what can we make of these observations? The first observation suggests in concrete terms why philosophers like Morris Weitz insist that there can be no analytic definition of terms like art and literature (if "literature" is to mean anything *imaginative creations not objectively identifiable with concrete external reality*

more than printed matter.) For terms like *literature* are terms we know how to use but not to define. We learn to apply such terms through the experience of reading certain kinds of texts, and the general term is in effect a cluster-concept that suffices when some of a wide variety of "family resemblances" are present. There are conditions for using the term *literature*, but they vary, and specific features of the object are not necessary to justify its use. It is apparent, for example, that texts which initially served other primary functions will probably not have the same basic features of those written as literature. But there are other aspects of my two observations which suggest that the case of definition is not as simple as Weitz makes it. While analytic definition of objective features might be impossible, there may be shared properties in the procedures that take place once the term *literature* is evoked that enable us to describe how the term is used. As Maurice Mandelbaum points out, the common features justifying terms like *art* and *literature* need not be "specific, directly exhibited" features: the common properties can be "relational attributes" which emerge from our sense of a common origin (as with a family) or, I would add, common procedures evoked.[3]

Both of my initial observations suggest the presence of common conventions established by the fact that society takes a text as a literary one. When we take the Bible primarily as literature, for example, we accept the fact that it no longer serves as an explanation of the empirical world or univocal guide to conduct. We shift our attention from its explanatory to its performative functions and treat it as an act of trying to explain and interpret experience—to be assessed not in terms of truth and falsity but by the emotional and intellectual qualities it exhibits as a way of relating to the empirical world. The case of the Bible, in fact, is very similar to what happens when we adapt Ginsberg or surrealist writing to literary conventions. The general procedures remain constant despite the wide variety of objective features and intentions.

It is, of course, much easier to claim that a procedural
definition is possible than to give one. But before I attempt one it
will help to examine two powerful but opposed recent treatments of the question, "What is literature?" in order to provide a
sense of the problems and issues involved and to demonstrate
the importance of my initial observations. The first essay, E.D.
Hirsch's "Some Aims of Criticism," illustrates some of the
humanistic implications inherent in Weitz's rejection of specific
features as a necessary condition of a work's being literary.[4]
Hirsch sees his position as an Arnoldian one: he argues that
modern criticism cannot adequately realize its aim of demon-
strating the moral role of literature because it remains trapped in
a nineteenth-century vision of "literature" as an essentially aesthetic concept. The New Critics are a case in point. They were
committed to showing the moral values of literature, but they
insisted that literary works had first to be appreciated in terms of
their essence as aesthetic artifacts (42). They felt it a betrayal of
literature simply to assess the direct moral and religious claims
some writers clearly intended to make (51). The need for aesthetic categories arises, Hirsch claims, from our mistakenly
taking "literature" as a concept entailing some essential, distinguishing aesthetic qualities. That equation, however, emerged
only in the nineteenth century and has no ontological basis. The
proper formulation is that "aesthetic categories are intrinsic to
aesthetic inquiries, but not to the nature of literary works" (52).
And we can not have an adequate educational program for
literary studies until we learn to supplement aesthetic inquiry
with procedures for analyzing basic instrumental and moral
values that writers intend to achieve through their work.

It is difficult to assess Hirsch's claims because they are on the
one hand so simple and apparently obvious once made and, on
the other, so revolutionary to those of us who learned how to
read from the New Critics. On an abstract level, I think, he
confuses two notions of essence—the idea of determining qual-

ities, which he rightly rejects, and the idea of conventional procedures characterizing a term, which I still think necessary to
explain the specific instrumental values and modes of assess-
ment associated with literary texts. Hirsch insists that the only
logical task of criticism is "to construct meaning" (51), but the
meanings we construct will depend on the procedures we think
appropriate. It would be easier to judge his argument if one
could be sure what he means by "aesthetic categories." Does the
term refer primarily to the use of formal and rhetorical analytic
methods, or is he after bigger game and claiming that our general attitude toward the texts we call literature is wrong? It
seems that he is making the stronger claim that even what may
loosely be called an aesthetic attitude is not necessarily a proper
way to approach texts written before the nineteenth century.
Here it is difficult to marshal sufficient evidence, or even to
know what would be sufficient evidence, to refute or support
his claim. Can we really be sure that religious poets like Milton
and Herbert did not intend their works to be aesthetic versions
of religious experience? If they did not, they certainly went to a
great deal of hardly explicable trouble. And even if we knew
their intentions, why should we believe that their intentions
would overcome the power of convention any more than
Ginsberg or the Surrealists can today? Moreover, it will not
suffice to show that the term *literature* had no aesthetic implications before the nineteenth century. One would have to examine
all the related terms—poem, romance, story, even essay—in
order to show no common aesthetic assumptions. This is on the
face of it unlikely at least for poetry, and, as Thomas McFarland
makes clear, the term *poetry* was a widely used one to describe
utterances that invoked aesthetic (but not formal) responses.[5]
And if we go back to classical defenses of poetry, we find Sidney
quite explicit on the conventions that fictional discourse evokes
and we see Milton, the poet who would be least satisfied with a
sheerly aesthetic response, nonetheless defining the poetic

function with special emphasis on displaying the generalizable qualities of an experience seen as a process:

> "Whatsoever in religion is holy and sublime, in virtue amiable or grave, whatsoever hath passion or admiration in all the changes of that which is called fortune, or the wily subtelties and refluxes of man's thoughts, all these things with a solid and treatable smoothness to paint out and describe."[6]

What gives literature its instrumental value is the capacity it has developed in us to take a variety of statements and consider them as ways of being in the world, irrespective of their value in describing its objective structure.

Richard Ohmann's essay, "Speech Acts and the Definition of Literature," takes an opposite position from Hirsch's, largely to achieve a similar defense of the humane, and not simply formal, values in literary texts. Where Hirsch feels the need to deny that literature can be analytically defined, Ohmann rests his case on the possibility of giving it a new analytic definition that explains why many of the properties attributed to literature in previous definitions had some truth. Literature, he argues, may be defined as a species of the genus "discourse" and differentiated from other members of that genus by the particular kind of linguistic act it presents:

> A literary work is a discourse whose sentences lack the illocutionary forces that would normally attach to them. Its illocutionary force is mimetic. By "mimetic," I mean purportedly imitative. Specifically a literary work purportedly imitates (or reports) a series of speech acts, which in fact have no other existence. By doing so, it leads the reader to imagine a speaker, a situation, a set of ancillary events, and so on. Thus one might say that the literary work is mimetic in an extended sense also: it "imitates" not only an action (Aristotle's term), but an indefinitely detailed imaginary setting for its quasi-speech-acts.[7]

This definition, he claims, integrates the valid insights in other definitions of literature: (1) it shows how literature can be called mimetic—not because it copies experience but because it directs us to recreate imaginatively a world in which the speech acts presented would be significant; (2) it shows how literature is distinct from referential discourse because it structures possible references into an imaginary world; (3) it shows that the emotive properties of literary discourse derive from the reader's need to place the illocutionary act in a full dramatic situation; (4) it shows how literature can be seen as autonomous play since the speech acts lack their usual force and do not involve author or reader in real obligations and responsibilities; (5) finally it shows why we tend to define literature as discourse where implicit meanings predominate since the utterances are freed from normal illocutionary work and thus invite us simply to contemplate the complexities of the experience presented.

Ohmann's attempted definition ignores many of the facts Hirsch tried to explain, for both men are arguing within the impossible parameters established by the dream of analytic definition, and thus neither can be adequate to the various ways literature relates to reality. The theory of literary discourse from the point of view of illocutionary force, for example, ignores authorial intentions which are clearly present as objective features in certain texts. The *Oresteia, Paradise Regained,* and the *Kreutzer Sonata* obviously aim to modify the beliefs and the behavior of their readers. (They might not succeed, but no analysis of objective features can explain why.) Other texts, like the examples I have mentioned in my second observation, obviously seek to avoid imitating illocutions, or imitating anything, in their quest for immediate presentation of feelings. In both cases Ohmann is right in his description of what happens to the force the author wants to give the utterance, but he cannot explain why apparently objective features do not take hold as they were intended. For he insists that literature can be defined as a "natural class" of objects, and hence is committed to the "directly exhibited" features of works. The extreme result of such a position is that he is forced to deny that *In Cold Blood* or the New Journalism can be literature at all because both claim to describe a real world and not to imitate the act of description. Claims about the "nature" of certain types of objects make ideologues of us all.

Hirsch asserts that there is no common feature of literary texts, Ohmann that there is one; yet both end up denying obvious truths. The reason, I think, is that neither heeds the distinction in recent philosophy between "natural" and "institutional" facts. Thus, for them, either an object can be defined in terms of objective features or it has at best the loose identity of a family-resemblance concept. Institutional facts, however, can be defined in a different way provided that we understand their nature. Institutional facts depend for their existence on rules and procedures developed by a society and can only be understood by recognizing how the procedures are established. We cannot, for example, understand chess by observing common features in every game; we must learn the rules and come to understand something of the strategy by which the rules are used. We must, in short, see the kind of predicates a society employs when the game is being played. With chess or with literature, we can easily apply Wittgenstein's dictum, "Only someone who knows how to do something with it can significantly ask a name."[8] In these cases we do not derive names from objects but learn what the object is by seeing how names are applied and predicates given. We know what literature is when we know what we characteristically learn to do when we are told a text is a literary one. And one of the things we learn to do when we read is to alter certain authorial intentions and at times to impose features like coherence in texts which do not clearly possess it. Ohmann unwittingly (one might say ironically if his text were literary) admits as much when he criticizes other treatments of natural defining features of a literary text as pointing not to what tells us the work is literature, but rather to the facts which we recognize as a consequence of our knowing the texts to *be* literary works (6, 8).

A procedural definition of literature has a good deal in common with "response" theories of aesthetics, for it defines both the nature of the literary object and its implicit purposiveness in terms of the kinds of response the text produces. But a procedural theory has two advantages. It does not require that the theorist explain the various aspects of response in terms of specific recurrent properties in literary texts. Such an explanation may be possible, but a procedural theory is content to argue that the essential properties of literary response are created by education and exposure rather than by necessary and sufficient conditions in the object. And as a consequence, a procedural theory need not be bothered by differences in response. It tries only to establish the kinds of questions one asks of a text and the qualities he tends to look for. It suggests the paths people follow in responding to what they take as literary utterances and does not pretend to determine the various places those paths lead. The second advantage follows naturally. A procedural approach explains why it is so difficult to specify analytic definitions of literature, and it also suggests why there are borderline cases. Social conventions in general are not susceptible to logical analysis, because we do not learn terms like *literature* or procedures for reading it in the same way we do the rules of mathematics. We learn by example and by imitating teachers and critics, so that we tend to have a much richer fund of information and behavioral strategies than we can easily explain. When we read a text, we have implicitly operating a history of other texts and of questions we put often without being self-conscious about them. The competent reader is like a trained athlete, whose skills far outweigh his explanatory powers and whose actions combine required moves with a continual possibility for free improvisation.

Once it is shown that literary works invoke conventions by being rather than by imitating illocutionary acts, it is fairly easy to show the kind of procedures invoked, though only in a general way since, as history indicates, they take myriad individual forms. The basic step is to distinguish two sets of procedures—one consisting of general purposes sought and questions asked, and the other constituting specific ways of adapting these purposes and questions when there are signs we are dealing with a particular genre, mode, or historical period. Again it is difficult to define the different approaches required by specific genres, but we can easily recognize misreadings once we have learned by samples and examples what the procedures are. Rather than try to delineate these procedures, I will try to give an example that will show in what ways they are present. Let us imagine someone actually asking a question that might require us to define literature. Suppose he asks, "Is Spenser really literature?" or, "How can you say Olson's poems or Robbe-Grillet's novels are literature; they seem nonsense to me?" Obviously it would not be very helpful to say, "Of course they are; literature has the following properties and I can point out each one in a given text." Our questioner is not asking us to apply a definition; he is asking us to show him how the text can be approached with the same general questions and purposes he applies to other texts. But we can not immediately give these general answers. We must make him familiar with the specific questions. Suppose we send him out to read several Robbe-Grillet novels and some (good) criticism. He might still be unable to explain why these works are literary, but the question diminishes as his ability to read the texts increases. He no longer requires the guidance of the more general conventions because he has learned to respond to more particular keys. The question, "Is this literature?" gives way to more particular ones like, "Why does Robbe-Grillet present this specific description in this part of the novel?" What seemed a theoretical problem gets resolved on a very practical level because the general conditions were not in doubt, only a problem of applying them.[9]

We need still, however, to suggest what the general conditions are—a problem very much like Augustine's attempt to define them. He felt he knew what it was until he tried to explain it; then time seemed unintelligible. For time, like literature, has no abstract existence; there are only specific situations in which we experience it in a variety of ways. We can nonetheless suggest an answer by examining what a literary education consists of. The general education of well-trained readers tends to develop a sense of what literature is by teaching them to read a set of canonical texts—Homer, Vergil, Shakespeare, selected works of lyric poetry and representative novels. These texts develop two basic expectations—that we should be able to sympathize with the conditions, actions, feelings, and thoughts of the principal characters and that we should be able to reflect upon the potential general significance of their actions, feelings, etc., by considering the rhetorical and structural patterns informing the text. Now it is precisely to be able to carry on both activities that we need to become familiar with the specific conventions of genres, styles, and periods. And it is in direct proportion to our developing facility to carry on these activities with a text that we cease to worry whether it is literature. In difficult cases like Robbe-Grillet, we must learn to locate our sympathies with the novelistic voice rather than with the characters and we must see how the thematic patterns function primarily as ironic counterpoints to traditional themes. An enemy twin, however, is still a twin, once we recognize his paternity.

There are three consequences of my proposed definition of general procedures. First it is impossible to draw a sharp line between descriptive and normative uses of the term *literature*. For the descriptive sense of the term depends ultimately on applying procedures we learn from exposure to canonical texts. To rephrase T.S. Eliot's well-known interrelation of tradition and individual talent, new literary creations depend on the canon for their identity, while at the same time, by forcing us to readapt the procedures we have learned, they also change the canon somewhat and open new possibilities for literary experience. Second, because the definition of literature depends on procedures and not on objective conditions shared by all texts, any theory of literature claiming general relevance must prove its explanatory powers on the loose grouping of canonical texts. Otherwise theories become mere analogues, providing explanatory contexts for specific kinds of texts. Finally, we can see that the provenance of the term literature grows problematic in proportion to the difficulty we have in applying the kind of response we learn to give these canonical texts. When we find it difficult to empathize with particular actors (as with the New Novel) or to discern formal patterns controlling our reflections on the significance of the action (as originally with naturalism or now with texts like in *In Cold Blood*), we withhold the name literature. It goes without saying then that what critics do is to show us how we can apply these procedures. We can see the New Novel as a drama of an author's struggle with signification in terms of a modern problematic of language and reference, or we can come to see how Capote arranges his actions to suggest their possible significance.

Wittgenstein suggests that when one is trying to define a term that derives its meaning from our ways of acting he try to clarify it by posing "intermediate cases." An intermediate case locates the phenomenon by reminding us of how it is distinguished from related activities. When the term in question is *literature*, we find that the argument from intermediate cases has the sanction of a long tradition which defined literature by contrasting it to history and philosophy. I shall conclude, then, by trying a different tack on an old issue. I shall contrast literature to the other two disciplines by examining what changes would occur if we were to treat philosophy and history *as* works of literature.

We notice first that a literary approach would involve a different perspective than is usual in these disciplines to what may loosely be called the characters in the work. In normal history, characters are seen as people uniquely defined by their specific traits, situations, choices, and the effects of their actions, while in philosophy, references to human cases are normally pure examples, shorn of individual traits.[10] A literary approach to the same texts tends, as Ohmann suggests, to see traces of universal attitudes toward experience in historical characters and to find moral principles at play in the relationship between actions and consequences. No reader of modern British philosophy will doubt the difference between its treatment of human characters in examples and literary treatments of character, but we might notice also that as philosophy becomes more psychological, for example in Sartre, the examples become almost more important and more revealing than the abstract arguments. In pure literary texts, characters tend to raise universal questions and attitudes while retaining our interest in them as individuals.

A second example, drawn from different senses we have of the author of a text and the status of his arguments, makes the differences more pronounced. In pure cases, we are not interested in the authorial stance of those who write history or philosophy; we abstract the descriptions or the arguments and measure them against what we can find as the facts or what we take to be the canons of coherent argument. And even when historians or philosophers do attend to the authorial stance and treat the argument as at least partially determined by that stance, they root the determining factors either in the author's historical situation or in the logical models or paradigms he employs. A literary approach, on the other hand, attends primarily to the specific ways the author's needs and purposes shape his argument. The critic notices, for example, the fear of a world without values which generates the systems of Kant and Hegel.[11] And he is not content with historical or logical explana-

tions; he wants to give the author's struggles to form and overcome his problems the status of a recurrent possibility for the
mind's activities. He is not content to describe an action; rather
he tries to indicate how the action itself becomes a possible type
or model not to be abstracted but to be generalized by developing the dramatic movement of the text as a characteristic means
men use to establish imaginative order. Thus instead of dismiss-
ing a work for its mistakes or blindness, he tries to show how
these problems are symptomatic of a particular attitude toward
experience. For the literary critic it is the blindness perhaps more
than the insight which allows him to construct his dramatic
treatment of various historical and philosophical perspectives.

We might generalize these differences in the following way:
the reader of history is satisfied when the author is erased and
his arguments and descriptions become necessary to gaining a
full picture of the situation, while the reader of philosophy desires to have all particulars absorbed into the objective criteria
for valid abstract arguments. The reader of literature tries to
perform both activities at once—to understand the dramatic
situation as a particular experience and to reflect upon the implicit activity of the author as he imposes his formal and thematic argument on the situation. This is the reason why literature
so often appears capable of being everywhere and nowhere, of
being more philosophical than history and more concrete than
philosophy, while at the same time being more empty than history and less rigorous, less useful than philosophy. Each of its
two basic actions tends in many cases to defer and displace the
other, so both became problematic. This inherent instability between the possible fullness of concrete universals and possible
reductions of literary images to mere fictions masking and sup-
plementing authorial desires constitutes one more inescapable
fact when we examine what we actually do when we take a text
as a literary one.

# NOTES

1. Morris Weitz, "The Role of Theory in Aesthetics," *Journal of Aesthetics and Art Criticism*, 15 (1956), 27-35. This is the classical argument against the possibility of analytically defining art.

2. I say that a procedural definition is a new approach to the question, "What is literature?", but it is by now quite common in general aesthetics. See especially F.E. Sparshott, *The Structure of Aesthetics* (Toronto: Univ. of Toronto Press, 1963), pp. 99-104, 431, and see the works by Dickie and Tilghman cited below. Jonathan Culler's *Structuralist Poetics* (Ithaca: Cornell Univ. Press, 1975), which I came upon after preparing much of this essay, shares my sense of procedures as determining what literature is and gives a very nice explanation of how structuralist techniques can show how these procedures work. Culler's concern, however, is more practical than mine and he really deals with the issue of convention only in discussing poetry.

3. Mandelbaum, "Family Resemblance and Generalizations Concerning the Arts," in Morris Weitz, ed., *Problems in Aesthetics* (New York: Macmillan, 1970), p. 187. For Mandelbaum the basic relational attribute uniting the arts is our awareness of the artist's intention to make a work of art, a genetic procedure rather than the one for which I argue, but my second observation above indicates some of the problem in taking intention as a norm. For another literary critique of Weitz see Meyer H. Abrams, "What's the Use of Theorizing about the Arts?" in Morton Bloomfield, ed., *In Search of Literary Theory* (Ithaca: Cornell Univ. Press, 1972), pp. 3-54.

4. E.D. Hirsch, "Some Aims of Criticism," in Frank Brady, John Palmer, and Martin Price, eds., *Literary Theory and Structure* (New Haven: Yale Univ. Press, 1973), pp. 41-62. I will cite this and the next essay I discuss by putting page numbers in parentheses in the text.

5. Thomas McFarland, "Poetry and the Poem: The Structure of Poetic Content," in *Literary Theory and Structure*, pp. 81-113.

6. For Sidney, "The Defense of Poesie," in Allan H. Gilbert, ed., *Literary Criticism: Plato to Dryden*, pp. 409-417, 439-440, and for Milton see the selection from *The Reason of Church Government* in Gilbert, ed., p. 590.

7. Ohmann, "Speech Acts and the Definition of Literature," *Philosophy and Rhetoric*, 4 (1971), 1-19, p. 14. This essay is the best and most philosophical of a series of essays Ohmann has written on the ways of using the concept of illocutionary acts to discuss literature. I discuss the

whole series at much greater length in "The Poem as Act: A Way to Reconcile Presentational and Mimetic Theories," *Iowa Review* 6 (1975), 103-124. There I also develop more fully the concept of "keying," mentioned later in this paper. For an interesting discussion of Ohmann, plus a claim for one further defining feature when a work does not fit Ohmann's category see Monroe Beardsley's essay in *Literary Theory and Structure*. And for the best treatment I know of analytically definable features in literature see Beardsley, "Aesthetic Theory and Educational Theory," in Ralph Smith, ed., *Aesthetic Concepts in Education* (Urbana: Univ. of Illinois Press, 1970), pp. 1-11. But even so good an attempt will not show that features like unity are a property of texts rather than a result of the fact that we are trained to relate the various elements to a coherent whole (even if the coherence is an image of incoherence) when we read a text labeled literary. On this point, see Culler's excellent discussion of how the claim that something is a poem invokes a set of conventional procedures, pp. 161-188. I might add the fact, so curious to one seeking analytic definitions, that there is nothing especially odd in our giving unified interpretations to unfinished poems like "Kubla Khan" or the second "Hyperion."

8. *Philosophical Investigations*, trans., G.E.M. Anscombe (New York: Macmillan, 1958), sec. 31.

9. I am using here a subtle argument developed by Stanley Cavell to show analogues between aesthetic experience and Wittgenstein's therapeutic model of philosophical questions being made to disappear. See "Aesthetic Problems of Modern Philosophy," in Max Black, ed., *Philosophy in America*, (Ithaca: Cornell University Press), pp. 83 ff. For the idea that questions like "What is literature?" are used primarily in contexts where a reader is puzzled about how to proceed, see B.R. Tilghman, "Wittgenstein, Games, and Art," *Journal of Aesthetics and Art Criticism*, 31 (1972-73), 519-524.

10. I am dividing up a series of cases that in practice exist as a continuum, but my case is evident when we consider the ideals of history and philosophy posed by many analytic philosophers. They state their demands as a need for rigor which eliminates literary and imaginary elements from these more "scientific" modes of discourse.

11. For a good example of differences between literary and philosophical treatments of the same texts, compare the discussions of Hegel in M. H. Abrams, *Natural Supernaturalism*, (New York: Norton, 1971) with those by Maurice Mandelbaum in *History, Man, and Reason* (Baltimore: Johns Hopkins University Press, 1971). Also consider Kenneth Burke's

lovely dramatistic readings of philosophical problems like the nature of substance in his *Grammar of Motives* (Berkeley: University of California Press, 1969). One might also consider what happens to philosophy when Jacques Derrida looks at it through the literary context of self-referential structures. See his "White Mythology: Metaphor in the Text of Philosophy," *New Literary History*, 6 (1974), 5-74. And finally, for a literary analysis of historians, see Hayden White, *Metahistory* (Baltimore: Johns Hopkins Univ. Press, 1973).

# Prolegomena Grammatologica: Literature as the Disembodiment of Speech

*Elias L. Rivers*

Despite the remarkable progress made during the past two centuries in our understanding of the history and structure of languages, we still have no comprehensive theory within which to organize all our knowledge of this central area of human culture. Comparative philology, from the nineteenth century on, has given us an increasingly firm grip upon the historical ramifications of certain major groups of languages and dialects: Indo-European, Far Eastern, Amerindian. Twentieth-century structural linguistics continues to clarify our vision of the synchronic hierarchies that exist within individual languages and within language systems in general. But the student of those linguistic artifacts known as works of literature has not yet developed satisfactory methods of analysis and synthesis. Philology and linguistics supply the literary scholar and critic with tools and models which he can hardly avoid using; but they obviously do not provide ready-made answers to all his problems. The study of language, in the broadest sense of the word, must include the study of literature, for literature uses language in peculiar ways and within special contexts. But structural linguistics has tended to neglect certain aspects of language—

semantic, sociological, psychological—which are essential to an understanding of its literary uses.

One of these neglected aspects of language is the difference between spoken and written systems, including the dialectical interplay between these two types of systems. In the case of written literature, which is most of what literature we have, this difference is fundamental. But historical philology depends upon written evidence, with no first-hand spoken data; and synchronic linguistics tries to ignore traditional writing systems, seen as a distortion of the "real" language, the spoken language upon which linguistics has concentrated. It is true, of course, that the human race spoke long before it wrote, and that the normal child easily learns to speak his "mother tongue" before he goes to school—if he does go—and laboriously learns to read and write—if he does learn. The *Urerlebnis* of spoken language can be considered a central part of "human nature"; the *Bildungserlebnis* of written language is at best a cultural "second nature." Hence linguists have tried to justify giving exclusive attention to the former and deliberately ignoring the latter. But the literary critic can no longer afford such ignorance.

Beginning with Champollion's decipherment of Egyptian hieroglyphics in 1822, a great deal has been discovered about the invention and evolution of systems of writing, which is a relatively recent development in human culture. We now know that, about 3000 B.C., Sumerian word-syllabic pictograms began their evolution toward cuneiform phonograms, most notably in the Akkadian syllabary of about 2500 B.C.[1] Similarly and almost simultaneously, Egyptian word-syllabic pictograms began their evolution toward phonograms and the Semitic syllabaries, or consonantal alphabets, dating from about 1700 B.C. The most important of these, the Phoenician syllabary (1000 B.C.), was eventually adapted, without fundamental changes, to transcribe other Semitic languages such as Hebrew (500 B.C.) and Arabic (500 A.D.). Much later, a similar but apparently independent development of Chinese word-syllabic pictograms, ideograms and phonograms, beginning about 1500 B.C., eventually gave rise to Japanese syllabaries (500 A.D.) and to modern Korean script. But, for European (and, hence, world-wide) culture, the crucial event was the contact, about 1000 B.C., between the Phoenician syllabary and certain Indo-European languages, both Anatolian and Hellenic; this contact between a Semitic writing system which recorded only consonants, and another family of languages with a radically different morphophonemic structure, resulted in the unique invention of the true alphabet, with both vowels and consonants. With its Latin and other derivatives, the Greek development and use of the alphabet is one of the most significant technological events underlying Western culture.

The impact of writing upon a traditional culture is not necessarily democratic.[2] The literate cleric or clerk may well represent the interests of a conservative minority, as he did in ancient Egypt or China. But even in such cases as these, the technical transformation of spoken language into script has a potentially revolutionary impact upon the culture, which previously could be transmitted only by oral tradition. The evanescent airy word could barely transcend time and space by laborious human repetition; the visible, portable word on stone or paper sustains itself through time and space in dehumanized silence. Mouth-to-ear contact with oral tradition, reinforced by face-to-face gestures of pride and shame, gave way, in part at least, to written codes of law, signed contracts and sacred texts. The homeostatic flexibility of oral legends tended to be displaced by rigidly fixed written records. Timeless ritualistic reenactment began to yield to linear historicity.

The invention of a writing system brings with it the disembodiment of language: the idiosyncratic physiological gestures of each person's *parole* are screened out by the abstraction of writing, which is a major step toward the discovery of the uniform underlying system of *langue*. The Greek alphabet, with its vowels and consonants, clearly anticipating the phonemic principle of structural linguistics, made possible the development of Greek grammar, rhetoric and logic, as well as that of historiography, literature and philosophy. In his *Prologue to Greek Literacy* (Cincinnati, 1971), Eric A. Havelock has imaginatively recreated the process which he calls "the transcription of the code of a non-literate culture," for example, the writing down of oral compositions traditionally attributed to Homer. This transcription represents, not one particular rhapsodic performance of the *Iliad* or *Odyssey*, but an ideal reconstruction of the traditional poetic *langue* which underlay many performative *paroles*.[3] We do not know how this transcription was accomplished, or how long the process lasted; textual critics apparently continued to consult rhapsodes even in Hellenistic times. But the fact is that Classic Greek culture had as its point of departure the juxtaposition of an unusually rich tradition of oral formulaic composition, transformed into written texts, and a powerful new potential for written composition; and such a juxtaposition was made possible by the inventive use of alphabetic writing. This juxtaposition explains Plato's critique of Homer; even though Plato paradoxically defended oral thought and discussion while composing written dialogues, he was always unambiguously opposed to the oral tradition of the rhapsodes, which he condemned as an anti-philosophical basis for the education of youth. But Greek philosophers and scientific historians, such as Thucydides, who depended more and more upon written composition, were never fully independent of the strong oral tradition institutionalized by the reciters of poetic texts and by the rhetoricians. The classical tradition of Greece and Rome preserved within itself an important oral dimension.[4]

Latin alphabetic culture began by being derivative. While Classical Greek literature was essentially monoglossic, Classical Latin literature was fundamentally bilingual: the immediate presence of literary Greek, in its Hellenistic sophistication, was felt constantly by Vergil, Horace and Cicero. Greek works were translated and imitated as models, and this greatly influenced the development of a Latin literary language.[5] The earlier poets, besides borrowing Greek words directly, deliberately revived Latin lexical and inflectional archaisms, collected rare dialectal terms, and invented compound words according to Greek models; Greek meters filtered the Latin language, excluding some traditional combinations of words and encouraging other less traditional combinations. By the time of Vergil, the adornments of Greek rhetorical composition had been assimilated into verse; balanced periods and similar devices are particularly noticeable in the speeches of Vergil's characters. In prose, Cicero not only helped establish a puristic and rationalistic grammatical code, but also invented the essential vocabulary of European abstract thought by translating Greek terms. Traditional parataxis gave way to Ciceronian hypotaxis, which maintained the same grammatical subject throughout long involved periods.

Now as soon as this classical literary style of written Latin became established as a conventional language, or sub-set of languages, used for epic, pastoral and satiric poetry and for rhetorical, philosophical and historical prose, a gap began to grow between that standardized literary language and the whole range of fluctuating and evolving vernaculars spoken in Italy and in other parts of the Roman Empire. The urbane and elegant restrictions of classical style excluded these "Vulgar Latin" vernaculars, which were never adequately recorded in writing. We can only try to reconstruct Vulgar Latin, both by working backward from the Romance languages, and by studying certain contemporary evidence found in the Roman grammarians, in popular farces and even in Cicero's own familiar letters. The famous banquet scene, or "Cena Trimalchionis," in Petronius's *Satyricon* gives us what seems to be a true "whiff of the gutter," socially, linguistically and literarily speaking.[6]

At the same time, there was nothing particularly unusual or

necessarily unstable in the polaric and complementary relationship between the classical written language, on the one hand,
and the less rigidly codified vernaculars, on the other. Such a
relationship constitutes a system which has been described and
analyzed by Charles Ferguson as "diglossia"[7]; it exists today not
only in German-speaking Switzerland, but in Haiti and in
China, in Greece and in the Arab world. Characteristically, an
individual first learns a vernacular at home and later learns the
standard written language at school. In diglossia, the written
language is thought of as the "real" language, and the vernaculars as illiterate corruptions. Neither prescriptive grammarians
nor descriptive linguists have ever studied adequately the
dialectical relationship between the two subsystems. With Fred
W. Householder, however, we must recognize that not only in
diglossic, but in all literate societies, an effective "primacy of
writing" becomes established.[8] Insofar as written and spoken
languages overlap, each linguistic sign has a double specification, or *significant*, one being phonemic or morphophonemic,
and the other orthographic or morphographemic; but the rules
are always much simpler for deriving the phonemic specification
from the graphemic specification than are the rules for moving
in the opposite direction. Hence the great stabilizing power of
writing within established literate cultures, whether protodi-
glossic, diglossic, or even bilingual, when only one of the two
languages has social prestige in writing.

The Roman Empire was coterminous with a diglossic or bilingual world of cultural communication. There was no primarily
linguistic cause for change. But, given a growing military and
political instability, this world could be transformed by the social
revolution of a Jewish sect called Christianity, which eventually
established a special variety of Vulgar Latin to replace the Classical standard. A lower-class secret society of biblical true believers developed a new anti-aristocratic and anti-pagan mode of
communal life, with its own jargon, neologisms and semantic

shifts. Coming from the eastern Mediterranean, Christianity's first language was a vulgar Greek vernacular, or koiné, the language of the New Testament, of St. Paul's Epistle to the Romans; for Roman Christians themselves were at first largely Greek-speaking slaves and immigrants. But translations soon came to be a necessity for Latin-speaking converts; and these translations were not elegant Classical versions, but clumsy literal ones, with many new Greek loan-words, and many Latin neologisms, invented to avoid established pagan usage. The ecclesiastical and liturgical use of this Christian dialect of Vulgar Latin gradually raised it from the gutter, giving it a special new dignity and sanctity, much to the disgust of Classical pagan aristocrats, who were being replaced by Christian bishops as the leaders of the new society.

Classical Latin then began to lose its reading public. The patristic writings of St. Augustine and other fathers of the Latin Church, along with St. Jerome's self-consciously philological revision of the Vulgate Bible, established a written ecumenical Latin as the new standard language of the Western world. Erich Auerbach has explained better than anyone else the stylistic revolution implicit in this shift.[9] The humility, or earthiness, of Christ's incarnation and crucifixion brought about an inversion of the Classical scale of aristocratic values: the lowest bodily aspects of life came to constitute, not low comedy, but sublime tragedy. The glory of physical suffering, or passion, was a radically new concept, expressible only in the radically new language of the Christian Church. This new Latin, very close to the vernaculars at first, was the basis of Europe's medieval diglossia or bilingualism.

Thanks to the work of philologists like Erich Auerbach, we have a general understanding of how the modern literary languages of Europe began to develop in the High Middle Ages. Insofar as the *chansons de geste* were oral compositions comparable to the poems attributed to Homer, there was a repetition of the primal Greek experience, leading to a new "transcription of an illiterate code." But, of course, the cultural situation now was quite different, for Western literacy had never been completely lost. In fact the Carolingian revival of a neoclassical written Latin which was further removed from the vernaculars seems to have made inevitable the eventual excision of pan-European diglossia. It was certainly inevitable by the twelfth century, when a new reading public began to demand literary works written, not in Latin, but in Provençal and Anglo-Norman. The Italian, Spanish and English vernaculars soon followed the French lead. Three or four centuries later the printing press and nationalism consolidated the standardization of the modern European languages.

Assuming now a general linguistic and cultural background of this sort, I submit that, as a point of departure for defining "literature," we would do well to take seriously the etymology of the word itself: the technique of inscribing alphabetic characters upon a flat surface. As long as Homer was a tribal tradition generating oral composition-performances, there was no γραμματική, *litteratura*, or literature in our sense of the word. Like Plato, we all pay lip-service to our oral traditions, but when we sit down to write, we are influenced primarily by what we have read, not by what we have heard. The orthography of French or English reflects, not a direct phonetic transcription of the spoken language, but a literate tradition which is more immediately semantic or morphemic than phonetic or phonemic. It is perhaps true, in some sense, that the ultimate language of immediate reality is still the oral mother tongue: the intimate language of the family, learned by the child at home. But when the child leaves home and goes to grammar school, he undergoes a fundamental *rite de passage:* he leaves his mother and baby-talk behind in order to join a traditionally male world of writing, which is not so deeply serious, in a primary emotional way, but which for that very reason can provide an artificial medium for the fictitious play of literature. This written language is a relatively abstract and autonomous system; it can be read silently, without phonetic articulation, like the Chinese ideogram whose meaning is known directly, regardless of its various possible pronunciations in Canton, Peking or Tokyo. The writer of literature is no longer the mouthpiece of traditional authority, like his oral counterpart, but is an individual who plays around with his own authority, dramatizing his role as reader and writer. He may often draw also upon the vernaculars with which he happens to be familiar, even his own mother tongue; but oral phrases, when once written down, function in a new, self-consciously literary context. The process of written composition may still be in some sense oral or auditory, though it permits revisions, something always ruled out of oral composition as a public performance. But the fixed text is essentially disembodied language, and the reader, not the writer, is now the performer who re-enacts that text. Cervantes said that "the pen is the tongue of the soul." And Borges adds:

> One now practices silent reading, an auspicious symptom. There are now inaudible readers of poetry. Between this stealthy capacity and a purely ideographic system of writing—the direct communication, not of sounds, but of experiences—there is an indefinite distance, but one that is forever less protracted than future time. [10]

## NOTES

1. See especially I. J. Gelb, *A Study of Writing: The Foundations of Grammatology* (University of Chicago Press, 1952). See also M. Cohen, *Le grande invention de l'écriture et son évolution* (Paris, 1959); H. Jensen, *Die Schrift in Vergangenheit und Gegenwart* (Berlin, 1958).

2. See especially Jack Goody, ed., *Literacy in Traditional Societies* (Cambridge University Press, 1968).

3. Better known for his important *Preface to Plato* (Harvard University Press, 1963), Havelock draws upon the oralistic theories of Milman Parry and Albert Lord; see especially the latter's *Singer of Tales* (Harvard University Press, 1960).

4. For a summary of one aspect of this tradition, see chapter 2 ("The Oral Heritage of Written Narrative") and Chapter 3 ("The Classical Heritage of Modern Narrative") of R. Scholes and R. Kellogg, *The Nature of Narrative* (Oxford University Press, 1966).

5. See especially L. R. Palmer, *The Latin Language* (London, 1954), for a history of the establishment and disintegration of Classical Latin.

6. In addition to Palmer (my note 5), see especially the brilliant analysis by Erich Auerbach in Chapter 2 of his *Mimesis: The Representation of Reality in Western Literature* (Princeton University Press, 1953).

7. C. A. Ferguson, "Diglossia," *Word,* 15 (1959), 325-40.

8. "The Primacy of Writing," in his *Linguistic Speculations* (Cambridge University Press, 1971), pp. 244-64. See also J. F. Kavanagh and I. G. Mattingly, editors, *Language by Ear and by Eye: The Relationships Between Speech and Reading* (Massachusetts Institute of Technology Press, 1972).

9. See especially Chapter 1 ("Sermo humilis" and appendix) of E. Auerbach, *Literary Language and Its Public in Late Latin Antiquity and the Middle Ages* (New York, 1965); see also his *Mimesis* (my note 6).

10. Quoted in Spanish (my translation) by Thomas R. Hart in *Velocities of Change: Critical Essays from Modern Language Notes,* ed. Richard Macksey (The Johns Hopkins University Press, 1974), p. 287.

# The Social Definition of Literature

## *Richard Ohmann*

There is a descriptive sense of the term *literature* and an honorific one. If you are using *literature* the first way, you may speak of bad literature. If you are using it the second way, you may not; rather, you would say that a bad book is sub-literary, not literature at all.

A few years ago I tried to anchor the descriptive concept of literature to a particular kind of speech act.[1] In doing so, I rejected attempts to explicate the concept by referring it to linguistic features of the text itself; instead, I held that works of imaginative literature differ from other discourses in the relationship that obtains between author and reader (or between speaker and hearer). It is something like a contract—a matter of understanding that the rules for accomplishing speech acts are altered. In other words, the descriptive sense of *literature* is rooted in social relationships.

So is the honorific sense. I doubt that the point needs arguing. Plainly the sense of what is beautiful or excellent differs from one epoch to another and from one society to another. So do the methods of establishing worth. Each society chooses by some means those new works it holds to have merit, and it will preserve a few of these over a longer time as part of its canonical literary culture. The English chose *Paradise Lost* by means very different from those the Athenians used to select the *Oresteia*, and different again from those an earlier English society used to select the *Canterbury Tales*. The means by which a canon is transmitted over generations also change: witness the influence in America of college curricula and academic criticism in establishing what American literature is, compared to their negligible role a hundred years ago.

In short, the definition of Literature, capital L, is a social process. In it, as in all social processes, some groups participate more actively than others; some do not participate at all. The exercise of power is involved in the process; therefore, so is conflict. We don't generally notice the power and the conflict except when some previously weak or silent group seeks a share of the power: for example, when, in the 1960s, American blacks and their supporters insisted that black literature be included in school and college curricula, or when they openly contested the inclusion of William Styron's *Confessions of Nat Turner* in the canon.[2] But I think that the social definition of literature is always, among other things, a contest for cultural dominance, even if in our society it is often muted—carried on behind the scenes, or in the seemingly neutral marketplace. If I am right, the only way to study the definition of "literature," in the honorific sense, is to look at the actual process quite specifically, for it will differ not only from society to society and from one age to the next, but within a society, from genre to genre: witness the relative unimportance of profit and the book market (central in defining our fiction) to the definition of poetry. In this essay I propose to look at the process of determining what will be considered good fiction in our society, as one example of what I mean. My treatment will be both schematic and brief, but I hope it will suggest the kind of social inquiry needed to answer the question, "What is literature?"

People read books silently, and often in isolation, but reading is nonetheless a social act. As one study concludes:

> Book reading in adult life is sustained . . . by interpersonal situations which minimize the individual's isolation from others. To persist over the years, the act of book reading must be incorporated . . . into a social context. Reading a book becomes meaningful when, after completion, it is shared with others. . . . Social integration . . . sustains a persistent engagement with books. Social isolation, in contrast, is likely to lead to the abandonment of books.[3]

Simone Beserman found, in her study of best sellers, that frequent reading of these books is correlated with social interaction—in particular, with the desire to rise in the society. Upwardly mobile second- and third-generation Americans are heavy readers of best sellers.[4]

As you would expect, given the way reading is embedded in and reinforced by social relations, networks of friends and family also contribute in determining which books will be widely read. In her survey, Beserman found that 58 percent of those who read a particular best seller do so upon recommendation of a friend or relative. (Of course these word-of-mouth chains originate somewhere—more of this later.) Who are these people, so crucial to a book's success? Beserman found that they are of better than average education (most have finished college), relatively well-to-do, many of them professionals, in middle life, upwardly mobile, living near New York or oriented, especially through the *New York Times*, to New York cultural life.

These people are responsive to novels where they discover the values in which they believe, or where they find needed moral guidance. Saul Bellow's remark, "What Americans want to learn from their writers is how to live,"[5] finds support in Philip Ennis' study, *Adult Book Reading in the United States*. He found that three of the main interests people carry into their reading are a "search for personal meaning, for some kind of map to the moral landscape," a need to "reinforce or celebrate beliefs already held, or, when shaken by events, to provide support in some personal crisis," and a wish to keep up "with the book talk of friends and neighbors."[6] In effect, then, the values and beliefs of a small group of upper middle class people play a disproportionate role in deciding what novels will be widely read in America.

To underscore their influence, consider two other facts. First, if a novel does not become a best seller within three or four weeks of publication, it is quite unlikely to reach a large readership later on. In the 1960s, only a very few books that were slow starters eventually became best sellers (in paperback, not hardback). I know of three: *Catch-22*, *Call It Sleep*, and *I Never Promised You a Rose Garden*, to which we may add the early novels of Vonnegut, which were not published in hard covers, and—if we count its 1970s revival in connection with the film—*One Flew Over the Cuckoo's Nest*. To look at the process the other way around, once a new book does make the *Times* list, many other people buy it (and book store managers around the country stock it) *because* it is a best seller. The process is cumulative. So the early buyers of hardcover books exercise a crucial role in selecting the books that the rest of the country's readers will buy.

Second, best sellerdom is much more important than is suggested by the figures for hardbound sales through bookstores. *Love Story*, for instance, the leading best seller of the decade (in all forms), sold only 450,000 hardback copies in bookstores, but over 700,000 through book clubs, 2,500,000 through the *Reader's Digest*, 6,500,000 in the *Ladies' Home Journal*, and over 9,000,000 in paperback—not to mention library circulation or the millions of people who saw the film. Books are adopted by clubs, paperback publishers, film producers, etc., in large part because they are best sellers or because those investing in subsidiary rights think them likely to be so. As Victor Navasky rather wryly said,

Publishers got out of the business of *selling* hardcover books ten or fifteen years ago. The idea now is to publish hardcover books so that they can be reviewed or promoted on television in order to sell paperback rights, movie rights, book club rights, comic book rights, serialization rights, international satellite rights, Barbie doll rights, etc.[7]

The phenomenon of the best seller is of small economic and cultural significance in itself, but of great significance in triggering reproduction and consumption of the story in other forms.

A small group of relatively homogeneous readers, then, has a great deal of influence at this stage in the social definition of literature. But of course these people do not make *their* decisions freely among the thousands of novels completed each year. They choose among the smaller number actually published; this fact points to a significant role, in the definition of literature, for literary agents and editors at the major houses. Since it is an obvious one, I'll not comment further upon it, except to say that as profitability in publishing has come to hinge more and more on the achievement of best sellerdom for a few books, the leading agents and editors increasingly earn their keep by spotting (and pushing) novels that look like best sellers—a nearly closed circle of marketing and consumption, the simultaneous exploitation and creation of taste, familiar to anyone who has studied marketplace culture under monopoly capitalism.

But plainly, influential readers do not even choose among all novels published. They choose among the few that come to their attention in an urgent or attractive way. How does that happen? To suggest the shape of an answer, I shall consider the extraordinary role of the *New York Times*. The *Times Book Review* has about a million and a half readers, several times the audience of any other literary periodical. Among them are most book store managers, deciding what to stock, and librarians deciding what to buy, not to mention the well-to-do, well-educated east coasters who lead in establishing hardback best sellers. The single most important boost a novel can get is a prominent review in the Sunday *Times*—better a favorable one than an unfavorable one, but better an unfavorable one than none at all.

Ads complement the reviews; or perhaps the word is "inundate": two-thirds of the space in the *Times Book Review* goes to ads. According to Richard Kostelanetz, most publishers spend more than half their advertising budgets for space in this journal.[8] They often place ads in such a way as to reinforce a good *Times* review, or counteract a bad one with favorable quotations from reviews in other periodicals. And of course reviews and ads are further reinforced by the *Times* best seller list itself, since, as I have already mentioned, the appearance of a title there stimulates many more sales. Apparently the publishers' faith in the *Times* is not misplaced. Beserman asked early readers of *Love Story* where they heard of the book. Most read it on recommendation of another person; Beserman then spoke to *that* person, and so on back to the beginning of the chain of verbal endorsements. There, in more than half the instances, she found the *Times*.[9] (This in spite of the quite unusual impact of Segal's appearance on the "Today" show the day of publication—Barbara Walters said the book made her cry all night; Harper was immediately swamped with orders—and of the novel's appearance in the *Ladies' Home Journal* just before book publication.)

The influence of the *Times Book Review* leads publicity departments to direct much of their pre-publication effort toward persuading the *Book Review*'s editors that a particular novel is important. It is hard to estimate the power of this suasion, but one thing can be measured: the correlation between advertising in the *Book Review* and being reviewed there. A 1968 study concluded, perhaps unsurprisingly, that the largest advertisers get disproportionately large amounts of review space. Among the large advertisers, for instance:

|                | Pages of ads | Pages of reviews |
|----------------|:------------:|:----------------:|
| Random House   | 74           | 58               |
| Harper         | 29           | 22               |
| Little, Brown  | 29           | 21               |

And the smaller ones:

|            | Pages of ads | Pages of reviews |
|------------|:------------:|:----------------:|
| Dutton     | 16           | 4                |
| Lippincott | 16           | 4                |
| Harvard    | 9            | "negligible"     |

During the same year Random House (including Knopf and Pantheon) had nearly three times as many books mentioned in the feature, "New and Recommended," as Doubleday or Harper, both of which houses publish as many books as the Random House group.[10]

In short, a small group of book buyers forms a screen through which novels pass on their way to commercial success, a handful of agents and editors picks the novels that will compete for the notice of those buyers, and a tight network of advertisers and reviewers organized around the *New York Times Book Review* selects from these a few to be recognized as compelling, important, "talked-about."

So far I have been speaking of a process that leads to a mass readership for a handful of books each year. But most of these are never regarded as literature, in the honorific sense, and do not live long in popularity or memory. Books like *Love Story, The Godfather, Jonathan Livingston Seagull,* and the novels of Susann, Robbins, Wallace, Wouk, Michener, and Uris run a predictable course. They have large hardback sales for a few months, tapering off to a trickle in a year or so. Meanwhile, they are reprinted in paper covers and enjoy two or three years of popularity (often stoked by a film version). After that they disappear, or remain in print to be bought in small numbers by, for instance, newly won fans of Wallace who want to go back and read his earlier books.

There is a similar pattern for mysteries, science fiction, and other specialized genres.

But a few novels survive, and continue (in paper covers) to attract buyers and readers for a longer time. How does this happen? To answer that the *best* novels survive is, from the perspective of this essay, to beg the question; I am trying to ascertain, precisely, how our society attributes excellence, book by book. Excellence is a constantly changing, socially chosen value. Who decides (and how) that some novels are worth reading and discussing year after year, while most are not? In the remainder of this essay I hope to hint at the way such a judgment takes form.

First, one more word about the *Times Book Review*. I have argued that it leads in forming the mass audience for fiction. It also begins, I believe, the process of distinguishing between ephemeral popular novels and those to be taken seriously over a longer period of time. There is a sharp difference in impact between, say, Martin Levin's favorable but mildly condescending (and brief) review of *Love Story* and the kind of front page review by an Alfred Kazin or an Irving Howe that asks readers to regard a new novel as literature, and that has so often helped give the stamp of highbrow approval to books by Bellow, Malamud, Updike, Roth, Doctorow, etc. Cultural leaders read the *Times Book Review* too: not only professors, but (according to Julie Hoover and Charles Kadushin) 75 percent of our elite intellectuals.[11] By reaching these circles, a major *Times* review can help put a novel on the cultural agenda and insure that other journals will have to take it seriously.

Among those journals, a few carry special weight in forming cultural judgments. A survey of leading intellectuals showed that just eight journals — the *New York Review of Books*, the *New Republic*, the *New York Times Book Review*, the *New Yorker*, *Commentary*, *Saturday Review*, *Partisan Review*, and *Harpers* — received almost half the participants' "votes" in response to various questions about influence and importance.[12] In effect, these periodicals are both a communication network among the influentials (where they review one another's books), and an avenue of access to a wider cultural leadership. The elite, writing in these journals, largely determine which books are seriously debated and which ones permanently valued, as well as what ideas are kept alive, circulated, discussed. Kadushin and his colleagues concluded, from their studies of our intellectual elite and influential journals, that the "top intellectual journals constitute the American equivalent of an Oxbridge establishment, and have served as one of the main gatekeepers for new talent and new ideas."[13]

A novel must win at least the divided approval of these arbiters in order to remain in the universe of cultural discourse, once past the notoriety of best sellerdom. The career of Love Story is a good example of failure to do so. After some initial favorable reviews (and enormous publicity on television and in other media), the intellectuals began cutting it down to size. In the elite journals, it was either panned or ignored. William Styron and the rest of the National Book Award fiction panel threatened to quit if it were not removed from the list of candidates. And who reads it today, or will read it tomorrow, except on an excursion into the archives of popular culture?

In talking about the Times Book Review, I suggested a close alliance between reviewing and profit, literary and monetary values. The example of the New York Review of Books suffices to show that a similar alliance exists on at least one rampart of higher literary culture. This journal, far and away the most influential among intellectuals (in answer to Kadushin's questions, it was mentioned almost twice as often as the New Republic, its nearest competitor[14]) was founded by Jason Epstein, a vice president of Random House, and is co-edited by his wife, Barbara Epstein. It may be more than coincidental that in 1968 almost one-fourth of the books granted full reviews in this journal were published by Random House (again, including Knopf and Pantheon)—more than the combined total of books from Viking, Grove, Holt, Harper, Houghton Mifflin, Oxford, Doubleday, Macmillan, and Harvard so honored. Or that in the same year one-fourth of the *reviewers* had books in print with Random House, and that a third of those were reviewing other Random House books, mainly favorably.[15] Or that over a five-year period more than half the regular reviewers (ten or more appearances) were Random House authors.[16] This is not to deny the intellectual strength of the *New York Review*—only to suggest that it may sometimes deploy that strength in ways consistent with the financial interest of Random House. One need not subscribe to conspiracy theories in order to see, almost everywhere one looks in the milieu of publishing and reviewing, linkages of fellowship and common interest. Kostelanetz' book is a rich, if somewhat overdrawn, account of this.

If a novel gets certified as important in the court of the prestigious journals, it is likely to draw the attention of academic critics in more specialized and sedate journals like *Contemporary Literature*, and by this route make its way into college and perhaps eventually school curricula, where the very context— course title, academic setting, methodology—gives it de facto recognition as literature. This final step is all but necessary: the college classroom and its counterpart, the academic journal, have become in our society the final arbiters of literary merit, and even of survival. It is hard to think of a novel more than 25 years old, aside from specialist fiction and *Gone with the Wind*, that still commands a large readership outside of school and college.

I have drawn a sketch, then, of the course a novel must run in order to lodge itself in our culture as literature, in the honorific sense. It is selected, in turn, by an agent, an editor, a publicity department, a review editor (especially the one at the Sunday *Times*), the New York metropolitan book buyers whose patronage is necessary to commercial success, critics writing for gatekeeping intellectual journals, academic critics, and college teachers. Obviously the sequence is not rigid, and some steps may on occasion be omitted entirely (as I have indicated with respect to *Catch-22* and *One Flew Over the Cuckoo's Nest*). But I believe that the pattern has become more and more regular in recent years, as publishing has been increasingly drawn into the sphere of monopoly capital (with RCA acquiring Random House; ITT, Howard Sams; Time, Inc., Little, Brown; CBS, Holt; Xerox, Ginn; and so on throughout almost the whole industry). And monopoly capital has changed this industry much as it has changed the automobile and the toothpaste industries: by placing much greater emphasis on marketing and predictability of profits.[17]

It is not my purpose here to discuss the consequences for *Literature* of these changes. In closing I would just note one fact and offer one speculation. The fact: that agents, editors, reviewers, buyers of hardback novels, taste-making intellectuals, critics, and professors all belong to roughly the same class, and stand in similar relationships to the bourgeoisie. The speculation: that these arbiters also have similar esthetic values and ideological orientations, which confine the attribution of excellence and hence the definition of literature within set but invisible limits of form and content. If so, that would give our literature a firm place within what Gramsci called hegemony—the hegemony, in this case, of the American dominant class.

## NOTES

1. Richard Ohmann, "Speech Acts and the Definition of Literature," *Philosophy and Rhetoric* 4 (1971). See also John Searle, "The Logical Status of Fictional Discourse," *New Literary History*, 1975. For a critique

of this approach (one with which I disagree), see Stanley Fish, "How to Do Things with Austin and Searle: Speech Act Theory and Literary Criticism," *Modern Language Notes*, 1976. Mary Pratt's *Toward a Speech Act Theory of Literary Discourse* (Bloomington: Indiana University Press, 1977) carries the discussion forward in a most valuable way.

2. John Henrik Clarke, ed., *William Styron's Nat Turner; Ten Black Writers Respond* (Boston: Beacon Press, 1968).

3. Jan Hajda, *An American Paradox: People and Books in a Metropolis* (Unpublished Ph.D. dissertation, sociology, University of Chicago, 1963), p. 218; quoted in Elizabeth Warner McElroy, *Subject Variety in Adult Book Reading* (Unpublished M.A. dissertation, sociology, University of Chicago, 1967).

4. Simone Beserman, *Le best-seller aux Etats-Unis de 1961 à 1970: étude litteraire et sociologique* (Unpublished dissertation, University of Paris, n.d. [1975?]), pp. 280-92.

5. "Saul Bellow of Chicago," an interview conducted by Jason Epstein, *New York Times Book Review*, May 9, 1971, p. 16.

6. A National Opinion Research Center report, University of Chicago, 1965; p. 25. Other main needs are (1) escape, which also implies a relationship between reading a book and the rest of one's social life (what one is escaping *from*), and (2) information, which I suspect is a need less often fulfilled by *novels* now than in the time of Defoe and Richardson.

7. Victor Navasky, "Studies in Animal Behavior," *New York Times Book Review*, Feb. 25, 1973, p. 2.

8. Richard Kostelanetz, *The End of Intelligent Writing; Literary Politics in America* (New York: Sheed and Ward, 1974), p. 207. Kostelanetz' estimate is confirmed by some of Beserman's interviews. Allan Green, who handles advertising for a number of publishers, including Viking, told her in 1971 that on the average, 50 to 60 percent of the budget went to the *Times Book Review* and another 10 to 20 percent to the daily *Times*. M. Stuart Harris, head of publicity at Harper, said he ordinarily channels 90 percent into the *Times* at the outset, though once a book's success is assured he distributes advertising more broadly (Beserman, p. 120).

9. Beserman, p. 168.

10. Kostelanetz, p. 209; based on reports in Harry Smith's *The Newsletter*, July 30, 1969 and Dec. 8, 1971.

11. Julie Hoover and Charles Kadushin, "Influential Intellectual Journals: A Very Private Club," *Change*, March, 1972, p. 41.

12. Charles Kadushin, Julie Hoover, and Monique Tichy, "How and

Where to Find the Intellectual Elite in the United States," *Public Opinion Quarterly*, Spring, 1971. For the method used to identify an intellectual elite, see Charles Kadushin, "Who Are the Elite Intellectuals?," *Public Interest*, Fall, 1972.

13. Kadushin, Hoover, and Tichy, p. 17.

14. Kadushin, Hoover, and Tichy, p. 9.

15. Kostelanetz, pp. 107-08; based on Harry Smith's *The Newsletter*, March 5, 1969.

16. Kostelanetz, p. 110.

17. For an account of this process that attributes it more to industrialism than to capitalism, see John Kenneth Galbraith's *The New Industrial State* (Boston: Houghton-Mifflin Company, 1967). I prefer the analysis in Paul A. Baran and Paul M. Sweezy, *Monopoly Capital* (New York: Monthly Review Press, 1966).

# Literary Works Express
# Propositions

## *Robert J. Matthews*

In literature no less than in the other arts, the nature of criticism
and the nature of the works which are the objects of criticism are
linked in a most intimate way: what sorts of things we may
justifiably say about literary works depends on what sorts of
things they are, and what sorts of things literary works are depends on what sorts of things we may justifiably say about
them. Explicit theoretical recognition of this mutual dependence
has been only partial. Philosophers and critics have long recognized the dependence of one's theory of the nature of literary
criticism ("critical theory") on one's theory of the nature of the
literary work ("literary theory"); however, they have been less
ready to recognize the dependence of literary theory on critical
theory. Rather they have tended to think of the work as an
independently existing entity whose aesthetically significant
properties are inherent. The aesthetic properties of a work have
been thought to be no more dependent on what is said of that
work than are its physical properties.

I am not going to defend here the claim that there is a mutual
dependence of the art work and its criticism; rather I shall attempt only to suggest in very general terms a way of thinking

about literary works that provides a conceptually adequate basis for both critical theory and literary theory. The crux of my proposal is the replacement of meanings by *propositions* as the primitive elements of critical analysis. The theoretical import of the proposed replacement is its emphasis on the art-productive nature of critical praxis. The discursive strategy of my paper exploits the recognized dependence of critical theory on literary theory: I argue from the impracticability of received critical theory to the conclusion that received literary theory is untenable; from there I go on to propose a propositional theory of the literary work which, I claim, provides the correct sort of abstract entity as the object of critical concern.

If one were to speculate *a priori* as to the view of criticism that a consumer culture like our own would construct for itself, one might imagine something like this: works of art are consumer goods, produced by artists and marketed by critics. These salesmen-critics might on occasion be guilty of various professional failings and weaknesses, ranging from simple ignorance of the merchandise to gross exaggeration of its worth; yet when they perform their task properly, they provide an indispensable service to the art consumer: the critic enables the consumer to choose his merchandise intelligently by informing him truthfully of the essential properties of the art-good. In addition to this reportorial function, the ideal salesman-critic would provide comparative evaluations of the different goods that were available, informing the consumer which was the "best buy." Of course, critics might do other things, some of which might even diminish their usefulness to the consumer; nevertheless, their essential activities would involve explicating and evaluating works of art.

Now, in a society possessed of such a view of criticism, much metacritical discussion would be directed toward cautioning against unscrupulous practices that obstruct the proper task of criticism. Thus, for example, critics would be cautioned against an Intentional Fallacy, which consists in focusing on the intentions of the producer rather than on the product itself. Also to be avoided would be the Affective Fallacy of thinking that the value attached to a product by consumers is indicative of its true worth. Marxist and Freudian critics would have to be warned against a Genetic Fallacy that consists in a belief that the history of production, be it socioeconomic or psychobiographical, is relevant to an evaluation of the art-good. Other failings could be added to this list; however, the point should be clear: criticism would lack a Better Business Bureau only in name.

My speculations as to the view of criticism that our society might be expected to construct for itself are certainly sketchy; nevertheless, it does seem to me that the view one finds expounded in recent decades, especially by "New Critics" and their progeny, has strong affinities with the caricature I am presenting here. Critics *are* typically seen as neither producers nor consumers, but rather as middlemen whose job it is to report on (and evaluate) the essential properties of works of art. Indeed, there has been fierce resistance to the suggestion that critics might play a part in the production of these works. Metacriticism *has* often amounted to nothing more than codes of business ethics. How else are we to interpret the metacritical preoccupation with critical fallacies to the nearly total exclusion of any effort to characterize critical praxis? And when critics and philosophers *have* attempted to provide such characterizations, what have we received but accounts that privilege reporting on and evaluating works of art? Existing critical theory has thus made a virtue out of simplicity: pursued properly, the business of criticism is exceedingly simple; only when this business is pursued improperly does it become complex and difficult to understand. Hence, insofar as critical theory is concerned with the *proper* task of criticism, that theory will itself be exceedingly simple.

But if, to carry my speculations a bit further, the ideal critic would focus exclusively on the art-good itself, elucidating its essential properties, then what precisely would be the nature of those properties? This much is clear: whatever their nature, they would have to be *inherent* in the work itself. They would have to satisfy other conditions as well, some of which might differ from one art form to another. Yet for the case of literary works, there would be only one serious contender: *meanings*. For no other property of linguistic tokens would appear to have the requisite degree of abstractness. But the choice of meanings would be a good one: while clearly vague enough to be serviceable, the notion would have a theoretical counterpart in linguistics that promised an eventual explication. Thus, even if critics did not now know precisely (or even roughly) what meanings were, they eventually would. But in the meantime, critics could continue to provide what they called "explications of meaning." Critical praxis would be secure, even if critical theory were incomplete. The important business of criticism need not wait for the development of theory, any more than other businesses have had to wait for the development of economics.

It is hard to exaggerate our long preoccupation with meaning, or at least with something critics call "meaning." For the last fifty years (a period whose beginning is marked roughly by the appearance of I. A. Richards' *Practical Criticism*), critical and metacritical thought alike have been little more than extended meditations on the subject. And understandably so, since under the pen of New Criticism literature itself came to be defined in terms of meaning. The precise nature of literary meaning has been the subject of much debate; however, the privileged position of the concept has not been questioned. Nor, until recently, has there been serious questioning of the corollary view that the proper task of criticism is the disclosure of this meaning.[1] Yet, despite this preoccupation with meaning, one discerns only with greatest difficulty instances of those meanings that the critic, speaking as metacritic, takes to be the essence of literary works and hence the object of his scrutiny. Of course, one does discern *explications of meaning,* which supposedly explicate the "meaning" of the work under consideration; however, it is not at all clear how these presentations of the critic are related to inherent properties of that work.

The disparity between meanings actually inherent in the work and those "meanings" discerned by critics is most evident in instances of criticism in which there has been a conscious attempt to employ a concept of literary meaning that does construe such meaning as an inherent property of linguistic tokens. One is struck by the inability of the critic to present those "meanings" that we have come to expect without first abandoning the theoretically rigorous construal of meaning in favor of a much looser, informal one.[2] And in those cases where the critic seems to have been successful, close examination reveals a pervasive metaphorization of the theoretical concept. The "meanings" of the praxis are not those of the theory.

This impracticability of what might be called the "metacriticism of meaning" does not establish its untenability; however, recent developments in linguistic theory do raise serious doubt. Proponents of this metacritical program, it will be recalled, look to linguists to provide a theory of meaning upon which an adequate theory of criticism might eventually be erected. But although they have left the task of constructing this theory of meaning to linguists, they have nonetheless stipulated that this theory must satisfy one crucial condition: the theory must provide for the explication of the "meaning" of a literary work *solely* in terms of the meaning of the sentences comprising the literary text, which will in turn be explicable in terms of the syntactic structure of these sentences in conjunction with the lexical meanings of the sentences' constituents. (Let us call this the "inherence condition.") I emphasize the word 'solely' because it is only through the assumed sufficiency of the text alone to

determine the work's "meaning" that we preserve the requirement that literary works be evaluated on the basis of *inherent*
qualities. But this is precisely where a serious difficulty arises.
Linguistics is not going to provide a theory of the sort
envisioned here. Semantic theory can provide an account of
sentence meaning that will explain the meaning of a sentence in
terms of the syntactic structure of this sentence in conjunction
with the lexical meanings of its constituents. But it cannot provide an account of literary "meaning" as a function of the meanings of the sentences comprising the literary text.[3] The problem
is not, as so-called "text grammarians" have argued, that existing linguistic theory has mistakenly chosen sentences rather
than texts as the basic unit of linguistic analysis. Text grammars
are no more capable of meeting the "inherence condition" described above than are sentence grammars. The problem is
rather this: the "meanings" that critics claim to discern in literary works are not, strictly speaking, meanings at all, but *proposi-*
*tions,* a different sort of abstract entity. But propositions, unlike
meanings, are not inherent in sentences or texts, since the proposition expressed by a sentence is a function of the *context* of
expression. Thus, insofar as critical theory presents itself as a
theory of the actual praxis of critics, that theory *is* untenable. It
postulates the wrong sort of abstract entity as the object of critical concern.

The proper characterization of propositions is beyond the
scope of our present discussion; however, this much should be
noted by way of explication. Propositions are the *contents* of
so-called propositional attitudes and of speech acts. That is, they
are the sort of thing we specify when we answer questions of the
sort "What did he say?" "What did he promise?" "What does he
believe?" and the like. They are also the sort of thing that is
shared when two individuals believe (imagine, suspect, hope,
etc.) the same thing or when they say (deny, promise, demand,
etc.) the same thing. Propositions might be said to provide the

nexus between thought and language; for if I express my belief
that, for example, received critical theory is confused by saying
"received critical theory is confused," the proposition expressed
by that sentence is the content of both my belief-state and of my
speech act. Although propositions are abstract objects that represent truth conditions, they should not be confused with assertions that make true or false representations of this world. This
is only one use to which propositions may be put. To use the
idiom of possible worlds, propositions are rules for picking out a
set of worlds—namely, the set of all worlds for which the proposition takes the value true. But to have picked out such a set of
worlds is not necessarily to represent the actual world as being a
member of that set; indeed, the question need not arise. We
often have occasion to represent a set of worlds that clearly does
not contain the actual world as a member; fiction is only one case
among many.[4]

The notion introduced above of the proposition expressed by
a sentence is important to our present discussion, because the
distinction between meanings and propositions can best be understood in terms of it. Consider the sentence, "I am hungry,"
said first by me and then by you. Clearly the meaning of the
sentence does not change with the speaker, though the proposition expressed does. Only when *I* utter the sentence does it
express the proposition that Robert Matthews is hungry. Uttered by you, the sentence expresses a different proposition. But
not only can the same sentence be used to express different
propositions without change of meaning; different sentences,
having different meanings, can be used to express the same
proposition. Thus, I could have expressed the proposition that I
did by uttering the sentence, "Robert Matthews is hungry."
Sentences and the propositions expressed by them are clearly
not identical; nor are the meanings of sentences correlated one-
to-one with the propositions that they can express. Rather they
are related as follows: the meaning of a sentence is an abstract

entity much like a mathematical function that determines the proposition expressed by that sentence in a context as a function of certain elements of that context. Thus, whereas meaning *is* an inherent property of sentences (and hence of texts), the propositions expressed are not. Propositions are properties of pairs of sentences and contexts.

But what grounds are there for believing that critics are concerned with propositions rather than with meanings? First, there is the tendency of critics to treat literary works as *utterances*, as a form of *discourse*, sometimes to the point of postulating a virtual speaker (e.g., the "dramatic speaker"). Yet clearly sentences or texts are not themselves utterances, but only what is uttered. There is, however, a clear sense in which propositions might be identified with utterances: utterances are often individuated on the basis of the proposition expressed; thus, we report in *oratio obliqua* what someone said (i.e., his utterance) by specifying the proposition expressed by his uttering a sentence in a context. Second, critics typically treat literary works as suggesting or implying certain things; however, it is propositions, not sentences or their meanings, that suggest or imply other propositions. Third, critics invariably specify an interpretation for all referring expressions in a literary text. Thus, for example, Wordsworth's "A Slumber did my spirit seal" is for Cleanth Brooks a poem about the dramatic speaker's lost love, for F.W. Bateson a poem about Lucy, for Coleridge a poem about Dorothy Wordsworth; while for others it is a poem, not about some female persona, but about creative spirit or mind. Yet none of these interpretations is dictated by the text itself; it is not part of the meaning of the poem that the pronoun 'she' take any of these objects as its referent. In each case the interpreter has presumed a context within which he has embedded the text of the poem; however, such a contextualization of the literary text by the critic would be required only if the critic is concerned with propositions rather than meanings. Finally, critical preoccupation with the fictional worlds and characters generated by most literary works presupposes the propositional character of those works, since fictional worlds, like possible worlds, are defined over propositions. That is, sets of propositions specify sets of worlds.[5]

In addition to these and other features of critical praxis that seem to support my contention that critics are concerned with propositions rather than meanings, one can also point to terminological ambiguities in received critical theory. In virtually every case, the ambiguity serves to mask an otherwise implausible account of critical praxis. Thus, for example, the metacritical claim that critics are concerned with meaning is preserved only by appeal to a notion of "utterance meaning," which allows the critic to smuggle in the suppressed notion of context while at the same time preserving the pretense of being concerned only with an inherent property of literary texts. But as is often the case with *ad hoc* adjustments to theory, a price must be paid elsewhere. In this case the theory becomes saddled with the problem of the utterer: if criticism is concerned with utterance meaning, then literary works are utterances of some sort. But if this is true, then who are their utterers? Failing any adequate answer, the *reductio* of this position is not long in coming: literary works are unuttered utterances (which is to say, not utterances at all)!

My proposal that we replace meanings by propositions as the primitive elements of critical analysis has the not insignificant virtue of providing the *correct* sort of abstract entity for critical theory. But this is not all. Adoption of the proposal would effect an important redirection of metacritical attention. Because the proposition expressed by a sentence is an explicit function of the *context* of expression, critical theory under a propositional paradigm would accord increased theoretical importance to the art-institutional context within which a literary work expresses the propositions that it does. The replacement of meanings by propositions would, as a result, have a profound impact on our conception of literature and, derivatively, on our conception of literary criticism. For if, as seems likely, the art-institutional context is not determined solely by the artist producing the text, but is partly determined by the contextualizing labor of critics, then the notion that critics are non-productive middlemen would have to be rejected. They too would have a hand in determining the aesthetically significant characteristics of literary works. The proper task of critics could no longer be thought of as simply reporting on and evaluating works of art. For it is, I take it, a conceptual truth about reporting that one can report only pre-existing facts. But if the effect of these so-called "reportings" is to determine at least partially the work being "reported on," then these "reportings" would not be reportings at all. The utterances of critics would have, to use J. L. Austin's terminology, a *performative* aspect.

The all-important details of my proposal remain to be filled in; however, my concern here has been simply to suggest that the aesthetically significant characteristics of literary works are not unchanging meanings but are rather the particular propositions expressed by a work in a particular context. My proposal not only recognizes the art-institutional character of literary works, but does so in a way that promises to make clear the respective contributions of text and context to the determination of the work. Hermeneutical theorists have long insisted that works of art are in some manner a product not only of an artist but also of a critical tradition. A propositional theory promises an explanation of the latter's role: by modifying the art-institutional context of which it is a part, the critical tradition associated with a literary work is able to modify the work itself. Of course, the precise way in which critical praxis modifies this context will have to be spelled out, but this is a task that must be left for another time.

## NOTES

1. For a discussion of the underlying philosophical issues, see Joseph Margolis, "Robust Relativism," *Journal of Aesthetics and Art Criticism* XXXV (Fall, 1976), pp. 37-46; and my "Describing and Interpreting a Work of Art," *Journal of Aesthetics and Art Criticism* (forthcoming, 1977).

2. See, for example, J.J. Katz, *Semantic Theory* (New York, 1972); or David Lewis, "General Semantics," *The Semantics of Natural Language,* edited by G. Harman and D. Davidson (Dordrecht-Holland, 1972), pp. 169-218.

3. I especially have in mind recent structuralist criticism, which purportedly discerns these "meanings" on the basis of a strictly linguistic analysis of the literary text in question.

4. The theoretical framework that I am presenting here is similar to that presented in Robert C. Stalnaker's published work. See, in particular, his "Propositions," *Issues in the Philosophy of Language,* edited by Alfred F. MacKay and Daniel D. Merrill (New Haven, 1976), pp. 79-91; "Possible Worlds," *Nous* 10 (1976), pp. 65-75; and "Pragmatics," *The Semantics of Natural Languages* (op. cit.), pp. 380-397.

5. Nicholas Wolterstorff, "Worlds of Works of Art," *Journal of Aesthetics and Art Criticism* XXXV (Winter, 1976), pp. 121-132.

# 3

## *Literature:*
## *Acts, Effects, and Artifacts*

# The Literary Work: Its Structure, Unity, and Distinction from Forms of Non-Literary Expression

## *Joseph Strelka*

As a rule Anglo-Saxon literary theory employs two different concepts when attempting to define the object of literary investigations. At the base of this division lies an insight into the true nature of literature deeper than that usually encountered in other languages and literary theories. A literary work in its broadest sense consists of certain fictional qualities on the one hand and certain poetic qualities on the other. Both these elements are then joined with non-literary linguistic elements and fused in the work itself to form new expressive units. In most cases it is easier to distinguish the fictional element which is characterized by plot and related motifs than it is to draw the border between works of non-literary languages and those which possess literary qualities. Ancient Indian literary theory attempted to clarify this distinction through the use of the concept "kavya." But since "kavya" means approximately the same as "verse" it can hardly serve to classify the special intensive language and the peculiarly literary properties of such genres as the essay and the aphorism. Be that as it may, for the sake of precision a single comprehensive concept will be employed here to denote a generally valid separation of literary and non-literary

115

forms. Although it has no tradition in English literary theory, the concept of the "literary work" would correspond rather well to the German "literarisches Werk" or the Russian "slovesnost." This concept of course also subsumes oral literary traditions, its etymological derivation from "litera" notwithstanding.

## 1. DELINEATIONS

The object of literary investigations is the linguistic work of art or simply linguistic art *per se*. Since Kant there has been no doubt that the literary work presents an aesthetic phenomenon *sui generis* which may not be confused with empirical reality or its direct depiction. For this reason, attempts to set literature off from non-literary linguistic phenomena have always emphasized the language artistry of literature in the narrow sense. The language of science, technical literature, and colloquial language—even when it expresses feelings rather than thoughts—are all denotative and depictional and refer to empirical facts, whereas the literary work, according to Wolfgang Kayser,[1] evokes a reality all its own. René Wellek contrasted the "denotative" quality of scientific language with the "connotative" quality of literary language,[2] and in a later work Roland Barthes also maintained that in the literary work a "message dénoté" is joined by a "message connoté."[3] The language of the literary work is thus not only referential and descriptive, but also expressive in the particular sense that it communicates the author's inner stance, and the literary work has the mission of influencing the inner stance of the hearer or reader.

By itself, however, the mission of influencing or persuading a reader or hearer is scarcely a criterion for the uniqueness of the literary work. Just as anatomy texts in rhyme, which medical students prepare for the sake of easier memorization, cannot lay claim to being literary works, most sermons and judicial or political speeches are similarly excluded even though they often consciously employ rhetorical traditions in order to achieve a persuasive presentation. It would be a falsification of the matter and a mechanistic reduction if one were to conclude that a work did or did not constitute literary art on the basis of such external techniques. Individual proponents of Russian formalism, certain representatives of structuralism and, until recently, almost all champions of linguistics have nonetheless considered the question in just such mechanistic terms. In the period following World War II Max Wehrli[4] was still able to welcome the promised stimulation of literary science by an idealistic linguistics. For the present, however, this hoped-for fruitful encounter has given way to a confrontation with a new linguistics that has proved far less productive even though modern linguistics now lays claim to an all-encompassing validity. Jean Paulhan warned quite early against hoping for too much help in this connection from linguistics, and in the same context recalled once more literature's special character.[5] It was, however, Bateson who brought about a decisive clarification of the matter. By contrasting de Saussure's linguistic cycle with a roughly parallel literary cycle of his own, Bateson pinpointed the literary irrelevance of the former.[6] This, of course, by no means implies that a literary work does not consist of language nor that a certain linguistic understanding of what Hugo Friedrich called "primary word sense"[7] is not a component of the literary work. It makes little difference whether one proceeds from the assumption that the literary work contains additional language elements that distinguish it from a non-artistic linguistic product—as does Michael Riffaterre[8]—or whether one assumes with Radoslav Katičič that it contains fewer elements because in a special literary sense language possibilities have been restricted.[9] A certain distinction still remains, and it was Bateson who showed that the proper concern of literary science lies precisely in the concentration upon this distinction. Just as there is a horizontal or temporal unity in a literary work which one cannot deny without doing the work an injustice—a clear example would be arriving at a play only after the beginning of the second act or leaving before the fifth act—there is also a vertical unity that brings about a metamorphosis of those elements of language with which linguistics commonly deals. It is this vertical unity that extends into both pre- and post-linguistic realms. The basis of this distinction lies in the theme, at first only half-conscious, which leads to the construction of symbols through a combination of image and imagination in the author's creative fantasy and which ultimately emerges in its final form as the literary text.

An external definitional criterion such as the form of presentation, which Käte Hamburger declared as definitive,[10] may well suffice for the simplest and occasionally even for major cases. That is to say, it is obviously a decisive factor whether a linguistic work is written in the form of a poem, a drama, or a novel. Since there are always borderline cases, and since the current composition of literature and our perspectives on it are continually developing, a more finely differentiated criterion is undoubtedly most desirable. Wladimir Weidlé has provided this criterion by introducing the concept of mimesis in its pre-Socratic sense as a process that leads to a *poiesis*.[11] Weidlé makes a distinction here between mimetic and purely significative language signs. The former mean nothing more than what they express; the latter are references to something else. This does not imply that all components of literary language are mimetic in this particular sense. The mimetic element, however, constitutes the essential definitional criterion for literature. Mimesis in this sense represents that which it expresses in such a manner that the representation corresponds exactly to what has been said. It allows meaning to be perceived either in the acoustic form of literature or in the form of significance. Additionally, it is also possible for the meaning to be perceived in both the acoustic and the signifying form. Beyond the purely significative language of science one must distinguish between two different mimetic languages in literary art, the first consisting of expressive poetic values and the second consisting of fictional formations.

According to Weidlé the various modes of linguistic expression are not mutually exclusive. They should instead be viewed as a broad spectrum composed of gradual transitions. At the one end stands the language of Pindar or Hölderlin; at the other, that of Euclid or Boltzmann. The language of Ranke or Wölfflin lies somewhere in between. Their language, however, is actually much closer to Pindar's manner of speaking and perhaps should occupy a medial position between a restrictively defined artistic prose at the one end and written colloquial language at the other. In order to indicate these transitions from literary to non-literary phenomena theoreticians have often turned to an image of concentric circles. Max Wehrli, for example, establishes the following categories: language, literature, *belles lettres*, and poetry.[12] While Leo Pollmann does not deal with Wehrli's outermost circle, he posits a sphere corresponding to Wehrli's "literature" as the basis from which one proceeds to *belles lettres* and ultimately to poetry.[13]

As a practical matter, various critics allow varied degrees of latitude in drawing the line dividing literary and non-literary products. In all cases, however, it is the literary properties of language and not aesthetic value that determines the differentiating criterion. The only possible involvement of value judgment is found in dealing with the exclusion of trivial literature from the more limited range of that which is seriously literary. Bateson, for example, makes this attempt.[14] If one disregards certain extreme cases—the particularly narrow boundaries drawn by Benedetto Croce or, alternatively, the equally radical broad definitions that would include a whole series of descriptive prose forms—there is general agreement concerning a commonly-held objective recognition of what belongs in the realm of literature and what does not. Practically speaking, these boundaries are subject to development and expansion. Certainly in recent times essayistic prose in its broadest sense has come to be included within the circle of literary phenomena. Sengle's efforts are typical for this development in German-speaking areas.[15] It should nonetheless be kept in mind that not everything that terms itself essay or travel notes, diary, dialogue, or letter actually falls within the boundaries of literature. The designation as literature is reserved for that type of broadly defined literary prose that displays an essentially mimetic expressive manner, whereas instances of descriptive prose in the same genres but with a significative expressive manner lie outside literature's realm.

## 2. THE LITERARY WORK AS CONSTRUCT

When attempting to dissect a work analytically in order to reveal its individual elements in their mutual interaction, critics have found the most fruitful model to be the idea of a many-layered structure. But when Wolfgang Kayser speaks of the structural character of a literary work or when Günther Müller speaks simply of a linguistic construct,[16] neither critic has the concept in mind that Roman Ingarden posited in his seminal work. The same holds true for Wellek's description of the literary work as a system of norms consisting of several levels which in turn contain their own sub-levels.

In Ingarden's system the first level is that of the linguistic tone structure. This level does not refer to the sound or rhythmic qualities of isolated individual words, but rather of larger structures including their essential connection with their significance. This relation also includes the manner in which the meaning of these structures reflects back upon their tonal character. The linguistic tone level enriches and modifies the polyphony of a literary work with its own aesthetic values and at the same time presents the external, albeit necessary, shell for the second constituent level, that of meaning units. Here too, specific, concrete meanings are derived only from a larger context in which higher levels of meaning become apparent. The scope of this level reaches far beyond the intellectual presuppositions of a work's ✓ rational side and includes, above all, the manner of the various possible modes of depiction through factual correlations. The sense units of the meaning level lead subsequently to a determination of the manifold aspects in which the third level, that of depicted objects, finally appears. This level includes the "world" of the author, which is normally first perceived only in the work itself, and which should not be confused with the real world, occasional similarities notwithstanding. Depicted objects can only be represented in the work through its contents but cannot be grasped visually. For this reason the factor of respective viewpoints plays a significant role. Since this is not a matter of concrete viewpoints, but simply of certain schemata, Ingarden further defines a fourth level of schematicized viewpoints in the structure of a literary work.[17]

Nicolai Hartmann has defined still further levels, but one loses a certain clarity by moving to his system.[18] Ingarden had already, for example, considered what Hartmann terms schematicized views simply as part of his third level. That quibble notwithstanding, much would be gained by separating the linguistic level—which itself falls into a level of sound and a level of meaning—from the level of represented objects and factual correlations. This level is often missing, but when present it is the primary level where mimesis takes place, which in turn makes the language product into a work of literary art. It was in this connection that Northrop Frye postulated four symbolic levels as the constituent parts of the literary work.[19]

## 3. THE LITERARY WORK AS SYMBOL

Although for the sake of analysis one can distinguish individual levels of the literary work, the structure of the work still presents the reader with a unified totality. This is true not only in a vertical direction through the integral fusion of the work's various levels, but also in a horizontal direction through the order imposed by the sequence of the work's individual parts. Ingarden describes this as a construct possessing organic unity but at the same time he warns against taking the concept "organic" literally instead of metaphorically.[20] The profound misunderstanding Ingarden feared already looks back on a venerable history in literary theory and might perhaps best be circumvented by avoiding the organism concept entirely. The concept of the symbol is actually much better suited for describing the unified totality that characterizes the many-layered construct we know as the literary work. Ingarden avoids this concept only because he conceives it too restrictively. Critics from Vjačeslav Iv́anov[21] to Gaston Bachelard[22] and from Philip Wheelwright[23] to Käte Hamburger[24] have thus emphasized the symbolic character of the literary work. There is, to be sure, also the problem here of semantic misunderstandings since the symbol concept has occasionally been so broadly conceived—by Marshall Urban, for example[25]—that it has become almost meaningless for the present context, valuable observations concerning the symbolic form of literary language notwithstanding. The central problem, however, actually concerns itself less with the presence of literary symbols within a given literary work than with the symbolic properties of the literary work as a whole. In his morphological literary theory Horst Oppel raises the question of how existence realizes itself in the symbolic totality of the literary work.[26] This question points directly to the heart of the present investigation, and here again it was Weidlé who brought order out of the chaos of symbol definitions as applied to the literary work. According to Weidlé's view, the literary symbol in its literary-theoretical context does not mean what it has customarily signified for the Anglo-Saxon semanticists, the neopositivist philosophers, and the French and German linguists, i.e., a purely denotative sign, a representation that is purely conventional, unmotivated, and replaceable at will. For Weidlé the symbol means something closer to what it had meant for Goethe, a sense image, "the thing itself without being the thing and yet being the thing nonetheless."[27] In this sense the symbol provides an intersubjective reality of that which is intended and makes it perceptible.

Whereas the architectonic aspect represents the analytical character of the literary work, the symbolic character of literature stands for the synthetic perspective. Both aspects are important for a fruitful literary-theoretical approach. A phenomenological dissection of a work into its discrete layers can make individual structural elements evident within their structural context; the symbolic view underlines the vital fact of a literary work's unitary wholeness. Indeed, in the case of literary art the synthesizing power of the symbol has much to accomplish in its fusion of a work's various aspects and levels. Disregarding for the moment the levels of sounds, meaning units, and objectifications, one can recognize that this symbol concept—as Karl Tober emphasizes[28]—is also capable of unifying the levels of the historical-ontological and the literary-historical. Finally, this symbol concept is particularly well-suited for describing the position of the literary work as an existentially heteronomous aesthetic phenomenon with its own ontological value, a phenomenon that nonetheless remains connected with the real world, arises from the real world, and reflects back upon it.

## 4. CONSTITUENT ELEMENTS

Granted that Ingarden's levels already represent the constituent elements of the literary work,[29] his highly abstract analysis still needs to be more precisely executed and supplemented by concrete references. Ingarden himself made the first steps in this direction when he spoke of the literary work's metaphysical properties which lay outside his four levels. These properties are not identical with theological concepts but signify instead those special and rare experiential values that give life a particular direction and elevation and which might also be viewed as religious. On another occasion Ingarden spoke of the gleaming, doubly radiant qualities of the language in a literary work of art. As Jean Starobinski has recently indicated, these are the qualities of a work of art that mark it as the expression of particular forms of the imagination.[30] In this sense problems of sound, rhythm, and musicality are just as significant as those of the work's actual structure and the problems of form investigated by such critics as Wolfgang Kayser,[31] Emil Staiger,[32] and Rudolf Maier.[33] In treating forms of imagination Walter Muschg has distinguished a magical, a mystic, and a mythical phantasy. In line with this division he then posits three separate basic forms of poetic language which at the same time correspond to three basic stylistic attitudes.[34]

In the final analysis the question of what literary science actually deals with can only be partially answered by recognizing the essence of the literary work's absolute and total unity as a unique object of cognition *sui generis*. Even though one must always proceed in a concrete instance from the closed individual work, it is nonetheless the totality of all works of linguistic art, whether transmitted orally or in writing, that constitutes the entire object of a general literary science. Since, on the one hand, new works are always being written or discovered, and since, on the other hand, works can be lost or simply forgotten, ultimately we are not able to deal with a static, firmly defined phenomenon even in terms of the object itself.

# NOTES

1. Wolfgang Kayser: *Das sprachliche Kunstwerk*. Bern: Francke, 2d ed., 1951, pp. 12-18.
2. René Wellek, Austin Warren: *Theory of Literature*. New York: Harcourt, Brace & World, Inc., 1956, pp. 20-28.

3. Roland Barthes: L'analyse rhétorique. In: *Littérature et société*. Edited by the Institute of Sociology at the Université libre in Brussels. Bruxelles: Editions de l'Institut de Sociologie 1967, pp. 31-35.

4. Max Wehrli: *Allgemeine Literaturwissenschaft*. Bern: Francke 1951, pp. 45-47.

5. Jean Paulhan: *Clef de la Poésie*. Paris: Gallimard 1944.

6. Frederick W. Bateson: *The Scholar-Critic*. London: Routledge and Kegan Paul 1972, pp. 101-110.

7. Hugo Friedrich: Dichtung und die Methoden ihrer Deutung. In: Horst Enders (Ed.): *Die Werkinterpretation*. Darmstadt: Wissenschaftliche Buchgesellschaft 1967, p. 294.

8. Michael Riffaterre: Criteria for Style Analysis. In: Seymour Chatman and Samuel R. Levin (Ed.): *Essays on the Language of Literature*. Boston: Houghton Mifflin Company 1967, pp. 412-441.

9. Radoslav Katačič: Literary Theory and Linguistics. In: Zdenko Škreb (Ed.): *Umjetnost Riječi—The Art of the Word*. Zagreb: Jzdavački zavod Jugoslavenske akademije 1969, p. 75-88.

10. Käte Hamburger: *Logik der Dichtung*. Stuttgart: Klett 1968, p. 12.

11. Wladimir Weidlé: Die zwei Sprachen der Sprachkunst. In: *Jahrbuch fuer Aesthetik und Allgemeine Kunstwissenschaft.*Vol. XII/2, pp. 154-191.

12. Max Wehrli, op. cit., p. 51.

13. Leo Pollmann: *Literaturwissenschaft und Methode*. Frankfurt a.M.: Athenaeum 1971, vol. I, p. 33.

14. Frederick W. Bateson, op. cit., pp. 62-70.

15. Friedrich Sengle: *Vorschlaege zur Reform der literarischen Formenlehre*. Stuttgart: Metzler, 2d ed., 1969, pp. 12-13 and 18-19.

16. Günther Müller: Ueber die Seinsweise von Dichtung. In: *Deutsche Vierteljahrschrift fuer Literaturwissenschaft und Geistesgeschichte*, vol. 17 (1939), pp. 137-152.

17. Roman Ingarden: *Das literarische Kunstwerk*. Tuebingen: Niemeyer, 3d ed., 1965.

18. Nicolai Hartmann: *Aesthetik*. Berlin: De Gruyter 1953.

19. Northrop Frye: *Anatomy of Criticism*. New York: Atheneum 1966, p. 71-128.

20. Roman Ingarden, op. cit., pp. 25 and 319-21.

21. Vyacheslav Ívanov: Symbolism. In: *Russian Review*, vol. 26 (1966), pp. 24-34. Cf: René Wellek: Russian Formalism. In: *Arcadia*, vol. 6 (1961), pp. 175-186.

22. Gaston Bachelard: *La Psychanalyse du feu*. Paris: Gallimard 1938.

23. Philip Wheelwright: *The Burning Fountain*. Bloomington and Lon-

don: Indiana University Press, 2d ed., 1968, pp. 3-17, 32-55, and 124-185.

24. Käte Hamburger, op. cit., pp. 269-81. Cf. also Rudolf N. Maier: *Das Gedicht. Ueber die Natur der dichterischen Formen.* Duesseldorf: Schwann, 3d ed., 1963 and Joseph Strelka: *Vergleichende Literaturkritik.* Bern and Muenchen: Francke 1970, pp. 20-40.

25. Wilbur Marshall Urban: *Language and Reality.* New York: Macmillan 1939, pp. 46-48 and 399-628.

26. Horst Oppel: *Morphologische Literaturwissenschaft.* Darmstadt: Wissenschaftliche Buchgesellschaft 1967, p. 37.

27. Wladimir Weidlé, op. cit., pp. 160-161, 167, 168 note 19, 169 note 22, 170, and 185 note 34.

28. Karl Tober: *Urteile und Vorurteile ueber Literatur.* Stuttgart etc.: Kohlhammer 1970, pp. 17-18, 116-117. Cf. also Emil Winkler: *Das dichterische Kunstwerk.* Heidelberg: C. Winter 1924, pp. 8-12 and Rudolf N. Maier, op. cit., pp. 16-34.

29. Roman Ingarden, op. cit., pp. 310-319.

30. Jean Starobinski: Imagination. In: *Actes du IVe Congrès de l'Association Internationale de Littérature Comparé,* redigé par Francois Jost. The Hague—Paris: Mouton 1966, pp. 952-963.

31. Wolkgang Kayser, op. cit.

32. Emil Staiger: *Grundbegriffe der Poetik.* Zurich: Atlantis, 2d ed., 1951.

33. Rudolf N. Maier, op. cit. Cf. also Joseph Strelka, op. cit., pp. 42-46.

34. Walter Muschg: *Die dichterische Phantasie.* Bern and Muenchen: Francke 1964. Cf. also: Jacques Maritain: *Situation de la poésie.* Paris: Desclée de Brouwer 1938 and Joseph Strelka: *Die gelenkten Musen.* Wien: Europa Verlag 1971, pp. 249-275.

# The Mirror as Metaphor for Literature

## *James I. Wimsatt*

Perhaps the earliest recorded application of the mirror metaphor to literature is found in Aristotle's *Rhetoric*, where Alcidamas' characterization of the *Odyssey* as "a mirror fair of human life"[1] is listed among several examples of obscure, ineffective metaphors. This seems an inauspicious beginning for the image, especially since one may well sympathize with the Philosopher's judgement. How, it may be asked, can the story of Odysseus' and Telemachus' wanderings among realms of gold and islands of enchantresses be called a mirror of life? The image clearly would find no support from the prominent modern commentator on the "imitation of reality" in literature, Erich Auerbach. Using one of the most intimate domestic scenes in the *Odyssey* to dramatize his discussion, Auerbach concludes that Homer incorporates in his stories "few elements of historical development and psychological perspective," remaining "within the legendary with all his material."[2] In his terms the description of the *Odyssey* as a mirror of human life would make as little sense as it did to Aristotle.

Auerbach reserves the mirror metaphor for such a modern work as James Joyce's *Ulysses*, our twentieth-century *Odyssey*, which he calls "a mirror of Dublin, of Ireland, a mirror too of Europe and its millennia."[3] In *Ulysses* no doubt he sees "historical development and psychological perspective." Yet Aristotle and others might not understand Auerbach's mirror either, puzzled as to how the highly particular representation of Leopold Bloom's and Stephen Dedalus' day reflects Europe's history. It is true that Joyce might well have accepted both Auerbach's and Alcidamas' figures of speech, for he took seriously the parallel of his novel with Homer's epic, and he considered the *Odyssey* to have literature's "most beautiful, all embracing theme . . . greater, more human than that of *Hamlet, Don Quixote*, Dante, *Faust*";[4] Ulysses is his "complete man in literature."[5] But such Joycean pronouncements are as baffling ultimately as the critics' images, and in any event determining whether or not Joyce would have embraced the images begs the question of their intrinsic suitability, a question that I hope to answer in some fashion in this essay, while suggesting that the mirror metaphor has an impressive potential for characterizing, even defining, literature.

Except for picture metaphors, critics probably have employed the figure of the mirror more frequently than any other to characterize literature. Authors also, especially those of the medieval and Renaissance periods, by means of titles have attached the image to a large body of literature. Yet neither critics nor authors have gone very far in providing explicit rationale for such use of the metaphor; and scholars, despite their many surveys of mirror metaphors—including the recent encyclopedic *Speculum, Mirror und Looking-Glass* of Herbert Grabes[6]—have not considered its implications in any depth. The common assumption, it seems, is that the figure is serviceable for describing accuracy in representation—a "faithful" mirror, a "distorting" mirror—and that is the extent of its significance.[7] This assumption does not do justice to the individual uses of the image nor to the physical object known as a mirror. There is much more to mirrors, and usually involved in mirror metaphors, than faithfulness in reflection. A physical mirror's fixed boundaries, often framed, lend the enclosed images a certain completeness; behind the mirror's more or less shining surface there lurks an illusion of mysterious depths; and, most suggestively for literature, in its reflecting powers the mirror presents a paradox unique in the physical world—itself a physical entity, it takes on the appearance of other entities which it faces, imparting to their likenesses a gleaming new being while remaining essentially unchanged by them. In literary works likewise there are certain meaningful limits of inclusion, often an impression is conveyed that significance is hidden within the formal surface of representation, and there is effected a potentially remarkable transference of the subjects of representation from their original mundane materials to a new existence in verbal matter. Because of these qualities the mirror metaphor has a capability, often realized in practice, of suggesting that a work identifies and isolates important significance in the various and apparently random existence of this world.

Putting it somewhat differently, mirror metaphors describing literature often point to an apprehension of superior reality located in the verbal reflections of the subject matter. Users of the metaphor, it seems, generally perceive this higher reality as arising from one of three unions or fusions: of the universal with the particular, of the ideal with the actual, or of the spiritual with the mundane. In the first case the metaphor expresses the notion running through the history of criticism that William K. Wimsatt has identified as the "concrete universal," the idea that successful literature "presents the concrete and the universal, or the individual and the universal, or an object which in a mysterious and special way is both highly general and highly particular."[8] Intuition of such a union of qualities, we may postulate, prompts Alcidamas and Auerbach to describe the *Odyssey* and *Ulysses* as mirrors of life. Neither the return from Troy nor

Bloom's day, as a worldly phenomenon that might be directly apprehended, presents general truth. But in the reflection provided by the writer's words the critic senses or intuits general significance.

A similar explanation may clarify some famous applications of mirror metaphors to drama. It can square Samuel Johnson's statement in his Preface to Shakespeare, "This therefore is the praise of Shakespeare, that his drama is the mirror of life," with his neoclassic notions that the poet must present general truth. Bottom's hypothetical real-life counterpart has just so many stripes, but in the reflection the drama provides, while it does not distort, the number of stripes somehow loses its limiting power. The criterion of the concrete universal is implicit too in Hamlet's dictum that drama should "hold, as 'twere, the mirror up to nature, to show virtue her own feature, scorn her own image, and the very age and body of the time his form and pressure" (III, ii, 24-27). In the reflected image of the dramatist's mirror, which is focused on the particularities of the world, Hamlet tells us, there should appear abstractions: Scorn, Virtue, the Form of the Time.

The definition of comedy formerly ascribed to Cicero, quoted endlessly in the Renaissance,[9] supplies perhaps a source for Hamlet's and Johnson's pronouncements. It epitomizes the critics' use of the mirror figure to describe concrete universals. Comedy, the definition holds, is "imitatio vitae, speculum consuetudinis, imaginem veritatis"—"a copy of life, a mirror of custom, an image of truth." Here stands the mirror, mediating between and joining together the "copy of life," that is, the faithful reproduction of the details of existence, and the "image of truth," Verity in its abstract and general form. The paradox of the definition is concealed, while the concept of the concrete universal is neatly evoked, by the image.

Mirror metaphors in titles[10] likewise may suggest that universals appear in the presentation of particular entities. The twelfth-century *Speculum Stultorum*, the tale of Brunellus the ass, presumably produces an image of foolishness embodied. At other times "mirror" in a title seems to imply that the divine is made visible in a work, as in the encyclopedias of Vincent of Beauvais which probably are called "specula" because they embrace whole areas of existence and thereby display the divine plan and by extension divinity itself. Breadth of scope indeed seems characteristic of most works called mirrors. This element is certainly involved in the figure's applications to the *Odyssey* and to Joyce's novel. It seems also a major aspect of the many treatises with mirror titles that present exemplars, such as treatments of vice and virtue and all sorts of courtesy books—mirrors for sinners, mirrors for princes. These merit the metaphor because the ideals of kingship and virtue presumably appear in extensive, systematic considerations of the subjects. The sinner or the prince can use such a glass to conform his actual image to the exemplar presented or implied.

In the Middle Ages mirror titles most often were employed for expository, often religious, treatises; however, such titles increasingly came to be given to imaginative or semi-historical works like the Elizabethan drama *The Glass of Government* and the series of verse histories known as *The Mirror for Magistrates*. But long before the titles were so applied customarily, imaginative writings were composed on plans used for expository mirrors: Dante's *Purgatorio* is built largely on the scheme of the Seven Deadly Sins just as are confessional treatises—mirrors of sin and virtue—and Chaucer constructs the Prologue to the *Canterbury Tales* on an estates framework quite similar to those employed in literary analyses of society like Gower's *Mirror of Man (Miroir de l'Omme)*. Today many works to which the former age gave mirror titles often appear mere catalogs; the essential and transcendental, it seems, no longer show through simple expositions as they once did. On the other hand, the principle of systematic inclusiveness in the General Prologue and *Purgatorio* produced enduring literature from which universals or exemplars still shine. Most students of literature probably would not bridle at the statement that these works are mirrors in which Chaucer and Dante present the very form of society and of sin and virtue.

The fashion of mirror titles faded away. In the seventeenth century many "mirrors" were accorded a new metaphor, "anatomy."[11] This in turn went out of style, but the mode usually designated has remained vital. Plans that provide for systematic, inclusive description have continued to produce noteworthy literature. It is no casual irony by which Alexander Solzhenitsyn's *First Circle*, which leads the reader up and down the hierarchy of Mavrino Prison and in an orderly progression takes him from room to room of it—in so doing providing a mirror of Russia's prison system—draws its name from Dante's great mirror of hell. *One Day in the Life of Ivan Denisovich* is a mirror based on temporal inclusiveness. *Gulag Archipelago* in scope and plan is still another mirror. So also are Truman Capote's *In Cold Blood*, Pope's *Essay on Man*, and Burton's *Anatomy of Melancholy*. One may assert without absurdity, I think, that all of these, too, present universals or exemplars or even images of the divine (if somewhat perversely) by virtue of their reflective powers.

There is no certain contradiction in the rival claims of universality, ideality, or divinity. In one basic sense finding the ideal or the transcendent in accounts of worldly phenomena is comparable to finding universals in them. In all cases a superior reality not apparent in the concrete phenomena facing literature's mirror is apprehended in their verbal reflection. Furthermore, this apprehension can be of essentially the same reality; whether it is called a universal or an ideal or a piece of divinity can depend in large part on whether the one who is characterizing it is inclined toward Aristotelianism, Platonism, or mysticism.

Throughout the literary history of the West, the mirror metaphor is used to indicate the presence of superior reality in verbal accounts of mundane phenomena. The large number of diverse literary works to which the figure has been applied perhaps suggests, furthermore, that presentation of superior reality, whether in the form of concrete universals, exemplary actuality, or immanent divinity, is a characterizing aspect of all of literature. Since this notion accords with the elevated concept of literature held by many, and with my own intuition, it seems reasonable to hypothesize that there is in fact a "mirror aspect" basic to literature and that the concept of one can assist an understanding of literature's nature and scope.

Some perhaps will object that this notion of a "mirror aspect" ignores the more common usage of the metaphor—that usually and properly it signifies straightforward imitation. They may point to Stendhal's famous image in *Le Rouge et le noir* (ch. 8) of the novelist sending a mirror walking down the road. Clearly Stendhal has straightforward imitation in mind. As I have already shown, however, such usage is not representative of the familiar recorded applications of the figure to literature. Even Stendhal's resort to the mirror may indicate an unconscious recognition that a good novel provides something beyond mere record.[12]

Not only the mirror metaphors of criticism and of titles, but also many applications of the figure within the texts of literature support the appropriateness of the designation "mirror aspect," while also suggesting the possible range and depth of the concept. Within texts too mirror metaphors often signify that a higher reality is present in the reflections. Sometimes this reality involves the ideal and exemplary, as when Ophelia calls Hamlet "the glass of fashion" (III, i, 161), or fair White in Chaucer's *Book of the Duchess* is seen as "chef myrour of al the feste" (1. 974). Even more prominently, however, the mirror has been used within literature to identify the invisible presence of the spiritual and transcendent. Metaphors of this order occur in such a wide variety of writings that, while many may be related to specific philosophical and literary traditions—for instance, to late Platonism[13] or to St. Paul's heaven darkly-mirrored (I Cor., xiii. 12)—the basic motives for their use manifestly lie in the unique suggestive qualities of the mirror and its operation.

As illustration we might adduce three striking water mirrors from relatively recent but quite diverse writings. The first of these occurs in Solzhenitsyn's *Cancer Ward.* Old Dr. Oreshchenkov ponders the meaning of life. "The meaning of existence," he muses, is "to preserve untarnished, undisturbed and undistorted the image of eternity which each person is born with—as far as is possible.—Like a silver moon in a calm, still pond."[14] Here the silver moon and the pond, taken separately, are suggestive, but it is in the reflection, the moon's appearance in the pond, that eternity enters; that is the essential factor in Oreshchenkov's peculiarly literary, peculiarly poetic insight. In the second instance also, found in Robert Frost's *Spring Pools,*[15] reflection of the sky in water becomes an image for the transcendent in the earthly. The poet in early spring, looking at water standing in the woods, meditates that

> These pools that, though in forests, still reflect
> The total sky without defect,

are soon to have their unspotted images sullied by the "pentup" buds of the trees, which will "darken nature" by blotting out "these flowery waters and these watery flowers." An unheeding summer erases the heavenly reflections in spring pools.

Baudelaire's *L'Homme et la mer* provides the third water mirror, which differs from the others in that it shows the viewer his own image. His spiritual nature is revealed to "Homme libre" by the reflecting sea:

> La mer est ton miroir; tu contemples ton âme
> Dans la déroulement infini de sa lame.[16]

This image suggests some versions of the Narcissus story, where similar reflections of the observer's soul are in question.[17] But Baudelaire's figure is no mere late recurrence of the Narcissus myth; it is quite distinctive. Distinctiveness indeed characterizes all three metaphors. Among them they have notable similarities; in all three a natural body of water reflects worldly objects to human observers; but, paradoxically, through the water's reflection and the observation of the reflection, an effective expression of the supernatural is achieved. Yet it seems clear that no significant line of influence connects them, and that each arises in great part from the individual writer's perceptions.

In literary works most mirrors with a spiritual dimension are not made of water, of course. The narrator in Hawthorne's *House of the Seven Gables* expressly states the paradox of the transcendent mirror image in terms of the looking-glass. He finds himself drawn into a fantasy "by the quiver of the moonbeams . . . reflected in the looking-glass," which, he adds, *"is always a kind of window or door into the spiritual world."*[18] Mirrors are also openings to the other world for the French symbolist poets. Guy Michaud proclaims that "The mirror is the very symbol of symbolism. Creation is an immense scheme of mirrors, and the mirror is what permits passage from one world to another."[19] A passage between worlds similarly is effected by mirrors in a much earlier work of French literature, the *Roman de la Rose,* where the reflecting crystals in the Pool of Narcissus, a mirror within a mirror, open to Amant a whole Paradise of Love.[20]

Literary uses of the image of the mirror to suggest superior reality are manifold. For dozens more examples one need only inspect a collection of Petrarchan or Metaphysical poetry, where time and again the ideal form of the beloved is registered in the human mirrors of the lover's eyes or heart.[21] And no doubt every reader can find his own additional instances in texts far removed from those cited. The point particularly to be made

here is that the mirror metaphor is not most typically used to
describe simple imitation of surface reality. More characteristically it serves to suggest a deeper or higher reality, and it
is therefore quite appropriate for describing the property in literature by which one sees, or thinks or feels he sees, the universal, the ideal, or the spiritual—or perhaps all three together—in
verbal representations of particular worldly entities.

To be sure, even if one concedes that this hypothetical mirror
aspect characterizes writings which are literary, and that those
which lack it are not literary, most practical problems of differentiating the literary from the non-literary persist. The hypothesis provides no ready objective test of literature any more than
a stipulation that men are characterized by souls would enable a
Martian to recognize human beings at sight. The presence of a
mirror aspect has to be determined initially, just as the
classification literature has always had to be, by personal experience and testimony. The finding of it thus depends on, and will
vary with, both the qualities of the writing and the knowledge
and beliefs of the reader which are brought to bear on reading it.
On the other hand, the practical dependence on subjective ap-
prehensions does not rule out the objective existence of a mirror
aspect, and if the hypothesis will not directly solve practical
problems, it can help theoretical ones. It can tell us about the
nature of the peculiarly literary. Literature, it says, has something that is like a soul, not only in its intangibility, but also in its
superiority to and informing of the concrete entity to which it is
attached. Admittedly, it is like the soul too in that there is ample
latitude for debating whether it is real or illusory. Some may
admit its apparent presence without granting it a real existence.
Even admitting its seeming presence, of course, has significant
implications. At the same time I would suggest that it has
potential actuality in any given writing. The mirror analogy
holds. Simple reflection, as I have noted earlier, is not all one
gets from a mirror, and verbal reflectors provide images at least

as pregnant with meaning as vitreous reflectors. For compelling
reasons mirror metaphors often carry conviction that a physical
mirror can be an authentic opening to superior reality; for
Hawthorne's narrator it is always such a door. In characterizing
literature as well, mirror metaphors may designate the real presence of superior significance.

From what specifically does the mirror aspect of a writing
arise? All attempts to separate elements of form and content in a
work of literature invariably fail, so one must feel that any identifying feature will pertain to a complete entity. At the same time
no doubt some particular constituent or constituents in each
work, however inseparable, will account more than others for
the presence of superior reality in them. With some it may be
versification that especially conduces to an intuition of ideal
form; with others, characterization that signally presents the
universal in the most individualistic appearances; and with
others, subject matter—perhaps divine, perhaps intrinsically
human—that most evidently leads to insights transcending the
physical world. With one group of works at least we may be less
tentative about how a mirror aspect is produced and how the
concept might be usefully applied. As I have discussed, inclusive arrangement is a characteristic of many works that were
traditionally assigned mirror titles, and such arrangement seems
to conduce to production of a mirror aspect, quite notably even
in collections of facts and observation like *Gulag Archipelago* and
*Anatomy of Melancholy*. The mirror aspect hypothesis, then, can
be employed to explain how such writings have a place in the
center of literature rather than on the fringes where some, including Wellek and Warren, would place them.[22] Using the criterion of the mirror aspect—seen as the product of any of the full
variety of artistic means—one may find also that Froissart's
*Chronicles*, Augustine's *Confessions*, and Walpole's letters fit
comfortably into the most exclusive anthologies of literature.

Testing of this last suggestion, however, would require a

lengthier explication of the mirror aspect. For this essay the
attempt to present the hypothesis and posit its rationale and
viability must suffice. In the course of this attempt I have
analyzed historically the applications of mirror metaphors and
shown that they commonly depict the physical mirror and the
mirror of literature as no limited reflectors. My notion of the
mirror aspect, originating in analysis of the metaphor, simply
extends the figure's range in imputing to all of literature an
existence not bounded by its mundane materials. It sees literature as worthy of the most elevated conceptions of critics and
readers, with a scope quite beyond Merlin's wonderful mirror in
the *Faerie Queene:*

> It vertue had, to shew in perfect sight
> What ever thing was in the world contaynd,
> Betwixt the lowest earth and heavens hight.

[III, ii, Str. 19]

Writings with a mirror aspect have this faculty and more, for
besides showing "what is in the world contaynd" they present
also what by the world is signified. They lead us inside the
mirror into Looking-Glass House where appears what is behind, beneath, and within the ordinary perceptions of our
senses.

## NOTES

1. *The Rhetoric of Aristotle,* trans. Lane Cooper (New York: Appleton,
1932), p. 192.

2. *Mimesis: The Representation of Reality in Western Literature,* trans.
Willard R. Trask (Princeton, N. J.: Princeton Univ. Press, 1953), pp. 19,
23.

3. P. 547.

4. Quoted in Richard Ellman, *James Joyce* (New York: Oxford Univ. Press, 1959), p. 430.

5. P. 449.

6. *Speculum, Mirror und Looking-Glass* (Tübingen: Max Niemeyer, 1973).

7. For instance, Meyer H. Abrams, in his admirable *The Mirror and the Lamp* (London: Oxford Univ. Press, 1953), pp. 30-35, having identified the mirror metaphor as an "archetypal analogy" for literature, assumes in discussing it that the image typically presents literature as a reductive reflector.

8. *The Verbal Icon: Studies in the Meaning of Poetry* (Lexington, Ky.: Univ. of Kentucky Press, 1954), p. 71. Other critics have discussed in different terms approximately the same concept that Wimsatt identifies as the "concrete universal." See, e.g., René Wellek's discussion of "type" in theories of realism, *Concepts of Criticism*, ed. Stephen G. Nichols, Jr. (New Haven: Yale Univ. Press, 1963), pp. 238-39, 242-46.

9. Using the Ciceronian definition as a point of departure, Eugene Waith presents a valuable discussion of Renaissance comedy as mirror in "The Comic Mirror and the World of Glass," *Research Opportunities in Renaissance Drama*, 9 (1966), 16-23.

10. I discuss works with mirror titles as participating in a particular mode of medieval literature in *Allegory and Mirror* (New York: Pegasus, 1970), esp. pp. 28-31.

11. See Grabes, pp. 242-43.

12. Aside from Stendhal, Plato provides a notable source for the figure by which literature is presented as a simple reflector. See the survey of Plato's mirror images applied to literature in Richard McKeon, "Literary Criticism and the Concept of Imitation in Antiquity," *Modern Philology*, 34 (1936), 9-12. With Plato, of course, the image is frankly unflattering; he views the mirror and literature as both reflectors of reflections. Plato's followers, however, could readily convert his metaphor to literature's advantage, as did Bishop Hurd (quoted by Abrams, p. 33), who, citing Plato's mirror figure in the *Republic*, envisions the poet as reflecting directly the "original forms."

13. See *Alain de Lille: Anticlaudianus*, ed. Robert Bossuat (Paris: Vrin, 1955), II, pp. 293-309; VI, pp. 73-272. For discussion of relevant mirror-figures in the *Enneads* of Plotinus and Plato's *Timaeus*, see Gordon W. O'Brien, *Renaissance Poetics and the Problem of Power* (Chicago: Institute of Elizabethan Studies, 1956), pp. 21-23.

14. *Cancer Ward* (Harmondsworth, England: Penguin, 1971), p. 46.

15. *The Poetry of Robert Frost,* ed. Edward C. Lathem (New York: Holt, 1968), p. 245.

16. Quoted in Guy Michaud, "Le Thème du miroir dans le symbolisme français," *Cahiers de l'Association Internationale des Études Françaises,* 11 (1959), 199-216.

17. See Frederick Goldin, *The Mirror of Narcissus in the Courtly Love Lyric* (Ithaca, N. Y.: Cornell Univ. Press, 1967), pp. 31-37 and passim.

18. *Works* (Boston: Houghton, 1881), III, 332. Cited in Marjorie Elder, *Nathaniel Hawthorne: Transcendental Symbolist* (Columbus: Ohio State Univ. Press, 1969), p. 79. Italics mine.

19. *L'Oeuvre et ses techniques* (Paris: Nizet, 1957), p. 108.

20. Ed. Ernest Langlois, *Société des anciens textes français,* 5 vols. (Paris: Firmin-Didot, 1914-20), ll. 1537-82. Narcissus' fountain contrasts with the Mirror of Nature which Genius speaks of later, ll. 19899-906.

21. Grabes refers to many of these in surveying the mirror as "mode-metaphor" in the Middle Ages and Renaissance. See esp. pp. 86-92.

22. René Wellek and Austin Warren, *Theory of Literature,* 3rd ed. (New York; Harcourt, 1962), pp. 25-26.

# Native Readers of Fiction: A Speech-Act and Genre-Rule Approach to Defining Literature

## Robert L. Brown, Jr., and Martin Steinmann, Jr.

### INTRODUCTION

What is literature? But first: What is a theory? For questions about literature, unlike questions about particular works of literature, are theoretical questions. There are at least three possible answers—possible senses of *theory*.

In the first sense, a theory is a set of statements claiming to account for—to explain and predict—certain phenomena. A theory of English syntax, for example, claims to account for all native English speakers' ability to recognize and produce English sentences by making explicit their implicit knowledge of the syntactic rules that constitute all the sentences of English. In other words, the theory will specify the necessary and sufficient conditions for counting an utterance as a sentence.[1] A theory of literature in this sense of *theory*, then, claims to account for (among other phenomena) the ability of "native readers" of literature to recognize works of literature. It will specify both the necessary and sufficient conditions for counting a piece of discourse as a work of literature.

But there is a tradition, best represented in the later work of Ludwig Wittgenstein,[2] and most strikingly developed in literary theory by Morris Weitz,[3] that rejects this answer and proposes a second answer—a second sense of *theory*. In the first sense of *theory*, Weitz argues (Ch. 13), a theory of literature is logically impossible, for there are no necessary and sufficient conditions for counting a piece of discourse as a work of literature. The concept is "perennially debatable": every proposed condition "is always open to fundamental question, challenge, rejection, and replacement" (p. 307). No set of properties is shared by all pieces of discourse counted as works of literature; there is only a set of "family-resemblance" properties, some present in every work of literature, but none in all. Further, the concept is "perennially flexible": new conditions are always possible to accommodate works possessing not only some of these family-resemblance properties but other properties as well (pp. 307-08). Consequently, the argument goes, no answer to the question "What is literature?" can make a truth claim. And at best a theory of literature can only be a recommendation to give the greatest weight to certain conditions or properties (p. 309) or, as Charles L. Stevenson would put it, a persuasive definition.[4] M. H. Abrams, borrowing a term from Coleridge, says essentially the same thing: theories are "speculative instruments," and proposing them is "much like taking a stand."[5] Thus we need not, he concludes, choose among theories, selecting the one (if any) that we believe to be true or to have the greatest explanatory power. For theories in this second sense have no such power; all are—or at least can be—equally valid.[6]

Finally, we must glance at another rejection of theory in the first sense and a proposal of a third sense of *theory* related to the second. On this view, a descriptive-explanatory theory is logi-

cally possible, but not worth having: it is of no practical use. One
job of critics, this argument runs, is to interpret works of literature, and for a theory of literature to be useful in this enterprise
it must be an instrument for interpretation. A theory in the first
sense presupposes a phenomenon to be explained—native
readers' ability to recognize or interpret works of literature, say.
In the third sense, however, the existence of the
phenomenon—critics' interpreting works of literature—
presupposes the existence of the theory. On this view there are
no native readers of literature, no people who learn how to
interpret or recognize works of literature in the way that speakers learn their languages. The critic must mediate between the
works and the reader, and his pronouncements are an essential
part of the institution of literature. Seen this way, literary discourse is fundamentally different from other discourse.[7]

Our answer to the question "What is literature?" will, then, be
a theory in the first sense of *theory*. We recognize that the term
*literature* designates very different concepts, some of which are
indeed perennially flexible and debatable. But some are not. We
assume that for any work of literature there is or was a body of
native readers whose rule-based intuitions can be accounted for
explicitly. Our goal is disinterested and unpragmatic. It is not to
create or influence phenomena, but to understand one distinct
language phenomenon central in many definitions of literature.


## SPEECH ACTS AND LITERATURE

We approach the question, "What is literature?" from the perspective of speech-act theory, first introduced into the philosophy of language by J. L. Austin,[8] and developed by (among
others) John R. Searle.[9] On Searle's version of the theory, which
we follow, there are four sorts of speech act: (1) *utterance acts*—
uttering sentences; (2) *propositional acts*—using utterance acts to

refer to things and to predicate properties or relations of them, thus expressing propositions; (3) *illocutionary acts*—acts of asserting, questioning, promising, commanding, and so on; (4) *perlocutionary acts*—by performing utterance, propositional, and illocutionary acts, affecting hearers or readers: causing them to answer a question, to obey (or disobey) a command, to laugh or cry, and so on. A speaker or writer can perform an utterance act without performing the others (in testing a microphone or practicing typewriting), but not the others without performing an utterance act. Typically, he performs an utterance-propositional-illocutionary act, and along with it a perlocutionary act.[10]

Every utterance-propositional-illocutionary act is rule governed: to follow the rules is to perform the act. But, though perlocutionary acts are typically effects of such rule-governed acts, they are not themselves rule governed. Nor are they effects of such acts alone. They are effects also of the hearer's or reader's nature and nurture—intelligence, values, knowledge, and so on. Consequently, though perlocutionary acts are within the intentional control of the speaker or writer, no rules insure their success. As many perlocutionary acts as there are hearers or readers may be triggered by a single utterance-propositional-illocutionary act.[11]

Every utterance-propositional-illocutionary act, moreover, is governed by constitutive, not regulative rules. *Regulative* rules govern human behavior that exists independently of them. Rules of etiquette, for example, are usually regulative, for they govern eating (among other things), and people would eat even if there were no such rules. *Constitutive* rules, however, constitute, create, or define the very kind of behavior they govern; without them, it could not exist. The rules of chess, for instance, are constitutive, for they both define and govern chess playing: no rules of chess, no games of chess. The rules governing utterance acts—the grammatical (that is, syntactic, phonological, and semantic) rules of languages—are constitutive, for without them speakers or writers could not perform such acts. No grammatical rules, no speaking, writing, or interpreting English sentences. And so with the rules governing propositional and illocutionary acts. No rules, no referring and predicating, and no asserting, questioning, or commanding.

But not all constitutive rules governing speech acts are alike; rules governing utterance acts—grammatical rules—are different in kind from those governing propositional and illocutionary acts. Grammatical rules define the syntactic and phonological structure and the semantic potential of every sentence, but without regard to possible contexts or speaker intentions. By virtue of the grammatical rules of English, every native speaker recognizes that *Norman is a Mormon* is an English sentence and knows what it means, wherever and whenever he hears or reads it.[12]

Grammatical rules, then, define properties of *sentences*, linguistic objects. But rules governing propositional and illocutionary acts define the contextual and intentional conditions under which utterances of sentences *count as* propositional or illocutionary acts. Thus these rules link utterance acts to utterance conditions. One of the rules governing propositional acts, for example, is that, for a referring phrase in a sentence (*the man who broke the bank at Monte Carlo*, say) to count as actually referring, there must exist or have existed something that it identifies. There is, or was, one and only one man known to both speaker and hearer who broke the bank at Monte Carlo.[13] Similarly, the rules governing the illocutionary act of asserting are that, for utterance of a sentence expressing a certain proposition P to count as asserting P, the speaker must be committed to believing P, having evidence for the truth of P, and so on. Simply stated, the rules constituting propositional and illocutionary acts allow such social *acts* as committing oneself to believing propositions, or to having evidence for their truth. They allow private intentional states to become social, public facts.[14]

The question "What is literature?" is, we must note before going further, ambiguous; for *literature* has several senses, two relevant to literary theory. In one, literature is "writings having excellence of form or expression and expressing ideas of permanent or universal interest" (*Webster's Third*): *King Lear, De Rerum Natura, Wilhelm Meister,* and Mill's *On Liberty*—but not the works of Edgar Guest or Mickey Spillane, and not the *Congressional Record*. In the other sense, literature is imaginative literature, fictional discourse: *King Lear, Wilhelm Meister,* and the works of Edgar Guest and Mickey Spillane—but not *De Rerum Natura* or *On Liberty*, and not the *Congressional Record*. As these examples suggest, some discourses are literature in one sense, some in the other, some in both, and some in neither.

Clearly, literature in the first sense must be defined in perlocutionary-act terms; it is discourse that causes the reader to think well of it—to pronounce it excellent or interesting. And, since perlocutionary acts can, as we have seen, vary from reader to reader, discourse that one reader counts as literary, another reader may not. Because literature in this first sense is relativistic, our intention is to define literature in the second sense. What, then, is fictional discourse?

## FICTIONAL DISCOURSE

We begin our answer to this question with the heuristic assumptions that fictional discourse is distinct from nonfictional, that the differences between these two kinds of discourse are differences in constitutive rules, and that we can define or explain fictional discourse by describing the rules that constitute it and relating them to other rules of language.[15]

First, can fictional discourse be defined in grammatical (or utterance-act) terms? Is there a grammatical feature or set of such features—syntactic, phonological, graphic, or semantic—possessed by all fictional discourse but by no nonfictional? In the last thirty years or so, literary theorists have frequently assumed that there is. There is, they assume, a language of literature or of poetry in the broad sense. " . . . the language of poetry," Cleanth Brooks long ago wrote, "is the language of paradox."[16] For Jan Mukařovský, "Poetic language is a different form with a different function from that of the standard."[17] For Manfred Bierwisch, a poetic or literary theory is "a theory of the structure of literary texts or verbal works of art. . . ."[18]

Whether fictional discourse can be so defined is a large and complex issue that has spawned a vast bibliography, and here we can only suggest why we reject the assumption that fictional discourse can be explained grammatically. Most crucially, though it is easy to think of grammatical features that *some* fictional discourse, but no nonfictional, possesses, no one—to our knowledge—has thought of any that *all* fictional, and no nonfictional, possesses. The point of view of the omniscient narrator, for instance, is a semantic feature of some fictional discourse and of no nonfictional, but, of course, not of all fictional. Meter and rhyme are phonological features of some fictional discourse, but not of all; and, as Elizabeth Barrett Browning's *Sonnets from the Portuguese* testify, these features belong to nonfictional discourse as well. At best, phonological schemes and graphic ones (carmina figurata, technopaignia), as in concrete poetry and George Herbert's "Easter Wings," are clues to, or symptoms of, fictional discourse.[19] But they are unreliable ones: much fictional discourse is quite asymptomatic. Compare the first sentence of *Robinson Crusoe* ("I was born in the year 1632, in the City of York. . . .") with an early sentence of Mill's *Autobiography* ("I was born in London, on the 20th of May, 1806 . . . .").

Whether a discourse is fictional does not, then, depend upon what the speaker or writer says; it depends instead, we believe, upon how he intends the hearer or reader to take what he says. If we take William Carlos Williams' "Poem," for example, to be fictional discourse—

### Poem

As the cat
climbed over
the top of

the jamcloset
first the right
forefoot

carefully
then the hind
stepped down

into the pit of
the empty
flowerpot

that is surely not because of the sentence of which it consists: a multiply embedded declarative sentence of the most ordinary sort. Nor is it because of its division into lines, at best a symptom.[20] It is because we believe, or at least assume, that Williams intends us to take it to be that. The question is, What does Williams intend us to do, and what do we do, when we take "Poem" to be fictional discourse? More generally, what is it to take a discourse as fictional?

Briefly, to take a discourse as fictional is, as other writers have observed, to take it as an utterance act that pretends to be, but is not, a propositional act and an illocutionary act as well.[21] In performing an utterance act, the speaker or writer pretends to refer to things, to predicate properties or relations of them, and to perform an illocutionary act, but he does not really do so. And *pretend* is the key word. As Searle has pointed out, it is an intentional verb; the idea of intention is built into it; we cannot pretend unless we intend to pretend. And so fictionality has its source in the intentions of the speaker or writer.[22]

Williams' "Poem" might well be an assertion referring to a certain cat, a certain jamcloset, and so on, and predicating certain properties and relations of them. According to the illocutionary-act rules governing assertions, utterance of a declarative sentence in authentic language use commits the speaker or writer to believing the proposition he expresses is true. But, if we are native readers of fictional discourse—if we know the rules constituting it—and if we take "Poem" to be fictional discourse, then we know, or assume, that Williams has committed himself to nothing in uttering "Poem." Nor has he, we know, lied or otherwise misinformed us or written pointlessly; he could not have done so. Whether he really referred to a certain cat is, we know, an irrelevant question, as is the question of whether a certain cat truly has the properties Williams might seem to predicate of it. Our knowledge of the rules constituting fictional discourse tells us that utterances taken the way we take "Poem" are not bound by the rules constituting nonfictional discourse. "Poem" is not a commitment but a pretense of one.

A discourse *is* fictional because its speaker or writer intends it to be so. But it is *taken as* fictional only because the hearer or reader *decides* to take it so  Often this decision is informed—by a semantic feature like the point of view of an omniscient narrator or phonological or graphic symptoms, or by formulaic phrases like "Once upon a time . . .," or by explicit announcements like "A Novel" on the title page, or by external evidence like an author's letters. In the most interesting cases, however, the decision is arbitrary: nothing in or around the discourse is evidence of how its speaker or writer intended it to be taken. Lacking evidence of the speaker or writer's intentions—and this point is crucial—we must postulate them. For the decision to read a discourse as fictional or nonfictional is a decision to use one set of constitutive rules rather than another, and we really can't read it—interpret it—at all until we have made this decision.

Just what are the rules that constitute fictional discourse? The definition of fictional discourse as a pretended propositional and illocutionary act is a useful beginning. But it tells us little about the operation of the rules; in particular, it tells us nothing about the precise nature of the pretense, which is not quite so straightforward as our account thus far suggests. The key to the distinction between fictional and nonfictional discourse lies in whom we take to be the speaker or writer and whom we take to be the hearer or reader.

In nonfictional discourse, *I* refers to the speaker or writer, *you* to the hearer or reader. In conversation, these correlations are patent: the speaker speaks, and the hearer is identified by eye contact, gesture, and the like. In written nonfictional discourse—letters, notes, memoranda, and so on—there is some possibility for misinterpretation, for the text may be separated from its context or situation of utterance. But, spoken or written, nonfictional discourse has the same basic structure: one speaker or writer (or, as in the case of the present discourse, a team), a hearer or reader (or group of them), and a context providing a body of shared knowledge. Let's call such nonfictional discourse *situated discourse,* since the words are inextricably linked to a particular context upon which they depend for correct interpretation.[23]

Fictional discourse, on the other hand, is neither intended nor—by native readers of it—taken as situated discourse. If there is an *I,* it refers not to the actual speaker or writer, but rather to a fictive speaker or writer. And so with the *you*: it refers not to the actual reader with the book in his hand or to the hearer of the joke or fictional anecdote, but to a fictive hearer or reader. What the speaker or writer of a piece of fictional discourse pretends to do is to perform the utterance-propositional-illocutionary act of *reporting* the speech acts of a fictive speaker or writer to a fictive hearer or reader. What the actual hearer or reader does is to *overhear* these reported speech acts.

This is, of course, obvious in plays, dramatic monologues, and narrative fiction with first-person narrators. In "My Last Duchess"—

> That's my last Duchess painted on the wall,
> Looking as if she were alive. I call
> That piece a wonder now; Frà Pandolf's hands
> Worked busily a day, and there she stands.
> Will't please you sit and look at her?

Browning pretends to report the utterance-propositional-illocutionary acts of a fictive speaker (the Duke, the *I* of the poem) to a fictive hearer (the Count's emissary, the *you* of the poem), and the reader overhears him doing so.

But the unsituated nature of fictional discourse is less obvious when the difference between the persona and the actual writer or between the fictive audience and the actual readership is less blatant—in "tall tales," say, or in some lyric poetry. We might, for example, take Keats himself to be speaking the "Ode on Melancholy," thus taking the poem as a highly metaphoric maxim on depression. But surely *he* is not telling *us* not to make our "rosaries of yew-berries." Similarly, when reading *The Way We Live Now*, we can identify the reader with us and other actual readers ("Let the reader be introduced to Lady Carbury . . . as she sits at her writing table. . . ."). But the narrator is clearly not Trollope, an ordinary mortal; it is a fictive, godlike, omniscient narrator who knows for sure Lady Carbury's thoughts and feelings. Simply stated, situated discourse is always spoken *in propria persona*; fictional discourse never is.

Typically, then, fictional discourse has a layered structure very much like that of reported speech in situated, nonfictional discourse. The utterance of a sentence like, "John told Twyla that he heard Mary say she won't marry Fred," in nonfictional discourse is interpreted in layers of speakers and hearers, each speech-act layer assigned to the proper speaker. The person uttering the sentence takes responsibility for accurately reporting John's speech acts; John, for accurately reporting Mary's. The utterance of the very same sentence in fictional discourse would be interpreted in the same way, except for one crucial difference: the person uttering the sentence—the narrator of a novel, say—exists only within the fictional world of the discourse—about which, more shortly.

The actual speaker, then, *cannot* be bound to the commitments which would seem to follow from the speech acts reported in a piece of fictional discourse: he has not performed them at all. But, we must note, once the reader has accepted the pretense and entered into the fictional world of the discourse, the propositional-act and illocutionary-act rules obtain. If they did not, the reader could not recognize unreliable narrators and characters who lie, make insincere promises, or otherwise violate these rules.[24]

Our basic claim, then, is that there are two broad genres of discourse—nonfictional and fictional—and that, except for this pretense, both genres are constituted by the same rules: grammatical (or utterance-act) rules, propositional-act rules, and illocutionary-act rules. The reader interprets both genres of discourse in the same way, except that, in reading fictional discourse, he recognizes that the words-to-real-world link is missing. This view of things pleases Ockham's razor. To account for fictional discourse, we need not postulate a separate-but-equal set of linguistic rules; we need only postulate one rule—the pretense-of-reporting rule. The rule knowledge required to form or interpret fictional discourse is identical with that required for nonfictional—with the exception of this one rule. Let's call this rule a *genre rule* to distinguish it from grammatical, propositional-act, and illocutionary-act rules.[25]

There is yet another striking similarity between fictional and nonfictional discourse. Both of these broad genres interact with other genres of discourse, each constituted by one or more genre rules. Some of these other genres are subgenres of fictional discourse. Novels written from the point of view of the omniscient narrator are one such genre, and so are the ritual insults, "sounds," in black vernacular culture, whose rules William Labov has described.[26] Other genres are subgenres of nonfictional discourse. Scholarly articles, autobiography, and (perhaps) inaugural addresses are examples, but so is everyday conversation, whose rules H. Paul Grice has described.[27] Still others are not subgenres of either. As we have noted, sonnets can be either fictional or nonfictional discourse. Wordsworth's are fictional; Elizabeth Barrett Browning's, nonfictional; Shakespeare's in doubt. The genre rules that constitute sonnets— specifying phonological, semantic, and graphic features—are neutral to fictionality.

## EXTENDING THE ANALYSIS: FICTIONAL CHARACTERS AND FICTIONAL WORLDS

We have spoken of fictional worlds peopled with fictive speakers or writers, and with fictive hearers or readers—that is, with characters. The question remains: How does a fictional world come into being? Our answer is that it is created in much the same way that a nonfictional world is: by inferences that the hearer or reader makes from the text by using relevant knowledge—knowledge of grammatical, propositional-act, and illocutionary-act rules, of genre rules, of facts, and of empirical laws.[28]

An everyday language illustration: suppose a friend calls and opens the conversation with "Mary's here for the weekend." In using the proper name *Mary* he refers to a person mutually known, predicates her being "here," and so on. What goes on when a hearer recovers a reference—visualizing Mary from memories, say—is a matter for psycholinguistic investigation, a *perlocutionary effect* of a speech act, and necessarily idiosyncratic. But though an individual's cognitive processes in visualizing the referent of a referring term are private, the entire process is not. Consider the effect of *overhearing* a reference, of hearing a total stranger say to his hearer, "Mary's here for the weekend," for example. We can't attempt to visualize Mary; we lack the factual knowledge, but we can form solid inferences on the basis of our knowledge of speech-act rules. We can infer, for example, from the rule requiring belief in the thing referred to that the speaker believes that Mary exists, and believes that his hearer knows (or knows of) Mary. Each inference contributes to our conception of the speaker, his hearer, their relationship, and the world they share. And as soon as we move beyond the limited case of reference with proper names, the inferences we can describe are much richer. Anaïs Nin provides a useful example in the third volume of her diary; she writes that "At the Gotham Book Mart I met the old mystic Claude Bragdon. . . . He is a tall austere man, a rigid petrified man, like an ancient tree, or a petrified mummy." Knowing that diary is not a fictional genre, we can assume that Bragdon once existed, and that he was as she presents him in her complex identifying description: tall, rigid, and mummylike. Since we probably have no previous knowledge of Bragdon, her account alone creates our image of this part of the actual world. Were we so inclined, we might attempt to verify her statements, and were we to find that Bragdon was not as she describes, we could assume that she has lied or misled us. Erring and misleading, of course, are defects of nonfictional discourse, including diaries. We know this just because we know the relevant genre rules.[29]

How do things differ in fictional discourse? The relevant generalization is that *all* discourse creates a potential world by the action of the rules of language. The difference between fictional and nonfictional discourse is simply that, in the latter, speakers or writers are committed to insuring that the potential world corresponds to the actual world.[30] The same rules which commit a speaker or writer to the consequences of his speech in nonfictional discourse create the characters and world in fictional discourse. Producing and interpreting fictional discourse—like most authentic language use—involve a cooperative effort: speakers do not normally intend to mislead their hearers, and hearers do not normally intend to misinterpret.[31] Knowing this, writers or speakers of fictional discourse can assume that if an inference can be made from the speech of their fictional characters it will be made and, as part of the cooperative effort, form their discourses so that the readers or hearers will be able to infer all necessary information about the fictional world and the characters within it.[32] So, when William Carlos Williams' fictional speaker refers to a cat, a jamcloset, and a flowerpot, the readers infer the existence of these things within the ficational world created by the poem.

Not only do the characters in fictional discourse create parts of the fictional world; they also create themselves, through similar inference processes. We easily come to know the personality of even a distant third-person narrator. And so too in lyric poetry. In the first stanza of the "Ode on Melancholy," Keats' fictional persona makes three negative commands:

> No, no, go not to Lethe, neither twist
> Wolfsbane, tight-rooted for its poisonous wine;
> Nor suffer thy pale forehead to be kissed
> By nightshade, ruby grape of Proserpine. . . .

Negative commands have interesting "preparatory rules," illocutionary act rules specifying the conditions necessary if the illocutionary act is to have a point. Simply stated: do not command things which your hearer is likely to do in the normal course of events.[33] Thus to command someone *not* to do something, we must believe that he *would* do it, left to his own devices. Knowing this rule, we can infer that the persona believes his hearer likely to engage in the sorts of depressive behavior he figuratively proscribes.

But our inferences do not stop there. We probably go on to infer certain personality traits of the fictional hearer: that he is depressive, given to suicidal fantasies, and tempted to seek escapes, perhaps. And so too with the fictional speaker: since he describes the depressed state in such elegant detail, we might infer that he too has been depressed, and can provide wise counsel. As the poem progresses, our sense of both characters grows.

Crucially, the first inferences about the persona's view of his fictional hearer are based in part on linguistic rules; the psychological ones which follow are not, however. These are based on empirical generalizations—crude ones—about the behavior of depressives. The theoretical point is this: inference is not a necessarily linguistic operation; it is a logical process which may be contingently linguistic in cases where linguistic rules are the basis of the inference. The inference process involved in interpreting fictional discourse thus corresponds exactly to that of nonfictional discourse and, for that matter, to non-linguistic inference as well. Except in two crucial details: First, and obviously, all truth conditions are suspended: we are not disturbed to find that Sherlock Holmes' Baker Street address is and always was within the boundaries of a nonfictional London park. Second, normal inferences—linguistic and otherwise—can be blocked by the action of the fictional discourse rule: we do not infer from Lemuel Gulliver's reports of giants and talking horses that he is totally mad, as we surely would from equivalent nonfictional discourse. And so too with inferences based on linguistic rules: Claudius, in his initial speech in *Hamlet*, refers to Gertrude in the company of intimates as "our sometime sister, now our queen,/Th' imperial jointress to this warlike state." In everyday speech we can infer that a person who identifies a friend with a lengthy identifying description must be speaking to a hearer who is not acquainted with the person. Language follows a strict principle of economy: maximum communicative ends with minimum linguistic means. So where *Gertrude* will serve to refer, Claudius should use it. Yet we find nothing strange in his speech, and we infer nothing from it. Members of Shakespeare's audience—native readers—know that this is a concession to them, the overhearers; it serves to build the fictional world: it is exposition.

Our remarks have been brief and programmatic. But the answer we propose to the question "What is literature (that is, fictional discourse)?" should be clear: fictional discourse is discourse whose creation and interpretation are governed by three distinct types of constitutive rules. Fictional and nonfictional discourse share the grammatical and speech-act rules of the language. Fictional discourse differs logically and ontologically through the action of the genre rule of fictional discourse.

## NOTES

1. The most important theory of this kind has, of course, been developed by Noam Chomsky in, e.g., *Syntactic Structures* (The Hague: Mouton, 1957) and *Aspects of the Theory of Syntax* (Cambridge, Mass.: M.I.T. Press, 1965).

2. *Philosophical Investigations*, tr. G.E.M. Anscombe (Oxford: Blackwell, 1953), p. 32.

3. First in "The Role of Theory in Aesthetics," *Journal of Aesthetics and Art Criticism*, 15 (1956), 27-35; later in *Hamlet and the Philosophy of Literary Criticism* (Chicago: Univ. of Chicago Press, 1964), to which references are given here. Weitz's focus is the concept of tragedy; but his generalizations, he believes, hold for the concept of literature and other concepts central to poetics.

4. *Ethics and Language* (New Haven: Yale Univ. Press, 1944), Ch. 9.

5. "What is the Use of Theorizing About the Arts?" *In Search of Literary Theory*, ed. Morton W. Bloomfield (Ithaca: Cornell Univ. Press, 1972), p. 25.

6. For some criticisms of this view of theory, see Monroe C. Beardsley, review of *In Search of Literary Theory*, *Centrum*, 1 (1973), 77-81; Jonathan Culler, "Viewpoint," *Times Literary Supplement*, no. 30705 (1973), 266; Alan Donagan, *The Latter Philosophy of R.G. Collingwood* (Oxford: Clarendon Press, 1962), pp. 103-04; Martin Steinmann, Jr., "Cumulation, Revolution and Progress," *New Literary History*, 5 (1974), 477-90, and "Linguistics and Literary Criticism," *From Meaning to Sound*, ed. Hassan Sharifi (Lincoln: Univ. of Nebraska, 1975), pp. 205-09.

7. Many different theorists fall under this category—many of whom would not enjoy the others' company. This view is implicit in much of the New Criticism and in the product of that theory: the new readings which people the literary quarterlies. In another version it underlies much of the effort of the French Post Structuralists to provide a new hermeneutics—and with it, new literary forms.

8. *How to Do Things With Words* (Cambridge, Mass.: Harvard Univ. Press, 1962).

9. First in "What is a Speech Act?" *Philosophy in America*, ed. Max Black (Ithaca: Cornell Univ. Press, 1965), pp. 221-39, but fully presented in *Speech Acts: An Essay in the Philosophy in Language* (Cambridge: Cambridge Univ. Press, 1969). A more recent treatment of some of the details of illocutionary acts is found in "A Taxonomy of Illocutionary Acts," *Language, Mind, and Knowledge*, ed. Keith Gunderson (Minneapolis: Univ. of Minnesota Press, 1975), pp. 344-69.

10. Searle, *Speech Acts*, Ch. 2.

11. Searle, *Speech Acts*, Ch. 2.

12. Cf. H. Paul Grice, "Utterer's Meaning, Sentence-Meaning, and Word-Meaning," *Foundations of Language*, 4 (1968), 1-18; and Robert L. Brown, Jr. and Martin Steinmann, Jr., "Multiple Competences," Proceedings of the 4th Annual Colloquium on New Ways of Analysing Variation in English (N-WAVE IV), 28-30 November, 1975 (Washington D.C.: Georgetown Univ. Press, forthcoming).

13. Searle, *Speech Acts*, Ch. 4.

14. Searle, *Speech Acts*, Chs. 1 and 2.

15. A rare assumption, but one shared by Jonathan Culler, *Structuralist Poetics* (London: Routledge & Kegan Paul, 1975) and Tuen A. van Dijk, *Some Aspects of Text-Grammars* (The Hague: Mouton, 1972). Cf.

Robert L. Brown, Jr., review of the latter, *Centrum*, 1.2 (1973), 155-65.

16. *The Well Wrought Urn* (New York: Regnal and Hitchcock, 1947), p. 3.

17. "Standard Language and Poetic Language," *Linguistics and Literary Style*, ed. Donald C. Freeman (New York: Holt, Rinehart and Winston, 1970), p. 52.

18. "Poetics and Linguistics," in Freeman, p. 97.

19. Strictly speaking, many of these symptoms are not really properties of the text at all. Metric patterns, alliteration, assonance, and so on are imposed upon the stream of sound by application of grammatical and other rules. Cf. Culler, pp. 114-15.

20. Of course, Williams is challenging our conventional attitudes toward poetry, and probably doing many more things as well in this defiantly unpoetic poem, but none of these meanings or gestures bear on the basic logical question we address.

21. Searle, "The Logical Status of Fictional Discourse," *New Literary History*, 6 (1975), 319-20, and Richard Ohmann, "Speech Acts and the Definition of Literature," *Philosophy and Rhetoric*, 4 (1971).

22. Searle, "The Logical Status of Fictional Discourse."

23. For a more complete treatment of this question, see Robert L. Brown, Jr., "Intentions and the Contexts of Poetry," *Centrum*, 2.1 (1974), 55-66.

24. Our view of fictional discourse is quite conservative, including only the suspension of the consequences of speech acts for the actual speaker or writer. Other features of specific genres of fictional discourse—mode of reporting, structural patterns, content, and so on—are, we claim, constituted by other rules.

25. Brown and Steinmann, "Multiple Competences."

26. *Language in the Inner City* (Philadelphia: Univ. of Pennsylvania Press, 1972).

27. H. Paul Grice, "Logic and Conversation," in *Syntax and Semantics, Vol. 3: Speech Acts*, ed. Peter Cole and Jerry Morgan (New York: Academic Press, 1975), pp. 41-58.

28. Two relevant accounts of inference are Searle, "Indirect Speech Acts," in Cole and Morgan, pp. 59-82, and the text on which it is based: Grice, "Logic and Conversation."

29. Cf. Elizabeth Bruss, *Autobiographical Acts* (Baltimore: Johns Hopkins Univ. Press, 1976).

30. But, of course, they may still not do so. As with all language rules, genre rules are subject to misuse, to what linguistic theorists call "per-

formance errors." We know from the genre rules that the author is committed to making the words match the world, but we know from everyday experience that people's perceptions of the world vary greatly. And we know from common sense that people lie and mislead. The linguistic rules cannot, of course, guarantee the truth.

31. Grice, "Logic and Conversation."

32. No discourse, of course, encodes all of its meaning; every speaker or writer assumes some common knowledge between him and his hearer or reader. Cf. Brown, "Intentions and the Contexts of Poetry."

33. Searle, *Speech Acts*, pp. 66-7.

# Aesthetic Intentions and Fictive Illocutions

## *Monroe C. Beardsley*

The concept of literature is sometimes thought to be an insecure and sliding one, dependent in no crucial way on the nature of the discourses in question but rather on the attitudes or activities of those who discourse about them. For example, there is the view that the concept of literature, being comparatively modern, has no application to earlier writings: that "there have always been, it would seem, poems, stories, fictions of various kinds, but there has not always been literature,"[1]—because discourses were previously not classified in that way. But I don't suppose that literature began when the term did; if, for example, the earliest use (1879) of the term *brontosaurus* noted in the Supplement to the OED was indeed the earliest use, we would not want to say that the brontosaurus came into existence only long after it was extinct. René Wellek has traced with fascinating thoroughness the history of the term *literature* and corresponding terms in other languages,[2] and this is a history of ideas. But if we are going to allow for progress in literary theory, we must admit new terms marking hitherto unnoted differences which were nevertheless present before they were named.

There are also problems, I think, with the institutional

analysis of literature quite carefully worked out by John M. Ellis.[3] The essential idea is this: "Literary texts are defined as those
that are used by the society in such a way that *the text is not taken
as specifically relevant to the immediate context of its origin*" (p. 44). I
have tried elsewhere to articulate my doubts about the institutional analysis of art in general;[4] as applied to literature, it seems
to have both a special plausibility and special difficulties. Without pretending that this important proposal can be dismissed
with a short rebuttal, I offer a few remarks. To be "used by the
society," for Ellis, is to be used "by members of the community"
(p. 46)—but it is difficult to define the relevant (i.e., literary)
community without circularity. And what is it to "take" a discourse as not *specifically relevant* to its occasion? Ellis also says
(my emphasis) that when "the piece of language is no longer
regarded as one having interest *only* for its original utterer, those
addressed by him, and those (present or future) who have interest in that whole situation, it is being treated as literature" (p.
44). But suppose a present-day critic writes an essay on Hopkins' poem, "The Windhover." He or she notes that this poem
was written at the end of May, 1877, a few months before Hopkins' ordination (scheduled for that September), and with the
aid of passages culled from Hopkins' sermons and journals
concludes that this poem, especially in such words as "My heart
in hiding/Stirred for a bird," refers to his novitiate and his coming new service to God. This critic of course need not be regarding the poem as having interest *only* for those concerned with
Hopkins' religious activities; but it seems that he is taking the
text "as specifically relevant to the immediate context of its origin." If his fellow Hopkins-scholars follow him in this practice, it
would seem that the poem is, by Ellis' definition, no longer
literature. Such a consequence would be troubling.

There may be purposes for which it would be convenient to
have a concept of literature relativized to the interests of the
literary world at any given time, but I don't think that's the one

we have, or need most. True, discourses that at one time are used only in certain ways, and are not thought of as belonging in a class with epic poetry and tragic drama, may later be taken up and placed in that class. But we can, of course, interpret this development in various ways: for example, we may say that the literary status of the work was formerly overlooked (as perhaps with *Pilgrim's Progress*) or that the concept of literature (not just its current range of application) underwent a change. The movement from without to within the class of literary discourses seems to be one-way, after all; what was previously regarded as a paradigm of literature but is now ignored will not be called "nonliterature," but "poor literature."

Stanley Fish's conclusions about the literature/nonliterature distinction has affinities with Ellis' but are less easy to make out. "Literature is language," he says; "but it is language around which we have drawn a frame, a frame that indicates a decision to regard with a particular self-consciousness the resources language has always possessed."[5] "Literature is still a category," but is defined "simply by what we decide to put into it"—where "we" constitute a "community of readers or believers."

> Only such a view, I believe, can accommodate and reconcile the two intuitions that have for so long kept linguistic and literary theory apart; the intuition that there *is* a class of literary utterances, and the intuition that any piece of language can become a member of that class.

I don't know where the second intuition comes from, or who besides Professor Fish has had it; my intuition is that *no* discourse can *become* literature (unless by being rewritten) and that there are discourses that have no hope of being classified as literature. Not that intuition is worth much unless it can be explained and justified—in which case it will be more than an intuition.

What Fish means, apparently, is that any piece of discourse

can be treated, or approached, or considered as literature; and since it is this "attitude" (p. 52) that defines literature, any discourse can be literature. But there are two gaps in this argument, I think. First, that something can be considered as an X does not in general make it an X—to seek aesthetic satisfaction from a tulip is, in a way, to treat it as a work of art, but that does not make it a work of art. So some discourses may have literary merit and may appeal to literary interest without being literature. Second, there is a leap (which Ellis is more careful to avoid) from individual to group: even if any discourse could be considered as literature by someone, it does not follow that every discourse could be considered as literature by the literary "community"—if that is defined in such a way as to include scholars and accomplished readers. But in the absence of any very clear account of that community, this second point can't confidently be pressed.

Turning now to the question of finding, or devising, a satisfactory definition of literature, what can we say that is reasonably well established about this term? First it must be acknowledged that the term *literature* can be used to designate a quality understood to be desirable, and thus to single out some discourses for commendation of a certain kind. This is not surprising, because many common nouns can be used in a similar way ("This was a man!"); and perhaps a special aura of "the best that has been thought and said" lingers about the word "literature." I take it that literary criticism and literary theory have no need for this first use of *literature*. So, second: *literature* is also used as a collective term for a class of discourses—as elliptical for "literary works," the presumed primary (perhaps sole) concern of the critic and of the theorist.

A work, in the sense of a product, has got to be something deliberately made; *literary work* thus contains an essential reference to a maker. How much activity, how far directed, counts as making may be subject to dispute. A wholly aleatoric discourse—one composed by picking slips of paper out of a hat—can hardly be said to have been made deliberately, even though the acts of picking were deliberate: the resulting discourse was not envisioned as such in any way before it came into being. For my purpose here, it is perhaps sufficient to note that this is one element of vagueness in the concept of *literary work*, but it leaves a vast number of discourses plainly and safely inside the class.

A literary work is something produced intentionally, then; I think this has not been denied, except by the aleatoricists. But is it something produced by a distinctive intention? Is "literary work" to be understood as itself elliptical for "literary work of art"? After all the intense discussion by aestheticians in recent decades, the question, "What is art?" still provokes disagreement, and it would be fatal to the present limited enterprise to become entangled in that dispute. Still, I must commit myself in one way or another, in order to proceed. I am still of the opinion that we can identify something that may reasonably be called an "aesthetic intention"—that is, the intention to make something capable of affording aesthetic satisfaction to one who properly approaches it. There are very many problems about aesthetic satisfaction (and its connected concept, aesthetic experience), but if I may be permitted to set them aside, I wish to propose that a work of art (in general) is something deliberately made, in the making of which an aesthetic intention played a substantial part. Here is where I part company with the institutional concept of art: I'm willing to say that an amateur painter, for example, has produced a work of art (however deficient it may be) if he paints with the clear intention (perhaps mixed with other intentions, as intentions usually are) of producing a painting that is capable of providing some aesthetic satisfaction.

Evidently my qualification "substantial" marks a second vagueness in the boundary of "literary work (of art)," but it is one we can put up with, I think. For though it is the presence of a serious aesthetic intention that makes an act of discourse-producing into an act of literature-producing, and though we may at times have to accept the author's word in order to know his intention, in most cases we can infer the intention from the actual deed. When a discourse shows signs of concern for those features of it that affect its capacity to provide aesthetic satisfaction—when it is structured in suitable ways, has an expressive style, etc.—we may legitimately suppose that the author was interested in making something aesthetically worth having, even though his other intentions, including his dominant intention, were religious or philosophical or political. Of course a work that displays signs of an aesthetic intention will also ipso facto have some literary value—which may help to explain why "literature" is so readily used normatively and taken to be essentially normative. However, it is, on my view, not the presence of aesthetic merits per se but the aesthetic intention they evince that distinguishes literary works of art from other discourses.

One fault that may be found in my definition is that it does away with a "canon of literature," for which, as Alvin B. Kernan has noted, some would claim significance.[6] To them

> it is apparent that the numerous fictions of popular and mass culture are excluded so absolutely as to make it doubtful whether they are even of the same species as literature. *King Lear* and *Absalom, Absalom* are literature, while *Tarzan of the Apes* and *Gone With the Wind* are not. On this there is no question. . . .

Kernan reports this view with some ironic detachment, though not without regret that "we begin to drift away from it" (p. 39). There is a real problem here, I think: what are we to do with the category of "popular literature," which has had a considerable and rapidly growing scholarly vogue in recent years (along with an interest in popular arts in general)?

I believe that when we consider attentively the phenomenological differences between the experience of reading *Absalom, Absalom* and that of reading *Tarzan of the Apes*—or, more obviously, between *King Lear* and *Charlie's Aunt*, or between a dramatization of *The Golden Bowl* on public television and an episode of *Happy Days*—we are aware that some elements enter into entertainment that do not enter into our experience of the higher works of literary or dramatic art. For example, there are those appeals, noted so long ago by Richards, to "stock responses." But these elements are so inextricably entangled with other elements that are equally notable in the greater works—narrative devices and structures, figures of speech, basic humorous situations, verbal wit—that we do not seem to have crossed the border of literature. Certainly we can mark off, very loosely, those literary works that have (or have had) considerable popular appeal, owing to their comparative simplicity and ease of access and to their familiar subject matter, and call these examples of "popular literature," classifying them along with American primitive paintings, cigar-store-Indian sculpture, and various kinds of folk art, such as quilts and square dances and blues. But insofar as we can discern a clear aesthetic intention in works of all these diverse kinds, I see no need to deny them the general name of "art," even if we cannot rank them as art with the works of masters. Of course there will always be countless interesting cases on the border of popular and fine literature—"The Murders in the Rue Morgue," *Iolanthe*, *Christina's World*, "Upstairs, Downstairs."

John Searle has remarked:

> There used to be a school of literary critics who thought one should not consider the intentions of the author when examining a work of fiction. Perhaps there is some level of intention at which this extraordinary view is plausible; perhaps one should not consider an author's ulterior motives when analyzing his work, but at the most basic level it is absurd to suppose a critic can completely ignore the intentions of the author, since even so much as to identify a text as a novel, a poem, or even as a text is already to make a claim about the author's intentions.[7]

As many theorists use the term, and as I think it should be used, it does not seem to be true that to identify something as a *text* necessarily involves an appeal to any intention. If the utterance or inscription in question belongs to a class of utterances (a dict) or of inscriptions (a script) that is a well-formed character in some language, it is a text—though produced with no intention at all, as by a parrot or a computer. What about a novel or poem, then? These cases being more debatable, the statement of my own view becomes the more dogmatic, I'm afraid: given an English discourse, or text, I would say that considerations about intention are not logically requisite to a decision whether it is a poem.

Nor could they be, I think, since the sort of intention that could be relevant to writing a poem is the intention to write a poem.[8] But we cannot understand what it is to *intend* to write a poem unless we already understand what it is to *write* a poem. Therefore we cannot define *poem* without circularity in terms of "intention to write a poem." But we *can* define *literature* without circularity in terms of "aesthetic intention."

In short, it is a paradoxical consequence of the intentionalist definition of literature that literature becomes severed (logically) from the categories or genres that in fact make it up. This is odd, but not utterly unsettling, I think. It only means that though characteristically discourses that are poems will also be literary works of art, this is not logically necessary: there is no self-contradiction in saying that a poem (but not literature) has been produced automatically or accidentally or inadvertently or by mistake or by chance.

The problem of defining literature has been vastly complicated and illuminated in recent years by a new concept of fiction derived from J. L. Austin's widely-known doctrine of illocutionary acts. I have previously discussed this concept of fiction—essentially, that fiction is discourse in which there is a kind of representation, or make-believe performance, of illocutionary actions, but no such actions are actually performed.[9] And I commented on earlier presentations of this view by Marcia Eaton, Richard Ohmann, and myself. Since then, various others have contributed valuably to the development of the view: notably Searle, in the essay just quoted, Barbara Herrnstein Smith,[10] Martin Steinmann, Jr.,[11] and Stanley Fish.[12] The issue that concerns us here, on which these theorists are divided, is whether literature can be defined in terms of fiction, as analyzed in Austinian terms.

It is customary to introduce the concept of *illocutionary action* by examples, because, so far as I can discover, no one has yet proposed a satisfactory definition of this term. I shall offer a definition on which to base my discussion. There are certain accepted conventions, or rules, that have the power to make an action of one kind also an action of another kind. Thus given the set of legal rules codified in the law of contracts, the act of writing one's name on a certain piece of paper becomes the act of signing a contract. And given a set of regulations laid down in certain codes of military behavior, the act of raising one's hand to one's forehead in a certain way becomes the act of saluting. These conventions, if written out, might be somewhat complex: they would specify the conditions under which an action of type A becomes also an action of type B. For example, in the second case, it is requisite that the person performing the action belong to the armed services. A civilian can go through the motions and call it a salute, but that is only an imitation (or representation) of one.

In Alvin Goldman's terminology we can say that when the particular sort of hand-motion is performed under certain specifiable conditions (taking "conditions" in the broadest possible way to include physical, psychological, and social conditions), that action *conventionally generates* the act of saluting.[13] And the act of writing one's name will, also under specifiable conditions, conventionally generate the act of signing a contract.

Now we must introduce Austin's concept of *locutionary action:* that of uttering a sentence, or sentence-surrogate ("It looks like rain"). "Uttering" is taken very broadly here, too: it includes writing as well as speaking, and some gesturing. Among the act-generating conventions in a given society or group are those that apply specifically to locutionary actions; in virtue of them, a locutionary act, under appropriate conditions, will conventionally generate an act of another type. Thus, in the simplest sort of case, the (locutionary) act of saying the words "Hello, Dolly!" when uttered upon coming into the presence of Dolly, conventionally generates the (illocutionary) act of greeting Dolly. Illocutionary actions can thus be defined as those actions conventionally generated by locutionary actions.

Since the conditions for performing an illocutionary action—as stipulated in the convention that makes its generation possible—are generally multiple, it is possible to perform a locutionary action that fulfills some of those conditions but not others. And if certain words are generally used in performing an illocutionary act of that kind, then to utter those words without fulfilling all the conditions is to present something that is like—but not quite—that illocutionary act. Thus deception becomes possible—and also harmless pretending. It is only necessary to make clear that one or more of the requisite conditions are lacking, while at the same time inviting the receiver (the hearer or reader) to make-believe that they are present, in order to convert a genuine illocutionary action into a fictive one. So fictive discourse, on this view, is discourse in which there is a make-believe illocutionary action, but in fact no such action is performed.

For this play of language to work, the writer must supply enough material so that we can by suitable supplementation and reconstruction determine what illocutionary action *would* be recorded in the text if any were; we try to fit the most appropriate generating conventions.[14] But at the same time the writer must supply signals that the conventions cannot really be applied, since some essential condition is withheld. By such signals, full illocutionary status is denied. One of the unfilled needs of this theory of fiction is a systematic study of these signals. Some are obviously supplied in the form of labels: to call the work a "novel" is to withdraw assertiveness from its sentences, and may even be to show that, if regarded merely as a locutionary action, the writing of the work was deficient, since the writer, in using proper names, was not always referring. There are various internal marks of nonillocutionary status; if a book begins:

> In the center of the pine wood called Coilla Doraca there lived not long ago two Philosophers. They were wiser than anything in the world except the Salmon who lies in the pool of Glyn Cagny into which the nuts of knowledge fall from the hazel bush on the bank. He, of course, is the most profound of living creatures . . .

we know that we must not take this locution seriously as generating an illocutionary act. (*The Crock of Gold* is no doubt an extreme case.) But suppose we read:

> I caught this morning morning's minion, king-
> > dom of daylight's dauphin, dapple-dawn-drawn Falcon,
> > > in his riding
> Of the rolling level underneath him steady air . . .

We easily make out a speaker at some later hour of a particular day reporting the flight of a bird he observed early that morning. By pursuing this line of thought, we come to understand the poem's situation. The poem is at least a quasi-report. But is it more than that?

This example, surely a representative one, is of the sort that poses a fundamental and difficult issue: for if we conclude that this (undoubted) literary work is *not* fiction, then we cannot define literature simply, and neatly, as fictive discourses. True, this attempted identification has been attacked in various other ways, for example by Tzvetan Todorov.[15] But I don't think his arguments are quite to the point. He says that being fiction is not a *necessary* condition of literature because a discourse that is not fiction can be "viewed as literature" or "read 'as if' it were literature." But since reading a discourse as if it were literature does not make it literature the conclusion does not follow. He also says that being fiction is not a *sufficient* condition of literature because

> In Freud's "case histories," for example, the question whether all the misadventures of "little Hans" or the "wolf man" are true or not is irrelevant: their status is exactly that of fiction: all one is entitled to say of them is that they support or contradict Freud's thesis.

But surely if these case histories are fiction they can in no way "support" any of Freud's theories.[16] In fact, they are quite clearly assertive discourse, recording genuine illocutionary acts, and insofar as they are not true they are not fiction but error. So this second conclusion doesn't follow.

Dispute over the proposal to define literature as fiction has centered less on the question whether all fiction is literature than on the question whether all literature is fiction. To establish this second thesis requires something in the way of a general theory about what has to happen to locutionary acts when recorded as the substance of literary works—that somehow this embodiment cancels their capacity to generate genuine illocutionary acts, though of course without impairing their capacity to suggest the (fictional) illocutionary acts that the works can be said to represent.

The difficulty—and perhaps the impossibility—of supplying such a general theory may be emphasized by considering "The Windhover" once more. We find no label, such as "novel," to serve as an illocutionary-condition-removing signal. Is there in effect, in the literary community, a general (second-order) convention according to which framing a message in meter, or in highly packed language like Hopkins', withholds illocutionary status? If there is such a convention, many Hopkins specialists seem to be unaware of it. And to this argument (if it may be considered such), others might be added to cast doubt on the existence of any such convention. Perhaps we could not even know that this is a poem about Christ (despite the dedication "To Christ Our Lord"), if we did not take the poem as a genuine religious affirmation by Hopkins. (True, the word "Falcon" is capitalized, which seems to claim symbolic character, but that may not be enough.) Suppose we could (and can, for all I know) establish by external evidence that Hopkins did in fact see a falcon on that particular day (as we can establish Wordsworth's presence on Westminster Bridge on September 3, 1802); would not that tend to confirm the genuinely illocutionary character of this utterance? And even if he confessed that the bird was made up, but added that he chose it to convey his special feelings about his religious vocation and the glory of God, would we still be able to maintain that the poem is a fiction? John Reichert has argued effectively that Robert Frost's "Nothing Gold Can Stay" provides no grounds for saying "that the attitude expressed is the attitude of a speaker who is not to be identified with the author."[17]

Barbara Herrnstein Smith claims

that we could conceive of as mimetic discourse not only the representation of speech in drama, but also lyrics, epics, tales, and novels. Indeed, I wish to propose that this, the fictive representation of discourse, is precisely what defines that class of verbal compositions we have so much trouble naming and distinguishing, i.e., "imaginative literature" or "poetry in the broad sense."[18]

A poem is not the record of a "natural utterance" (her term that comes close to "illocutionary action"):

> The distinction lies . . . in a set of conventions shared by poet and reader, according to which certain identifiable linguistic structures are *taken* to be not the verbal acts they resemble, but representations of such acts. By this convention, Keats' ode "To Autumn" and Shakespeare's sonnets are precisely as fictive as "The Bishop Orders His Tomb" or Tennyson's "Ulysses." . . . To the objection, "But I know Wordsworth meant what he says in that poem," we must reply, "You mean he *would have* meant them if he *had* said them, but he is not saying them" (p. 271).

That conventions are essentially involved here is surely true, but when we have said so, we are still quite far from understanding the nature of fiction or of literature unless we can say much more exactly what such conventions look like and how they operate. "Whenever a discourse has properties P, Q, R, . . . it is to be read, not as the record of an illocutionary action but solely as a structure of meanings"—but what are those properties? Are they really "identifiable linguistic structures"? The question at issue, which we must be careful not to beg, is whether in fact there are any such properties that can be cited in a formalized convention of this sort. We could not say, for example, that if a discourse has pronounced aesthetic qualities, its illocutionary status is thereby withheld, for a compliment can be graceful, yet it is still a compliment. Why is a compliment in a Shakespeare sonnet—or a pantheistic claim in a poem by Wordsworth—not a genuine illocutionary action? I don't believe that Smith has told us.

Yet I must confess that I am extremely sympathetic to her point of view, and have not lost hope for its justification. This may seem quixotic, given that, whatever conclusion we may reach about lyric poems, we should still, I think, admit into the class of literary works many pieces of discursive prose (history, philosophy, personal essay, religious meditation, etc.) that are quite certainly records of illocutionary actions. So it would not be troubling to concede also that some lyric poems—perhaps including "The Windhover"—are in the same category of nonfiction. But Smith has some excellent remarks about the dangers of interpreting poems narrowly in terms of an actual or supposed occasion of composition. To sever the poem from its occasion (that is, to perceive and articulate a convention by which the poem is freed of illocutionary dependence on its occasion) is to make necessary room, not for idiosyncratic and subjective readings of the poem, but for the fullest attention to its meanings.

Perhaps we can say this much, at least: in publishing a poem, the writer himself abstracts the original text from the occasion of utterance and gives it a kind of impersonal public character; this second locutionary action (the act of issuing, as distinct from the act of writing) gives us no assurance that the writer has performed the purported illocutionary actions, and thus grants us permission (invites us?) to take the poem as a fiction.

If literature is defined as I have proposed, then fictionality does not enter into the definition at all—though it might be taken as the differentia of a subcategory of "imaginative literature." But it can, of course, be one of the most reliable marks, or indicia, of literature. A work of fiction that offers a coherent narrative, in which persons and places and actions are intelligibly connected and their connections shaped for interested contemplation, will testify to the role of an aesthetic intention in its composition. Indeed, almost any fictive discourse, by its nature, will be a literary work—so that fiction would be a sufficient, though not a necessary, condition of literature. I say "almost" because there are examples of extremely crude pornographic fiction in which it is practically impossible to discern an aesthetic intention, in the style or the characters or the ordering of events.

Those formal features of literature that have sometimes been taken as defining conditions of literature are also, on my view, to be regarded as indicia of literary status, insofar as they show aesthetic intention.[19] Of course not all concern with structure is aesthetic concern; but even logical clarity and rigor, in some contexts, can be understood and approved as contributions to the work's capacity to provide aesthetic satisfaction. One feature of discourse that has particularly commended itself as a defining condition of literature is semantic density, or multiplicity of meanings.[20] This, too, I now see, is at best a sufficient condition of literature, though not part of its definition. No doubt there are difficulties in getting hold of the concept of semantic density, and its usefulness may be limited; but I am inclined to think it is needed for defining the term "poem," and where it is present in a discourse to a marked degree, it is always evidence of attention to the work's aesthetic character, and hence a mark of literary status.

## NOTES

1. Alvin B. Kernan, "The Idea of Literature," *New Literary History* V, 1 (Autumn 1973): 31.

2. "Literature and its Cognates," in *The Dictionary of the History of Ideas*, New York : Scribners, 1973, III, pp. 81-89.

3. *The Theory of Literary Criticism: A Logical Analysis*, University of California Press, 1974, esp. ch. 2. I have discussed his proposal in a review, *Comparative Literature*, XXVIII, 2 (Spring 1976): 177-80. Cf. the remarks on literature as an institution by Christopher Butler, "What is a Literary Work?" *New Literary History* V, 1 (Autumn 1973): 17-29.

4. See "Is Art Essentially Institutional?" in Lars Aagaard-Mogensen, ed., *Culture and Art: An Anthology*, Nyborg: F. Lokkes Forlag and Atlantic Highlands: Humanities Press, 1976, pp. 194-209.

5. "How Ordinary is Ordinary Language?" *New Literary History* V, 1 (Autumn 1973): 52.

6. *Op. cit.*, p. 38.

7. "The Logical Status of Fictional Discourse," *New Literary History* VI, 2 (Winter 1975): 325.

8. See Ina Loewenberg, "Intentions: The Speaker and the Artist," *British Journal of Aesthetics*, 15 (1975): 45, 48.

9. See "The Concept of Literature," in Frank Brady, John Palmer, and Martin Price, eds., *Literary Theory and Structure*, Yale University Press, 1973.

10. "Poetry as Fiction," *New Literary History*, II, 2 (Winter 1971): 259-81; "Actions, Fictions, and the Ethics of Interpretation," *Centrum* III, 2 (Fall 1975): 117-20, and discussion.

11. "Native Readers of Fiction: A Speech-Act and Genre-Rule Approach to Defining Literature" (with Robert L. Brown, Jr.), in this volume; "Perlocutionary Acts and the Interpretation of Literature," *Centrum* III, 2 (Fall 1975): 112-16, and discussion.

12. "How to Do Things with Austin and Searle: Speech Act Theory and Literary Criticism," *Modern Language Notes* 91, 5 (October 1976): 983-1025; a small part was reprinted in *Centrum* III, 2 (Fall 1975): 107-11.

13. See *A Theory of Human Action*, Englewood Cliffs, N.J.: Prentice-Hall, 1970, ch. 2, esp. pp. 25-26.

14. Michael Hancher has a good discussion of this problem in "Understanding Poetic Speech Acts," *College English* XXXVI (February 1975): 632-39.

15. See "The Notion of Literature," *New Literary History* V, 1 (Autumn 1973): 7-8.

16. For a discussion of this and related points about Freud's case histories, see my essay "The Humanities and Human Understanding," in Thomas B. Stroup, ed., *The Humanities and the Understanding of Reality*, University of Kentucky Press, 1966.

17. "Monroe Beardsley and the Shape of Literary Theory," *College English* XXXIII (February 1972): 564. There are many thoughtfully made points in this essay—some of them I think quite conclusive—which I hope to discuss on another occasion.

18. "Poetry as Fiction," p. 268. Cf. "On the Margins of Discourse," *Critical Inquiry* I, 4 (June 1975): 769-98.

19. But see the discussion by Jurij Lotman, "The Content and Structure of the Concept of 'Literature,'" *A Journal for Descriptive Poetics and Theory of Literature* I, 2 (April 1976): 339-56.

20. See "The Concept of Literature," pp. 27-30.

# Literature as Illusion,
# as Metaphor, as Vision

## *Murray Krieger*

Yet may I by no means my wearied mind
Draw from the deer, but as she fleeth afore
Fainting I follow. I leave off therefore,
Since in a net I seek to hold the wind.
                    Sir Thomas Wyatt, "Whoso list to hunt"

I was tempted to use the general title of this volume as my own title here, except for my recognition of the fact that my colleagues in this undertaking might claim an equal interest in it and, like me, will have to resist. But there is these days a better reason to avoid the title, "What Is Literature?" Many theorists of late would argue that it is a question-begging question in that it assumes what must be demonstrated: the existence of an entity which must be established, since it is widely denied existence. In other words, it assumes the existence of a discrete body of things called literature which stands out there waiting to be defined. But much of the most influential theory these days, preferring the blanket term *écriture*, would refuse to grant that discriminable groups can be justified as having a separate status within the generic character of the act and product of writing. Consequently there can be permitted no privileged group of writings called literature. And the nominal act of creating such a group, as we critics have traditionally done, is converted into just another mythology which some recent semioticians would deconstruct. While not many years back even a Sartre could address himself to the question "What is literature?" current thinking suggests the question itself betrays a naive complacency in what it takes for granted.

So, rather than ask the question, I choose in my title to proceed aggressively to answer it, and in a way that affirms both the myth behind such a term as *literature* and literature itself functioning *as* a myth, though one sustained by us with an awareness—already demonstrated in my opening paragraph—of its deconstructability. So I proceed from one substitute noun for "literature" to the next: in claiming the literary work[1] to be an illusion, I am acknowledging our awareness of its make-believe, as-if reality, which is not to be confounded with the factual reality to which we may tend to relate it; in claiming it to be a metaphor, I am acknowledging that in it the two differentiated entities of normal discourse (signifier and signified) are made identical—though only by poetic fiat, not by propositional equation; and in claiming it to be a vision—an author's and, through him, his culture's—I am focusing upon our seeing, as distinguished from the thing apparently seen. Each of these definitional substitutes for "literature" emphasizes our skeptical willingness to undo literature's "reality," just as the nature of this defining process is meant to emphasize our skeptical willingness to undo the reification of "literature" as a definable entity.

In the limited space suggested for this essay I can barely—too barely—move assertively from one to the next defining characteristic, leaving it to my lengthier discussions elsewhere to argue for their preferability to other possible definitions.[2] But my brevity here may suggest too much assertiveness, too great a commitment to these defining characteristics as substantive entities themselves, although I am primarily interested in promoting the awareness of literature's illusionary nature. At each stage of my definition I mean to press our self-conscious myth-making, not our pretension to metaphysical discoveries.

I make one additional observation about this attempt at definition, whether one sees it as propaedeutic—implying that substantive arguments to support it may now follow—or as a conclusion of arguments made on other occasions. It is a confession of the obvious: that the definition has normative as well as descriptive elements, so that it opens the way, automatically as it were, to evaluation as well as mere identification of literary works. By virtue of satisfying the definition, a work qualifies as literature; but to qualify as literature, in accordance with this definition, is already to be judged as successful literature. In other words, the definition is prescriptive of how the individual piece of writing ought to function in the human economy if we are to accord it the honorific title of literature. If it so functions, then it must be both literature and satisfactory as literature. The interpretive analysis of the work thus smuggles in the evaluation as its inevitable companion. In this sense, there is no poor literature: if a work is poor, then it fails to qualify as literature in that it does not reveal the power to function in this way. So it is not truly literature, but is something else parading as literature. Obviously, any such prescriptive definition is woefully circular, assuming beforehand the characteristics for which it then searches and excluding whatever fails to conform. Only a total philosophical anthropology can systematically establish such functions and authorize such a defined and exclusive class, though the present essay is hardly the occasion for so elaborate a construction.

Of course, this defining process, conceived in a simple, common-sense way, presupposes that our substantive (in this case *literature*) does exist as an enclosing form for a number of entities out there (presumably individual pieces of "literature").

This would spring from a pre-structuralist (if not pre-Humean) naïveté which would assume that the existence of a signifier implied the equivalent existence of its signified. However, not only do the written works not fall into real classes for us to name, but the works exist as individuals for us only as a result of our illusionary act of reification out of our radically temporal experience of them. We know that it is the reader who must construct the object out of the sequential patterns given him. Yet he tries to be responsive, and such an attitude suggests a controlling thing he is being responsive to. He has only his actual experience to which he can refer, and yet out of this limited experience he must derive a normative experience and the object which that experience would project.

Even with these experience-bound qualifications, forced upon us by a sophisticated epistemological awareness, there is the pragmatic need—if we are to make the definition usable—to draw the line between literature and non-literature. I suggest it be drawn, in accordance with the characteristics I am offering here, by appealing to the phenomenological notion of intentionality. That is, there is the special kind of experience we intend as we confront this object, and we intend it because we intend this object as one having the discriminable features that sustain such intentionality. We must assume that we can on occasion be disappointed, and that sometimes the object will not be seen as sustaining what we intend it as being and doing, so that we can escape the circularity of inevitable self-confirmation. In such unfortunate cases it can be claimed that the object should more appropriately be sponsoring another sort of intentionality. It stands, in other words, outside the domain of the intentionality that produces the requiredness of the literary work: instead, it is functioning as a work of non-literature, of whatever sort in the particular case.

It must be granted that, in the practice of criticism, many works (one thinks, for example, of first-person, confessional works—Rousseau comes at once to mind) can be viewed as functioning (and functioning well) on either side of the line separating literature from non-literature, although—I would hope—the far greater number would turn out to be less ambidextrous. With the latter the placement within the intentional category would carry with it (as I have suggested) an implied judgment about the literary value of each. And the gray area constituted by the works more difficult to place may call attention to the imprecision inevitable to the grounds of our discriminations of intentionality—phenomenological and not realistic grounds, after all; but it does not undermine the definition so much as it makes it necessary for us to move beyond the definition as we use it to solve major critical problems, though each case remains open to argument. In the humanities, after all, definitions should be beginnings only, pointing toward opportunities rather than conclusions which would preclude further work and further uncertainty.

Given the definition as no more than a phenomenological postulate, it is little wonder that I see something mythic about our very naming of the literary work as literary, and even more so about the class of such works we term *literature*. But, as I define it, the work functions for us as a myth that—if we watch it closely enough—knows itself to be one. This characteristic is an inevitable accompaniment to our sense of it as a fiction, emanating from the work as an inner skepticism about itself and its peculiar status in being.

It is at this point that I see the cogency of E. H. Gombrich's work on illusion and self-reference[3] as illuminating our experience of literature as well as of the plastic arts. There is a peculiar unreality—or a strange reality peculiarly distanced from our own—about the characters and actions in literary works. As members of the audience we are not prompted to intrude ourselves into the action onstage during a dramatic performance any more than we would try to step into a painting. Further, the people out there on the stage are characters rather than real people, however much they may resemble the latter: those characters and the experiences they undergo have a repetitiveness, an inevitability (indeed an everlastingness) about them that transcends any single performance or silent reading. As Aristotle reminds us, their beginnings, middles, and ends—absolute in their relations among one another and in their capacity to begin the tale again—differ radically from our own mortal and contingent beginnings, middles, and ends. This is the sense in which the work is an illusion, only an appearance of a reality that it eludes, keeping for itself a freedom from chancy contingency, a freedom to play in its special immunity from *our* kind of death. And no sophisticated reader—however caught up he may be (and he *should* be) in the action—thinks it other than illusion, or confuses it with the dimensions of his own life. In its self-referential dimension the work itself reminds us of its make-believe status.

Perhaps the characters and action in a dramatic performance, based on the actors' impersonations of the characters and their actions, furnish the clearest example of literature's illusionary nature. But, though perhaps in less obvious ways, illusion functions similarly in the non-performing literary genres: the illusion of history or biography in the epic or in some prose fiction or the illusion of journal or confession or autobiography in lyric or first-person fiction. More prominently, there is the illusion of the normal use of language in all literature, but especially in the conventional lyric, where even the sounds of words, as sensuous elements, have an illusory aspect that is freely exploited. We must, that is, feel—as it were—the sensory appearance of the words, as it joins with common and uncommon meanings to create a use of language that is anything but common. Yet the illusion persists, though undercut every moment, that it is only the same old words that are being mouthed. And another dimension of reality is being evaded for an illusory world which at once takes itself seriously, *as if* it were reality, and yet shows us its awareness of its make-believe nature by being conscious of its artifice. I would argue, then, that the literary work is described more accurately as a self-referential illusion of reality than (as has been suggested since Aristotle) as an imitation of reality.

In no aspect of the work is its own apparent awareness of its illusionary nature more strikingly revealed than in its character as metaphor. I see each work as constituting itself and its relation to reality through a master metaphor that is co-extensive with its own body: that is, it seeks to reduce the muddled contingencies of normal experience to a controlled appearance under the formal rubric of its own reality. As metaphor it equates as it symbolizes, rendering the large and incomplete world out there as the small and complete representation which is the work. It is as if this reduced and perfectly coherent part could contain the unimaginable whole, without remainder. Thus the work's pretension is metonymic as well as metaphoric. Its every aspect conspires to make it a satisfying totalization which, as an apparition, gives us itself for the world. Our sense of the work's "corporeality" (to use Sigurd Burckhardt's term[4]) arises from the substance we attribute to it as its language and its events take on body that substitutes for our reality by becoming its own apparent reality. It transforms the motley materials it borrows from the world of normal discourse, having forced them to deviate from their common generic uses and converting them into elements of its own, now maximally exploited to create its reductive totality.

But if the metaphor, as the work itself, is an absolute reduction, in the security of its aesthetic completeness it also betrays from time to time an awareness that it is in the end only metaphor and not reality. Out of its words it creates its world as if it were our world, while the very perfection of its creation reminds us of all in our world which it is not. It creates its words out of our words, except that it seems to turn its signifiers into

the shapes of their own signifieds, into the inevitable product of
what had been an arbitrary series of relations; yet they are still
but words. If there is something miraculous about a literary
presentation that takes on body—about empty words filling
themselves with substance and persuading us of their
fullness—we know it can be a miracle only if we also know it
cannot happen. The world, the work, and the word seem one in
the master metaphor. Or rather the world seems enfolded in the
work which seems one with its word. But outside the terms of
the metaphor, alas, the world is not in the work, and the word,
as an illusion and an illusionary metaphor, is, like all miracles,
seen from an outside view as a deception. In the fictional self-
consciousness of its most metaphorical moment, the work rein-
forces our awareness of its duplicity. It encourages us to look at
it both ways—at its best, both ways at once.

In its most developed form in our finest works, the metaphor
is both complete in the reduction of everything to its terms and
utterly aware of itself as an inadequate measure of the world. As
Rosalie Colie describes the metaphor, in the very act of being
wholly established it "unmetaphors" itself.[5] As a myth it is a
totalized world, and as it demythifies itself it is not part of the
world—the unpatterned workaday world—at all. Thus it is both
a constructed emblem that contains the world and a deconstructed breath of air that does not begin to describe it. What it
denies about itself at no moment detracts from the fullness of
affirmation to which its every element contributes. Its paradoxical capacity to combine self-affirmation with self-denial—to see
itself as the world and to see the world as anything but itself—is
its most brilliant manifestation of its commitment to literature as
illusion, illusion as that so persuasive as-if reality which seems
to be all the reality there is while it reveals its merely make-
believe (dare we say counterfeit, even fraudulent?) character.

If literature is illusion, and that special manifestation of illusion which I have described as a metaphor, it is of course also

vision. But by now it should be obvious that I can see it as visionary not, as in romanticism, in any vatic or gnostic sense, but only in a sense—consistent with its inner skepticism—that would restrict the visionary to the merely illusionary. The emphasis is on a sustained seeing without any assurances about the existence of the seen. The illusion of reality which the metaphor creates for us is a reduced moment of vision, a reduced moment of a culture's vision of its reality as that vision (and hence *its* reality) is constituted for that culture by its poet. For through the metaphor is created the illusion of reality as vision. It is reality trimmed to the confines of aesthetic creativity and, through that creativity, aesthetic apprehension and then apprehension of the world itself as aesthetic. Through this sense of vision (even if illusory vision) we can see how even this self-deconstructing view of literature opens the aesthetic to broadly anthropological considerations. The very history of culture depends upon it.

But here again the reflexive character of illusion asserts itself, and we are reminded, even as the vision asserts itself, that the vision of the world may not after all be the world, indeed that it stands at odds with the world and is threatened with being engulfed by the world. Still, we return to the work to sustain the vision once again, frail and too delicate an emblem though it may finally prove to be, for while we renew its life we renew our own capacity for seeing.

There is one constant in this movement from illusion to metaphor to vision: it is the claim that the literary work borrows elements (words, thoughts, characters, actions) from the commonplace world and presents illusionary equivalents of them, except that these equivalents are severely transformed by the created microcosm that sustains and reshapes them. All that is minimally efficient or meaningful in "life" is maximally exploited into a total functionalism. What is arbitrary in a loose system of signifiers in which substitution seems uniformly permissible emerges in the illusionary artifact as both indispensable and inevitable. If the structuralist has reason to emphasize the gap in normal discourse between signifier and signified, the literary work challenges his analysis as in it the signifier fills itself with signified and thus itself becomes indispensable and inevitable. As it thus revives the possibility of a living language that can match words to our imaginations, literature discovers for itself the function of giving its culture words that permit it to speak as if for the first time. What a literature says is what it sees, even if what it says and sees is unsaid and unseen outside the enabling act provided by the aesthetic mode. For only *in* the seeing and saying can its world exist, can the signified survive in the signs that create as well as carry it—indeed, that embody it.

It should now be seen that, as must have been unavoidable, I have been providing not so much a definition of literature as a definition of the only sort of literature I believe I can justify. From the outset I warned that my proposed definition would be normative and even honorific, enclosing only those kinds of literary works which it is designed to find successful. Obviously, it prefers works of closed form, as in the critical tradition we can trace from Aristotle to post-Coleridgean organicism, to the exclusion from literature of so much else. But there is also in the definition the requirement for works to turn on themselves and their own closedness, and for them consequently to open to the world if only by negation. Thanks to self-reference—that self-consciousness which illusion reveals about what it is and is not—the totality of self-assertion for the sake of illusion is to be matched by the totality of self-immolation before an unyielding if unenclosable reality. Both are totalizations, although the simultaneous reversals of possibilities in them leave them free from the metaphysical consequences of holism. Further, however narrow one may think the inclusions permitted by my definition, it should be remembered that only the most uselessly non-restrictive nominal definition could try to include everything to which someone might wish to attribute the name of "literature." As in all other definitions, it comes down to a choice among exclusions.

I return also to another earlier warning: that this occasion would permit only a hasty summary of the elements of my proposed definition, with little opportunity to do more than state them baldly, essentially without argument. Yet what I have had to state baldly is a series of self-contradictory propositions about illusion and reality in literature, about both its self-enclosure and an awareness of its self-enclosure that opens it outward. The propositions, in denying themselves, deny their appropriateness as defining tools for this object of definition. I have tried to speak firmly, definitively, about the will-o'-the-wisp literature, whose very being undoes this mode of dealing with it. Its duplicitous way of functioning makes a myth of every claim. In taking itself lightly as discourse, it forces all discourse—even the theoretical—to take itself lightly in pursuit of literature. I feel like the lover in my epigraph from Wyatt, who cannot find the equipment appropriate to his beloved quarry, and finally retires, exhausted: "I leave off therefore, / Since in a net I seek to hold the wind."

## NOTES

1. The reader will note that I move easily—here and in the balance of this essay—from literature to the literary work and back again. The obvious assumption behind such a movement is the simple notion that literature refers to a class of works which we are lumping together for definitional purposes, so that what is found true of the single work is representative of what would be true of them all as a class. Clearly for other definers of literature (Northrop Frye is a most striking example) literature is more than this uncomplicated collective made up of sovereign individual works, but rather has its own life which transcends its individual manifestations. One of the chief values of this volume

should be its revelation of such differences in assumptions about the work and the larger entity we think of as a collection of such works.

2. Let me suggest, among other places, my *Theory of Criticism: A Tradition and its System* (Baltimore, 1976).

3. The obvious starting place for Gombrich (though he later goes off in many profitable directions) is *Art and Illusion: A Study in the Psychology of Pictorial Representation* (London, 1960).

4. *Shakespearean Meanings* (Princeton, 1968), pp. 22-46.

5. This is a central notion and a controlling methodological device in her brilliant study of Marvell, *"My Echoing Song": Andrew Marvell's Poetry of Criticism* (Princeton, 1970).

# "All Discourse Aspires to the Analytic Proposition"

## *Michael McCanles*

And fails. Is the truth of this assertion, or even its meaning, self-evident? I strongly suspect that neither is. Certainly, the statement "All discourse aspires to the analytic proposition" does not itself appear to be analytic. On the contrary, it presents itself in need of support, of development, as requiring in short much discourse to make it acceptable. If I want to elicit your assent to this statement, then I will have to show how it is true, nor would you demand less. But if, on the other hand, I really believe that it is true, then I must also believe that there is some logical connection between "discourse" and "aspires to the analytic proposition," that the meanings of the subject and the predicate in some way imply each other. In other words, I am claiming that this proposition exhibits some degree of analyticity. In the analytic proposition, like the law of noncontradiction, or the premises of Euclid's geometry, or the Substance-God equation in Spinoza's *Ethics*, the meaning of the predicate is already implied in the meaning of the subject. But in having said so much, have I not got myself into a contradiction? If an analytic proposition, by Kant's definition,[1] is one whose meaning and truth are open to intuitive grasp and assent, then obviously no further discourse is needed to explain it. Consequently, my discovery that I require further discussion to make my thesis proposition acceptable would seem to invalidate whatever degree of analyticity I claim for it. But then, my whole purpose in writing this discourse is to support my belief that my thesis statement does partake of something of the analytic. The contradiction I have got myself into is one which, I suggest, radically informs any expository discourse that attempts to argue coherently a central thesis: if I need to prove by discussion that my central assertion is analytic, then it is not analytic; but then to show how it is, in some degree, analytic is exactly the goal of my discussion.

What I have been doing just now is illustrating part of the point I want to make in the process of explaining it: namely, that any discourse that marshals itself coherently to argue a thesis proposition becomes at once a set of instruments supporting it and a set of obstacles blocking that support. Discourse—the extension into discursive space of syntactical strings linked together by various kinds of entailments—is a devolution away from that pure tautology of subject and predicate in the analytic proposition toward which, I propose, discourse as a whole aspires. "Discursive space" is an extension of Wittgenstein's notion of "logical space": "A tautology leaves open to reality the whole—the infinite whole—of logical space: a contradiction fills the whole of logical space leaving no point of it for reality."[2] It is between the two limiting (and empty) cases of tautology and contradictory propositions that all other statements occur.

The urge to exhaust a given subject in a discourse deducible from or leading toward a single, self-evident proposition is something so basic to human communication that we tend to take it for granted. It is the urge to exhaust all the entailments of all the propositions generated by the act of verbalizing the world or a piece of it, to saturate the available discursive space, answering all opponents and silencing all voices but one. It is

likewise the urge to write the ultimate Book embodying the final
language or code of the world, a code which presents itself as
the origin of all other codes (constituting all other competing
books), into which these codes may be translated, but which
itself requires no further translation.[3] However, a text can only
come into existence through selection from the total number of
texts made possible by the synchronic system of statements
available on a given subject. "Discursive space" is this synchron-
ically conceived field of meaning from which each text selects
those statements that can be formed into logically coherent
wholes. As on the phonemic, semantic, and syntactical levels,
so on the level of discourse: a text can come into existence only
by selecting from its funding system of available statements
some statements and rejecting others. And since this system
must consist not only of a set of semantically interrelated terms
but also their contraries, every text is potentially liable to having
to confront other, competing texts formed from those statements likewise generated by the same synchronic system, which
statements nevertheless contradict the first text.[4] One might
conclude, then, that the dialectical counterpart of the pursuit of
analytic statements is the disruption of analyticity by contradictory statements both *denied and implied* by the former.

Philosophizing such as Aristotle's, Descartes', Spinoza's or
Hegel's gives us historical examples of just this kind of pursuit
in action. Most of us, however, in seeking to argue a position
take for granted that we are not going to say the last word on it,
that there are other positions possible on the same subject. We
recognize that however much analyticity we claim for our theses
our arguments always involve a certain number of synthetic
statements open to response and modification. As modern discussions of analyticity have shown, the line between analytic
and synthetic propositions is not nearly as definite as Kant
thought it to be.[5] On the contrary, precise classification seems to
require rather several shadings of both, of what Yehoshua

Bar-Hillel calls degrees of analyticity.[6] The degree of analyticity assignable to a thesis depends of course on how exhaustive the supporting discourse can be. What I am saying, then, is that any discourse which seeks to argue the truth or probability of a thesis always, at least implicitly, aims at establishing some degree of analyticity in the relation between the subject of that thesis and whatever predicates the discourse attributes to that subject. For this reason I believe that it is useful to outline briefly here a model for discussing all verbal discourse, an ultimate limiting case crystallized purely in only a few instances, which nevertheless most other discourses fulfill in an incomplete, denser fashion.

This model conceives verbal discourse as always implicitly aspiring to a mode of communication where all that is said can be grasped in the instantaneous, intuitive recognition and assent usually limited, in theory at least, to analytic propositions. And discourse is envisioned here as coming into being through the failure of this aspiration. Since the main concern of this volume is with the question, "What is literature?" I am going to assume the identity of literature with fictions, and distinguish fictive from nonfictive discourse according to the different ways each fulfills this model. This distinction presupposes another one, this time between the ways fiction and nonfiction operate within the intextual as distinct from the contextual or intertextual realms. Intextually, fiction and nonfiction develop the consequences of failing to attain analyticity in essentially the same way. Intertextually, that is, in the ways text confronts other, potentially competing, texts that dwell in its own discursive space, fiction and nonfiction differ decisively.

To continue using my own argument as an example, I should note that in order to support my thesis I must make another statement; and in order to support this statement, I must make still others.[7] The mere act of extending my discourse through statements followed by still other statements needed to support these, fragments my original thesis statement into a sequential manifold of syntactic strings. In further specifying the line of argument advanced by previous statements, each succeeding statement modifies them in some way, and denies their implicit claim to being at that point the "final" one that need be made. And so, what we usually think of as well-formed discourse—a harmonious flow of logical entailments—discloses itself as actually a series of denials, of announcements that, "No, that's not quite it—we must say something further."

Each succeeding statement relates to a previous statement as what C. S. Peirce calls its interpretant. As Umberto Eco has developed Peirce's notion of interpretant, it refers first of all to the semantic markers which define a given word: roughly, the semantic markers of a term are words required to establish the word's meaning or intension.[8] But if we extend the relation of word and its interpretants from the semantic to the discursive level, we discover that the interpretant "also defines many kinds of proposition and argument which, beyond the rules provided by codes, explain, develop, interpret a given sign. In this sense one should even consider as interpretants all possible semiotic judgments that a code permits one to assert about a given semantic unit, as well as many factual judgments."[9] The beginning of the chain of interpretants (which is potentially infinite, since each interpretant is a word requiring still further interpretants) are the semantic markers that define a word. It might also be noted that interpretants stand in an analytic relation to the word they interpret, since they establish the various predicates that can be attached to the term as the term's meaning. Thus, in my thesis statement I assert that "aspires to the analytic proposition" is an interpretant of "discourse," and I am here seeking to argue that "discourse" analytically *means* (among other things) "aspires to the analytic proposition." In order to establish this analytic relation my discourse extends itself ever onward as an analytic chain of statements, each filling out the meaning of previous statements, and requiring still further statements to explain them. Thus my discourse *becomes discursive and dischronic* as it pursues a final interpretant, a statement that will conclude all and require no further interpretive statement. It would require no further statement because it would enclose within itself its own meaning; it would be a statement wherein the subject and predicate totally imply each other, and as such literally nothing more could be said about it. I am suggesting, in other words, that my discourse and any other discourse that seeks to establish the (analytic) truth of its governing, central statement pursues—always unsuccessfully—Derrida's myth of origins, a final statement subsuming all other statements in the text, but which itself neither requires nor allows any further statement to explain it.

If I am right and all argumentative discourse such as my own aspires to analyticity, that is, to a self-interpreting statement, then it becomes apparent that such discourse extends itself ever onward in pursuit of such a statement precisely because it never achieves it. In aspiring to analyticity it comes into existence as a continual chain in which no statement is the final one, no statement can close off the potentially infinite chain of statements, no statement is finally analytic. In short, discourse comes into being through the continual failure to achieve its own telos.

In this text that I am writing now, each statement replicates in its own place in the discursive syntagm my thesis proposition's claim to analytic finality, only to have that claim disallowed in the very act of extending its meaning. The whole tissue of my discourse reenacts the original fragmentation of the first statement of my text. For I find that I must say more and more in support of this central statement, while implicitly calling into question whatever degree of analytic truth my "saying more" claims for it. What I am writing here is a product of continual self-revisions, continual adducing of ever more interpretants. We might say, then, that this discourse is generated out of a primordial impulse to negate discourse. It is the failure of my aspiration to negate discourse, my failure to communicate instantaneously and intuitively the truth of a (putatively) self-evident statement, that calls my discourse into being.

As regards fictive discourse I want to make a similar suggestion. In a plot—fiction's analog to nonfictive argumentation—an agent moves an action aimed at a goal cognate to the analytic proposition. The agent's goal is to achieve a plotless, static, non-conflictual existence, wherein all counterpressures that actually or may potentially disturb this state are brought into univocal harmony with the agent's masterplan. In the process of moving toward this goal, the agent will have to confront a manifold of recalcitrant entities: other characters, the natural world, the limitations of language and thought—or, to put it summarily, the whole condition of living in the sequentialness and diversity of the time-space continuum. Consequently, every statement or gesture or action which the agent treats as an instrument toward the achievement of his ultimate goal, turns into or generates obstacles to that goal. He encounters other agents, for instance, who resist being brought wholly into orbit around his desires. These agents in turn initiate counteractions which require the first agent to meet these with still other actions, also bound to elicit still further counteractions. And so what is from the reader's or viewer's standpoint the progressive, forward movement of a plot is actually from the agent's viewpoint a regression backward along an ever-extending chain of instrumental acts become obstacles, requiring still further instrumental acts to remove them.[10]

Oedipus, in attempting to escape the predicted plot of his own life, continually enacts it. Lovelace, in order to achieve the love of Clarissa, performs acts which remove him further from her. The lyric poet, in verbalizing a moment of instantaneous intuitive recognition, finds he must confront the recalcitrance of words, syntax, and formal structure—entities which insidiously

offer themselves as instruments only to turn into stubborn obstacles in his hands. Even in such a work as *War and Peace* the
multiple plots cohere to present characters whose irritation at
the discursive "plottiness" of life commits them to much restless
movement in the interest of finally escaping movement. Think
of Pierre; Andrew; Andrew's father, Napoleon (whose irritation
at the opposition and the diversity of the world is blown up to
global proportions); Natasha's developing insight into what
"peace" might be, and so on. From the viewpoint stated here,
the title of the novel might traslate as: "much 'war' generated
out of an overriding desire for 'peace'." Even the Bible and its
English rewrite, *Paradise Lost,* that gives us the generative
grammar grounding the multitudinous performances of all
human history, display that history as the falling away from a
state of pure, timeless plotlessness into time, plot, division, and
discursion. And like human history in this, our most dominant
and all-encompassing myth, human discourse enacts a parallel
yearning to return to this state of discursionless communication,
an ultimate analytic text allowing no further interpretation. And
so if, as I said before, argumentative discourse is born out of the
urge to negate discourse, then in fictions plot is born out of the
desire to escape plot.

Between fiction and nonfiction the essential difference lies in
this: that nonfictive discourse always commits an act of aggression against the discursive space within which it dwells,
whereas fictive discourse does not. It would be the goal of Descartes or Hegel or Marx to make coextensive the discursive space
inhabited by their own statements, and the whole of possible
discursive space in general. The urge to create a "universal philosophy" is likewise the urge to "use up" all discursive space, so
that no other statements save those coherently flowing from the
original *données* of their systems could find a place in it. As the
anagogical extension of oral fixation, it is the urge, finally, to
swallow up the whole of reality in a single, vast tautology. The

history of human discourses has shown, of course, that the discursive space men have attempted to treat as limited is nevertheless always expanding, and that all attempts to make the discursive space of one discourse identical with the whole of all possible discursive space are necessarily doomed to failure. No matter how far a discourse may extend its imperialist aggression, there will always be still further reaches in which will gather counterdiscourses, opposing armies, guerrillas, and snipers that will seek to limit this aggression.

On the other hand, it is obvious that *Oedipus, Clarissa, The Romance of the Rose,* and "A Slumber did my Spirit Seal," have not called forth similar counterstatements. The reason why they have not is that fictive discourse creates a corresponding discursive space that is equally fictive, a space wherein potentially competing novels, poems, and plays may dwell but without calling into question the competing statements of still other fictional works. In the discursive space inhabited by fictions the law of noncontradiction is suspended, whereas in that inhabited by nonfictive arguments this law works with inexorable force. While Wordsworth's *Preface* to the *Lyrical Ballads* invades the discursive space marked out by Pope's *Preface to Shakespeare,* can we say the same of the *Lyrical Ballads* themselves *vis-à-vis* "The Essay on Man"? Does it make sense to say that T. S. Eliot's "Gerontion" invades the discursive space inhabited by Shelley's "Adonais" in the same way that the essays on the metaphysical poets invade that already occupied by *A Defence of Poetry?* These questions throw into relief the radically different ways in which fiction and nonfiction accommodate the contradictions inherent in the very act of discoursing. Intertextually, the arguments of philosophy, the physical sciences and social sciences encounter and seek to negate one another, while fictions with competing messages may dwell together without mutual aggression, because, as Sidney said, "the poet, he nothing affirms." Intextually, fiction differs from nonfiction, and perhaps has this advantage over it, that it may actively cultivate the contradictions inherent in discourse, whereas nonfiction must be overtly committed to overcoming these. Consequently, fiction may encompass and even provisionally conquer the dialectics concomitant with discursion, while nonfictive discourse remains always vulnerable to them in the act of aspiring to escape them.

One way of testing this distinction between fictions and nonfictions is to notice how we treat texts that have, in cultural contexts other than our own, made aggressive claims on the discursive space inhabited by other texts. Here, a wide variety of texts comes to mind: Mayan hymns, Egyptian tomb inscriptions, the Roman Catholic mass, reported Gnostic and Catharistic rituals; texts that carried out medieval controversies about universals: Edmund Burke's *Reflections on the French Revolution;* pre-Civil War abolitionist tracts; the *Corpus Hermeticum* by the legendary Hermes Trismegistus. What is common about these texts is that all of them claimed within the context in which they were composed dominance over other possible texts in the same discursive space. All claimed, in other words, to be taken "seriously" as embodying some sort of ultimate, final code of truth or moral value; while it is precisely this claim that we suspend when we confront them from our own present standpoint. Within this perspective, the quarrels between realists and nominalists we treat no differently than we treat the debates in Plato's dialogues or in Shaw's dramas. That is, we suspend the claims of these debates to existential import, and replace this claim with a disinterested contemplation of the presuppositions and structures of thought that funded these debates and drove them forward.

On the other hand, Plato's dialogues and Shaw's drama, to the extent we consider their ideological designs and claims on the reader, become nonfictions. The same would hold true for socialist novels of the thirties, examples of Soviet realism, or the novels of Ayn Rand: these putatively fictional texts partake of the aggression indigenous to nonfiction in the same way as overtly philosophical, scientific, or political texts. The difference

between fiction and nonfiction is not a matter of qualities, structures, or purposes allegedly indigenous to some texts and absent in others; it is, rather, a matter of how the reader himself
treats the text. He may or may not take account of the signals the
author places in the text to indicate how he wants the reader to
treat his work (e.g., in titles: "a novel," "a treatise on human
nature," or in the typographical layout of poetry, or in the symbolic notation of scientific texts). A novel by Henry James may
be taken as nonfictionally polemical (arguing the moral
superiority of altruistic self-abnegation in the same discursive
space inhabited by Ayn Rand's novels); while a treatise of Descartes may be taken as fictionally independent of competing
texts (the aesthetic beauty of the logical reduction of certainty to
the *cogito*).

Whether we personally agree with whatever truth a text
claims is irrelevant: I am not arguing that nonfiction is what we
take as true and fiction is what we take as false. Rather, I am
concerned with the ways in which we may (and do) allow or
suspend a text's truth-claims for purposes of analysis. If we
consider the truth-claims of a philosophical or scientific treatise
(as distinct, e.g., from the logical symmetry of its argument),
then we are treating it as nonfiction—and this does not mean
that we thereby personally commit ourselves to acquiescing in
or denying these claims. In short, what is nonfictional is any text
whose claim to embody an ultimate code of the world—
Derrida's myth of origins—we allow into our consideration;
while fiction is any text whose similar claim we choose to suspend.[11]

## NOTES

1. Kant's distinction between analytic and synthetic "judgments"
occurs in the Introduction to *The Critique of Pure Reason*. Cf. L. W. Beck's
two articles, "Can Kant's Synthetic Judgments Be Made Analytic?"

and, "Kant's Theory of Definition," in *Kant: A Collection of Critical Essays*, ed. Robert Paul Wolff (Garden City, N.Y.: Anchor Books, 1967), pp. 3-36.

2. *Tractatus Logico-Philosophicus*, trans. D. F. Pears and B. F. McGuinness (London: Routledge and Kegan Paul, 1963), 4.463, p. 69.

3. Cf. Jacques Derrida, "Structure, Sign, and Play in the Discourse of the Human Sciences," *The Structuralist Controversy: The Languages of Criticism and the Sciences of Man*, ed. Richard Macksey and Eugenio Donato (Baltimore: The Johns Hopkins Univ. Press, 1972), pp. 247-265, for an incisive critique of this urge. Derrida calls it the search for the realization of a "myth of origins," a closure on the potentially infinite circulation of texts wherein each text requires a second text to render its meaning, the second text requires a third text, and so on.

4. See A. J. Greimas, *Sémantique Structurale: Recherche de méthode* (Paris: Librairie Larousse, 1966) for a semantically-based model of discursive structure. Also Geoffrey Leech, *Semantics* (Harmondsworth: Penguin Books, 1974), chapter 12, "Semantic Equivalence and 'Deep Semantics'," pp. 263-290. Both Greimas and Leech feature componential analyses of meaning into binarily classified markers. The expansion of this kind of analysis into deep structure representational models of extended discourses is developed both by Greimas and by Teun A. van Dijk in *Some Aspects of Text Grammars: A Study in Theoretical Linguistics and Poetics* (The Hague and Paris: Mouton, 1972). Greimas, however, develops most completely the notion that well-formed discourse is a diachronic sequence of lexemes whose interrelations are determined by repetitions of the same semantic markers as well as of the contraries of these markers. I have in turn extended Greimas' approach to emphasize how a well-formed text, that is, one that abides by rules of semantic-logical presupposition, implication, and subordination, can be well-formed only through a process of selection/rejection from its own implied lexicon. If well-formedness, as I argue in my text, equals analyticity—each successive statement must feature terms whose semantic markers are identical with or implied by those of terms in previous statements—then this selection/rejection process requires further that the contraries of these markers must be rejected. As Greimas and Leech demonstrate, any term is connected to a number of other terms as its contraries, a relation registered in the fact that contrary terms are constituted out of markers classified as "+" and "−" respectively. Thus "man" is opposed to "woman" along a semantic axis whose poles are +MALE and −MALE respectively (or −FEMALE and +FEMALE); while "man" is opposed to "boy" along a semantic axis

whose poles are +ADULT and −ADULT respectively. The point I am making is that any well-formed discourse both rejects and implies other, probably several, possible texts funded by the same lexicon, and employing terms contrary to those featured in the first text. This is so since the lexicon is constituted of terms the meaning of which requires the inclusion of their opposites. Consequently, the pursuit of analyticity equals the rejection of all terms and propositions that contradict the line of semantic entailment in the text, which semantic entailment is constituted of repetitions of semantic markers or (non-contradictory) implications of semantic markers. And this rejection entails further the necessary risk of contradiction by other texts generated by the same lexicon because these other texts are already implied by the first text—implied, that is, through the mediation of the lexicon which these mutually-cancelling texts all share.

5. Recent critiques of analyticity derive from two articles: Morton G. White, "The Analytic and the Synthetic: an Untenable Dualism," in Sidney Hook, ed., *John Dewey: Philosopher of Science and Freedom* (New York: Barnes and Noble, Inc., 1967 [orig. pub. 1950]), pp. 316-331; and W. V. Quine, "Two Dogmas of Empiricism," *The Philosophical Review*, 60 (1951), 20-43. Like Yehoshua Bar-Hillel (see footnote 6), White finds that the distinction is one of degrees (330), as does Quine (43). Moreland Perkins and Irving Singer, "Analyticity," *The Journal of Philosophy*, 48 (1951), 485-497, argue that what constitutes analytic predication is actually a function of what a given group or society happens to believe is analytic, i.e., synonymy of meaning presupposes the phenomenological content given in a specific word or concept at any given time or place. This phenomenological approach to analyticity is discussed by Beck ("The Analytic and the Synthetic," pp. 7ff.), where he distinguishes between the logical criterion of analytic judgment ("its conformity to the law of contradiction") and the phenomenological criterion ("the issue of an inspection of what is found introspectively to be really thought in the concept of the subject"). Kant took for granted an "eternal" content for certain concepts, whereas when one emphasizes the element of assent one is confronted with the actual phenomenological content of the grasp of the analytic proposition, whatever may be granted or asserted regarding its logical content.

6. Yehoshua Bar-Hillel, "Degrees of Analyticity," *Philosophia*, 1 (1971), 1-20. Bar-Hillel emphasizes the testing of subjects to ascertain the degree of their "readiness to renounce the truth of a statement." Such an approach presupposes Perkins and Singer's assertion that, in

essence, those propositions are analytic which are thought to be analytic. It is actually in the discursive space opened up by these discussions that my own argument is made. For if analyticity is no longer limited to alleged (i.e., traditionally defined) tautologies, then we can now understand how arguments which otherwise would appear strictly synthetic nevertheless seek to establish a certain degree of analyticity for their major theses.

7. The word "statement" here does not mean a single sentence, although in specific instances a sentence might make up a single statement. I am referring rather to a segment of a text, rather than to a grammatical unit. I follow to some extent Michel Foucault, *The Archaeology of Knowledge*, trans. A. M. Sheridan Smith (New York: Pantheon Books, 1972), p. 87 and passim, in the meaning I want to attribute to "statement." Syntagmatically, a statement functions in relation to other statements preceding and following it according to entailments which are often (as I argue here) dialectical. Paradigmatically, a given statement can be isolated from those that surround it and can be defined against them, as one out of several possible statements that might have, but did not, enter into relation with these. Practically, the segmentation of a discourse into statements may differ from reader to reader.

8. Umberto Eco, *A Theory of Semiotics* (Bloomington: Indiana Univ. Press, 1976), p. 68: "the most fruitful hypothesis would seem to be that of conceiving the *interpretant as another representation which is referred to the same 'object.'* In other words, in order to establish what the interpretant of a sign is, it is necessary to name it by means of another sign which in turn has another interpretant to be named by another sign and so on."

9. *Ibid.*, p. 71.

10. The view of fictional plot which I summarize here I have already developed in full elsewhere: "Mythos and Dianoia: A Dialectical Methodology of Literary Form," *Literary Monographs 4*, Eric Rothstein (Madison, Milwaukee, and London: Univ. of Wisconsin Press, 1971), pp. 3-88; and *Dialectical Criticism and Renaissance Literature* (Berkeley, Los Angeles, and London: Univ. of California Press, 1975), pp. 214-227 in particular.

11. A similar and more developed argument for distinguishing fictive from nonfictive texts according to how they were treated in their own times, and how the present critic may treat them, is made by John M. Ellis, *The Theory of Literary Criticism: A Logical Analysis* (Berkeley, Los Angeles, London: University of California Press, 1974), pp. 112ff:

"Literary texts can be converted into nonliterary texts quite simply: since the use made of the one is quite different from the use made of the other and, since it is this use (not properties of the texts) which is defining, we can make a poem not a poem by so treating it. We can treat a poem of Goethe as a letter from him to Friederike Brion. It may well have functioned that way in its context of origin; and there is nothing logically wrong in doing this. . . . The one thing that is different about literary texts, then, is that they are not to be taken as part of the contexts of their origin; and to take them in this way is to annihilate exactly the thing that makes them literary texts. I am not making the point that this use is an inappropriate one, but the stronger point that the texts are actually made into something different by this use: they are just not literature misused, they are no longer literature at all. The process of a text becoming a literary text involves three stages: its originating in the context of its creator, its then being offered for use as literature, and its finally being accepted as such. In the final step, society makes the text into literature." Stanley E. Fish, in "How Ordinary is Ordinary Language?" *New Literary History* 5 (1973) 41-54, begins by attacking the assumption made by stylistics that "literature" is defined by language usage that deviates from "ordinary language," and concludes, "What characterizes literature then is not formal properties, but an attitude—always within our power to assume—toward properties that belong by constitutive right to language. . . . Literature is still a category, but it is an open category, not definable by fictionality, or by a disregard of propositional truth, or by a statistical predominance of tropes and figures, but simply by what we decide to put into it. The difference lies not in the language but in ourselves." Finally, it should be noted that this definition of the fiction/nonfiction distinction according to use rather than intrinsic properties looks—but with serious qualifications—toward the speech-act approach exemplified by the essay of Robert L. Brown and Martin Steinmann in this collection, and by John Searle in "The Logical Status of Fictional Discourse," *New Literary History* 6 (1975), 319-332. Speech-act theory's concern with distinguishing the total meaning of statements according to the uses to which they are intended, and the uses to which the same statements may be put in a fictional as apart from a nonfictional context, generates an approach that is similar to the one I have exemplified in my own essay. But to the extent that a speech-act definition of literature remains confined to the question of how authors may signal to readers the rules for understanding the specifically fictional speech-act, it still assumes certain constitutive and intrinsic properties inherent in texts as the guiding norm. Along with Ellis and Fish, I would wonder whether these rules are not rather within the discretion of the reader, independent of whatever signals the author may have planted in his text. To query how fictional texts communicate their own fictionality is a legitimate enterprise; but the range of such querying becomes illegitimate to the extent that it implies that we violate something intrinsic to the text when we put this communication in brackets and choose to suspend it.

# Literature as Transaction

## *Norman N. Holland*

Thou com'st in such a questionable shape
That I will speak to thee.

What is literature? A creature of Cartesian cleavage, I begin by thinking of a set of objects. "Literature" includes such airinesses as the posture of an actor or the vibrato of a rhapsode or nitty-gritties like the specks of carbon black that make up the paragraph you are reading. I want *res extensae,* a corpus of books I can touch and tuck away in one corner of a library apart from science, non-fiction, religion, or art. The trouble is that these different books will not stay put in the categories librarians give them. A private diary, even one written in a secret code like Pepys', shifts over into the category of literature when its pedestrian, slightly preposterous author subsides into historical respectability. *The Spectator,* once kept under "current periodicals" as the *Times* is today, comes to be assigned in literature courses. The radio plays of the 1930's and the fugitive songs of country fiddlers slide out of folklore into Literature with a capital Left.

Sometimes the word becomes simply an honorific. We can

praise any sermon, political speech, or advertisement by saying, "Ah, *that* is literature!"[1] Thus, Roland Barthes (in *Mythologies*) treats detergents, wrestling matches, the face of Greta Garbo, and the *Guide Bleu* as though they were literature by looking at them with the eyes of a literary critic. The criticism that results is superb, but it leads me to a paradox. How can one write literary criticism about that which is not literature? Liberal as I am in these matters, I find it a stretch to call detergents, wrestling matches, or the face of Garbo literature, and certainly I draw the line at the *Guide Bleu*.

When this first approximation, literature-as-thing, falls short, I swing, Cartesianly, to the opposite extreme. I begin thinking of literature as *res cogitans*, literature as a state of mind or point of view, instead of an object. That way, I need not say that the things—Pepys' *Diary*, *The Spectator*, or *The New York Times*— have changed when they are newly classified as literature. Rather, our attitudes toward them have. Barthes has not, like Christ at the marriage-feast, turned the water of the *Guide Bleu* into the wine of literature. He is simply asking us to look at that worthy series in a novel way. (Yes, my pun is intentional.) A second approximation then: *literature is not things but a way to comprehend things.*

This definition accords with Stanley Fish's, arrived at through a finely reasoned erasure of the distinction between literature and "ordinary language." "Literature is language around which we have drawn a frame, a frame that indicates a decision to regard with a peculiar self-consciousness the resources language has always possessed." "What characterizes literature then is not formal properties, but an attitude. . . ." "Literature is an open category, not definable by fictionality, or by a disregard of propositional truth, or by a statistical predominance of tropes and figures, but simply by what we decide to put into it. The difference lies not in the language, but in ourselves."[2]

I could equally well follow Morse Peckham and conclude that

literature is not a product but a process, not an object but a role we take.[3] English, alas, has no word for such a role, someone actively relating to a literary work. "Reader" excludes heard and spoken literature. "Member of the audience" is clumsy. Accordingly, I have been applying the *−ent* (for agent) and using "literent." *Literature, then, is being a literent.* Or, if you prefer, liter*a*nt.

I could also adopt a strategy invented by Roy Schafer for some of the confusing entities of psychoanalysis and say literature is not a noun but an adverb.[4] *Literature is perceiving literarily.* What does it mean, though, to perceive something "literarily"? What do "literents" do to become same?

Surely some part of it means not doing, not acting on the physical world in response to the literary event. If a dramatent at *Twelfth Night* shouts a warning to Malvolio against the letter, he is responding in an extra-literary way. Following J.L. Austin, Richard Ohmann uses the term "illocutionary" for occasions when language itself is an act, as in praying, bargaining, warning, contracting, welcoming, pleading, and the like. One can think of a literary work as a sequence of "felicitous illocutionary acts" without the ordinary consequences of such acts. The literent uses his knowledge of the right conditions for rightly performing such acts to infer things like who the speaker is, what roles he plays, what kind of society he lives in, whether he is reliable, or what relationship he intends to establish by his words. Such inferences may well heighten the reader's own social awareness, but he is responding "unliterarily" if he takes the prayers, bargainings, warnings, and so on, as cues for his own acts.[5]

Often critics announce what looking at something "literarily" means. Followers of F. R. Leavis customarily say that to respond to literature properly one must evaluate it, as, for example, by placing it in a tradition or a manifest of better and worse literary works. Other critics (or literary historians) demand that literents look through the work to the culture that produced the literary work or its author or its popularity. Other critics insist that, "The primary understanding of any work of literature has to be based on an assumption of its unity."[6]

Different critical schools define "literents" and "literarily" differently. Different cultures also pose different demands. Shakespeare is a towering figure to English literents, but the French have never found in him the orderly overstatement so characteristic of their national life and letters. Different eras also slant the literary point of view differently. Neo-classic literents asked Shakespeare to provide poetic justice, "beauties," and unchanging aspects of human nature. His Romantic and later nineteenth-century audiences saw his plays as portrayals of particular events outside the text: fictions made history.

Classic or Romantic, French or English, extrinsic or intrinsic, evaluative or formalist, however, looking at something literarily always seems to involve some effort to "make sense" out of it. That effort can range from the critic's highly disciplined search for the "right" tradition to the casual laugher's finding a "point" in a joke. As humans, we seem to need to make sense of what we hear, although (as I have suggested some time ago[7]), we also seem able to satisfy that need for a "point" by almost any kind of interpretive strategy.

In short, we have more or less come round to the familiar idea that "literature," "literarily," and "literent" simply name conventions. "All aesthetics," concludes Fish, "are local and conventional rather than universal, reflecting a collective decision as to what will count as literature, a decision that will be in force only so long as a community of readers or believers (it is very much an act of faith) continues to abide by it."[8]

Peckham reminds us that it is an individual who follows or changes the convention: a work of art is "an occasion for a human being to perform the art-perceiving role in the artistic situation."[9] We can elaborate that role into the many relations a literent may have: literent to text; literent to author; literent to a character; literent to an image or episode; literent to a critic; literent to many critics; literent to culture; literent as critic, and many more. For each of these relationships, our culture may say certain stringencies are appropriate. More important, for each of them, *each of us* may say certain stringencies are appropriate.

Therefore, we can go beyond "convention." We invoke a complex mixture of the communal and the personal when we call something literature, perceive it literarily, or become its literents. My very consciousness that I am beginning such an act groups the thing with other works that other people have called literature. It calls that naming into question. My "literarily" claims that you will respond to it as I have. It argues for this work the status of sharability. In the same way, when I try to "make sense" of something literarily, I draw on a social, intellectual, or moral background that associates me with a community of like-minded people. I draw on other literary experience, hence other events that other people have called literature. In other words, we use the word *literature* as we use words like *science, art,* or *religion* to establish a community involving both things and people and the transactions between them. But always, each of us uses these words and creates these communities in his or her personal way.

Thus *my* "literarily" involves three things: convention; making sense of the text; and not acting in response to it. *You,* dear literent, will have to decide for yourself whether you can share these three. You might cry down convention and appeal to total individuality. You might be, with Susan Sontag, against interpretation; you might call for an erotics of literature rather than a hermeneutic. You could point out that the criterion of inaction fits capitalist art in which the maker in the studio-factory of Hollywood or even the poet's proverbial garret is alienated both from his product and his literents, while in a socialist setting, like China, the audience can expect to act immediately on the work.

Such criteria are, finally, personal or, more precisely, ways one person defines himself by means of his community. But even with so flexible a definition can one look "literarily" at a sonata or a statue or a stalagmite? Whatever else "literarily" involves, it must mean dealing with language. Barthes can write literary criticism about detergents and Garbo because he puts them into words.

Barthes, like all writers, reconciles his individual style of language and perception with the more or less communal system which is language and culture at large. He explains this bridging by the deductivism of Saussurean and later semiotics: signs are a fixed code linking sound to concept. Cultural events can be "read" by means of a similar "code" (even though the reading takes the individuality and talent of a Barthes!). This deductive formulation merely asserts a code without proving or articulating it, and it has little support from professional linguists. I do indeed want some proof that the exquisitely mute face of Garbo or the grunts and groans of *le catch* speak to me in some fixed code I happen to share with Roland Barthes.

Chomskyan and post-Chomskyan linguistics go beyond the idea of a deductive code. They strongly suggest (but do not yet prove) that individuals bring complex hypotheses to bear *both* in the speaking (or generating) *and* in the hearing (or interpretation) of sentences. Interpreting a sentence, even a single word, involves some sort of undoing of transformations, and that in turn may involve de-transforming all the other words in the sentence. Conversely, creating a sentence requires the active transformation of unitary thoughts, and the choice of transformations will express the writer's or the speaker's personality.[10] We *transact* sentences: *trans* + *agere,* to do through, to complete.

"Literarily," then, means a transaction in which we bring hypotheses to bear on a linguistic event. Some of these hypotheses are small linguistic interpretations of particular sentences. Some are large cultural notions about literature, speakers, plots, characters, genres, society, and the like. And some are quite personal. But my second approximation must take all into account: Literature is transacting literarily, that is, through linguistic hypotheses and cultural conventions (such as evaluating or not acting in response) *personally applied.*

"Personally applied." Different people will look for different things when they look literarily, and these different things will express their several personalities. Indeed, I have found that one can state the principles by which literents' personalities affect their literary perceptions quite precisely.

Each of us is a mixture of sameness and difference, continuity and change, that we call identity. I understand your sameness, the essential you, by seeing it persist through change. Conversely, I understand changes in you by seeing them against what has not changed. One way of conceptualizing that dialectic—there may be others, but this I have found the most effective—is to think of identity as a theme and variations like a work of music or literature. I can look identity-ly at a person just as I can look literarily at a text. I can draw on ideas of Heinz Lichtenstein and use the term "identity theme" for the continuing core of personality that I see a person bringing to each new experience. I can understand change and differences as variations played on that theme, so that I understand each action as embodying the theme by being a variation on it (just as each variation in sonata-form embodies the theme by its very difference from it). I can see in each action both change and continuity.[11]

Reading is one of those actions, and I can articulate still more precisely the way we involve texts in the creative variation of our identities. We bring to a text certain expectations—some cognitive, like literary and linguistic hypotheses, others the deeper roots of those hypotheses, typically a pattern of related wishes and fears. We try to find in the text a match to those expectations, because we need to make the text the kind of world we live in relation to. In the clinical sense, we "defend against" or "adapt" the text: that is, we shape and change it until, to the degree we need that certainty, it is the kind of setting in which we can gratify our wishes and defeat our fears. The defense enables us to invest the events, people, and words of the text with our fantasies, which, as intellectual beings, we transform into coherent, significant experience, thus confirming the whole transaction.[12]

Defense, expectation, fantasy, transformation—DEFT—they draw meaning from the clinical language of psychoanalysis, but they have larger senses as well. Our expectations place the literary work in the sequence of our wishes and fears, in other words, in time, while our transformation of the work toward significance attaches it to themes that transcend the immediate concerns of the moment. Defenses define what we will let into ourselves from outside, while fantasies are what we project from within toward that outside. Understood psychoanalytically, then, the literary transaction takes place at the intersection of time and timelessness and of self and others. To look at something literarily is to transact it between the world of meaning and the world of action (as, indeed, Aristotle hinted in his re- marks on literature *vis-à-vis* history and philosophy).

Yet these principles by which we re-create our identities through literary transactions apply to many things besides perceiving literarily. They constitute a general theory of the way personality enters into the perception of external realities. They describe the re-creation of externals into communities of shared transaction. The psychology of literents is also the psychology of voters, believers, athletes and spectators, producers and consumers.

Similarly, the linguistic hypotheses we bring to the literary transaction are not limited to that one relationship. At its deepest level, transformational grammar shows that any language makes use of three elementary transformational processes: adjunction, substitution, and deletion.[13]

In a general way, these processes correspond to the elementary operations of arithmetic. Adjunction is addition, deletion resembles subtraction, and substitution is like the equal sign. Similarly, these three processes bear a striking resemblance to what I believe to be basic processes of the mind as revealed by ego psychology. Adjunction resembles condensation. Deletion plus adjunction is like displacement (and displacement to a null equals deletion *tout court*). Substitution corresponds to symbolization, in the psychoanalytic context, a special kind of displacement.[14]

Thus, we find what, in a way, we should have expected to find: that "transacting literarily" is continuous with other human activities. (After all, we *are* continuous, aren't we?) Everything *can* be looked at literarily as Roland Barthes so elegantly demonstrates, even the *Guide Bleu*. Yet this very admissiveness suggests something is lacking in this second definition as a definition. "How can one write literary criticism about that which is not literature?" I feel a third approximation is called for, something that will set literature off from other human experiences, even if we grant that it is closely related to them.

So far, I have defined literature wholly from the literent's point of view, yet obviously some objects lend themselves to being transacted literarily more than others. Poem, story, play, and (I would say) film or happening will reward my quest, and sonata, sculpture, or stalagmite will not. *Paradise Lost* or even Pepys' *Diary* will requite my literary love more than *Consumer Reports*, and Bartlett's *Familiar* more than the daily stock quotations. To be sure, I *can* look literarily even at commercial and numerical writings, aiming at them my characteristic DEFT, including linguistic, cultural, or even semiotic hypotheses. Nevertheless, other kinds of writing will yield more to my literary inquiry.

I am not trying to smuggle back the objective definition of literature as thing that I first rejected. I am insisting that we not divide either literature or the rest of the world Cartesianly into

things and states of mind. The paradigm that more truly expresses twentieth century discoveries in science and letters is:
one cannot separate the two. Fundamental reality is the field of
interactions between selves and others.

In other words, the literary transaction has two directions:
from literent to text and from text to literent. I inquire, and the
text responds, and I develop my inquiry accordingly. The transaction is cybernetic. The failure to take into account the way
texts favor some relations and hypotheses over others renders
accounts of literature as "subjective" just as deficient as "objective" accounts that leave out the literent. "Subjective" and "objective" each tell only half the transaction.[15]

The text carries out its half by changing the consequences of
my action. Suppose I am reading, "A slumber did my spirit
seal." My tendency may be to read the poem as a pantheistic
triumph over death, as death's defeat of life, as a study in guilt,
or as an example of castration symbolism.[16] No matter which,
the word "diurnal" adds consequences to my choice. I may feel
"diurnal" is a scientific abstraction, a solemn Latinism, or a pun
on "die" and "urn," yet I will have to fit one or another of those
readings into my total transaction of the lyric or else give up my
membership in a certain community of learned literents or my
commitment to the poem as a whole.

The literary transaction is like a contract: you are always free
to break it, but when you signed it, you changed the price of that
freedom. Notice that neither text, contract, nor poem finally
controls my transaction, however. We humans are always,
paradoxically, both free and bound to choose.

The materials in the text simply provide ways I *may* respond.
An omission gives me a chance to deny any unpleasant reality or
to project a fantasy of my own into the gap. I can use change in
point of view to displace eagerly to the new one or to try to hold
onto the old. A cut from long shot to close-up makes it possible
for me to feel sudden intimacy or a jarring closeness. In practice,

if literents were controlled by texts or constrained by critical principles, we would find far more agreement about meanings than we do. In principle, we are free to be as crazy as we want and, in fact, very good criticism is written in that vein (although I will mention no names).

One has to redefine text, in order to discuss literary theory realistically, as text-in-relation-to-a-person, just as the word literent defines a person as person-in-relation-to-a-text. And thus we come to a third approximation, one that will accommodate both Pepys' *Diary* and Barthes' detergents. To perceive literarily is to transact literature through personally applied linguistic hypotheses and cultural conventions. Then, *literature is transacting literarily, which is rewarded*. And, of course, I grasp the reward through the same DEFTing, hypotheses, and conventions as I grasp the text.

In short, I think we approach a potentially literary thing prepared to replenish it with a set of inquiries or hypotheses. Questions like: Can I interpret this film as language, using the same kinds of transformations and undoings of transformations with which I perceive other language? When I respond to this *poésie concrète* as literature am I placing myself within a community of like-minded literents? Does this piece of journalism fit among other works that I and others call literature? Do I "make sense" of this play extrinsically in terms of a social and personal context around it, or intrinsically in terms of thematic and psychological unities I find within it? Is this polemic asking me to act on the physical world? Is this diary freely available for my fantasies? Finally, how does this text, this potential, answer my inquiries? For just as I choose the questions, I weigh the answers.

At the highest level, then, in transacting literature I assert in symbolic form my human freedom to choose my own destiny. I re-assert my free, personal re-creation of self and text precisely by requiring of the text consequences for my freedom. I plunge

# NORMAN H. HOLLAND

myself into a dialectic; yet, however the text replies, I retain final
responsibility, for I am aways free—and bound—to do with the
materials of the work what will express my inner nature. I cannot do otherwise. I am always both free and bound both to
ignore and to heed the text, conventions, other critics, common
sense, literary history, or the dictionary. I am both free and
bound to mutter to myself against all pressures and constraints,
my own inner certainty, *Eppur si muove!* And simultaneously to
hesitate and to wonder (if I choose to), can the term *literature*
include so small and macaronic a pun?

## NOTES

1. Thomas J. Roberts ingeniously suggests that we give such words as
"fiction" a meaning shaped like a T, of two overlapping bars. One bar is
fiction by virtue of its author's intention; the other is fiction by virtue of
our wish to admire the book in question. *When is Something Fiction?*
(Carbondale: Southern Illinois Univ. Press, 1972).

2. "How Ordinary is Ordinary Language?", *New Literary History*, 5
(1973), 41-54, 52.

3. Morse Peckham, *Man's Rage for Chaos: Biology, Behavior, and the Arts*
(Philadelphia: Chilton, 1965).

4. *A New Language for Psychoanalysis* (New Haven and London: Yale
Univ. Press, 1976).

5. Richard Ohmann, "Literature as Act," *Approaches to Poetics*, ed.
Seymour Chatman, English Institute Essays (New York: Columbia
Univ. Press 1973), pp. 81-107, 97-98. See also his "Speech, Literature,
and the Space Between," *New Literary History*, 4 (1972), 47-63.

6. Northrop Frye, "Literary Criticism," in *The Aims and Methods of
Scholarship in Modern Languages and Literatures,* ed. James Thorpe (New
York: Modern Language Association, 1963), p. 63.

7. *The Dynamics of Literary Response* (New York: Oxford Univ. Press,
1968), p. 185.

8. Fish, p. 52.

9. Peckham, p. 66.

10. See my "Prose and Minds: A Psychoanalytic Approach to Non-Fiction," in *The Art of Victorian Prose*, ed. George Levine and William Madden (New York: Oxford Univ. Press, 1968), pp. 314-337. See also my forthcoming "What Can a Concept of Identity Add to Psycholinguistics?" in *Psychiatry and the Humanities*, III (1978).

11. See my *Poems in Persons* (New York: Norton, 1973) and *5 Readers Reading* (New Haven: Yale Univ, Press, 1975), both drawing on such articles of Lichtenstein's as "Identity and Sexuality: A Study of Their Interrelationship in Man," *Journal of the American Psychoanalytic Association*, 9 (1961), 179-260.

12. See my "Unity Identity Text Self," *PMLA*, 90 (1975), 813-22.

13. Roderick A. Jacobs and Peter S. Rosenbaum, *English Transformational Grammar* (Waltham, Mass.: Blaisdell, 1968), pp. 26-28.

14. See my "Defence, Displacement and the Ego's Algebra," *International Journal of Psycho-Analysis*, 54 (1973), 247-57.

15. See my "The New Paradigm: Subjective or Transactive?", *New Literary History*, 7 (1976), 335-46.

16. See my "Literary Criticism and Three Phases of Psychoanalysis," *Critical Inquiry*, 3 (1976), 221-33.

# "Literature":
# Disjunction and Redundancy

## *Morse Peckham*

Most definitions of literature emanate from high cultural levels and are most readily subsumed under the category of, in a loose sense, philosophical behavior. The most interesting feature of such definitions is their instability. As new cultural stages emerge, definitions of literature are innovated in response to cultural change—to emerging interests, ideologies, philosophies, issues, and so on. Such efforts at definition are almost invariably normative, a phenomenon that is evident from the changing ascriptions of value granted to particular works. Either the work can be made or cannot be made, or is or is not made, to serve the emerging situation. If adaptation is accomplished, a work to which value has traditionally been ascribed will continue to be valued. If not, then the value ascription is withdrawn. At any given time, of course, some individuals, unaware of or resistant to the emergent culture, will continue to make the traditional ascriptions. It is evident that high cultural definitions are unlikely to be more than temporarily satisfying, since their interest is not in defining literature but in comprehending and establishing an emergent culture. To be sure, in the short range, a spurious stability will appear, since if there is no significant cultural change, the definitions of the most recently emerging culture will tend to stabilize, but a new cultural upheaval will force their abandonment.

What is needed is, first, a field definition of literature, a field that will be established non-normatively and will begin by accepting as literature whatever anyone says is literature or some sub-category of literature—poetry, fiction, informal essay, etc. Such a field definition is non-normative and includes within its boundaries not only literary works emanating from a high cultural level but also the infinitely greater bulk of literary discourse found at all other levels: Edna Ferber, Ella Wheeler Wilcox, Edgar Rice Burroughs, pornographic fiction, jokes, limericks, and so on. What would be excluded are works in which verbal behavior is but one of several to many semiotic systems—plays, movies, operas, comic books. That the scripts of such works can be considered apart from the other semiotic systems in the original is an interesting point to which it will be useful to return, for it shows that the advantage of a field definition is the blurred character of the boundaries of such definitions.

Nevertheless, though a field definition is useful, "field" remains a metaphor, but "literature" is a category. The question is whether it is a conjunctive or a disjunctive category, whether all works of literature may reasonably be said to have at least one internal attribute in common, or whether this statement may not be reasonably made.[1]

There is little question that virtually all definitions of "literature" assume that it is properly to be regarded as a conjunctive category, that all works of literature, whether a dirty joke or *Paradise Lost*, have in common an immanent and defining attribute; that is, other modes of discourse are without that attribute. Without trying to claim exhaustiveness, I think that most definitions can be boiled down to the following types.

First is the definition based upon the assertion of a common psychological or subjective origin. Thus literature has for some time been defined as a product of, or expression of, the imagination. Since it is easily demonstrated that certain other types of discourse—philosophy, science, history—are equally products of the imagination, this difficulty is countered by saying that literature is a verbal product of the "creative imagination." But this strategy does not seem to help much. Consider Immanuel Wallerstein's appeal to "the empirical evidence" in his recent *The Modern World-System: Capitalist Agriculture and the Origins of the European World-Economy in the Sixteenth Century.* Now the fact of the matter is that if "empirical evidence" means here what it does to, let us say, a physicist, or a chemist, or even a few sociologists, Wallerstein does not have any. What he does have are documents and certain artifacts, such as ploughs, which are by no means self-explanatory. Moreover, his book is not based even upon very much of his own examination of such historical documents but upon the research of others. This is not to denigrate a fine scholar and a book of considerable importance, but rather to point out that, guided by Marx, Wallerstein has certainly produced a discourse marked by what anyone would call a product of the "historical imagination." But is it "creative"? If "creative" is taken in its most extreme and narrow sense, the mark of discourse which has no correspondence in anything, verbal or non-verbal, outside of the literary discourse in question, then the question remains unanswerable, for we do not know whether Wallerstein's thesis indeed has any relation whatsoever to what really happened. There is no doubt that a good many competent historians will disagree with him entirely. In short, it has proved impossible to confine the term "creative" to any particular mode of behavior.

This leads us to the second type of definition, one based upon content. This usually takes the form of a claim for some kind of semantic autonomy, most frequently appearing in the form of a claim for literature of a unique kind of "truth." When inquiry is made as to what this "truth" is, it usually turns out that literature exemplifies some philosophical or moral truth or that it furnishes an ineffable or otherwise unutterable truth. It can be experienced by the individual reader but cannot be communicated. It is reasonably obvious that what is going on here is an effort to ascribe value to literature—and in practice, only some works of literature, ordinarily a rather small class—by using the highly eulogistic term "truth." It is quite obviously normative and just as obviously the product of a high cultural level, though not the highest. From another point of view, that of the total non-normatively-defined "field of literature," the semantic content of literature is infinitely varied. No one semantic function can be said to be a defining attribute of literature. Literature is a semantic field in which anything goes.

The third kind of definition concerns itself with the formal aspect. Literature is said to have unity and coherence. (Or "aesthetic" unity, a formulation so question-begging that it is not worth discussing.) Even if this were so, they cannot be defining attributes, for surely other kinds of discourse may be reasonably said to be marked by the same attributes. Further, any perceptual field (and literature is such, for it consists of discourse perceived either by eye or by ear) is unified and coherent if the criteria are sufficiently loose; and none is, if the criteria are sufficiently stringent. Unity and coherence are matters of judgment, a fact easily demonstrated by the enormous amount of disagreement. How many articles have been written and even published on the unity and coherence of *Beowulf!* Nevertheless, a formal definition does have some possibilities. There is little doubt that literature can present a degree of incoherence, of disunity, or incomprehensible relationships to be found in no other kind of discourse. Poetry, for example, can conform to or violate the syntactic norms of the language in which it is written. A fictional character can be thoroughly inconsistent or incoherent. Indeed consistency of character increases as the importance of the character in the work decreases, and as the cultural level of the work is lowered. Plots can be resolved or left unresolved. Two stanzas of the same poem may be quite contradictory. And so on. This definition is at least promising. If the norms of linguistic behavior are behaviorally maintained, rather than genetically maintained, and such behavioral maintenance certainly seems to be the case, then it can be said that the violations of linguistic norms to be found in literature are socially permitted. This leads in the direction of some kind of socio-cultural definition of literature.

A fourth kind of definition, of minor importance but worth mentioning, is the dysfunctional. It is said that there are elements in literature or there are attributes of literature which are superfluous to its semantic function, to what is being said in, or by, the work. "Grace, elegance, charm, power" are words commonly used to designate this superfluous dysfunctional attribute, but the most common term is probably "style." Literature, then, is discourse marked by "style." That this is a normative definition is indicated by the extremely various efforts to state what that "style" amounts to. On the other hand, one often enough hears of some works that they have no style (the fiction of Balzac, for example) but are certainly works of literature. Yet this definition has possibilities, for it is often said that certain non-literary works, such as those of Buffon, are so marked by literary style that they are "really" works of literature. This is promising, for at least it shows the fuzziness and instability in the boundaries of the field of literature.

No doubt there are other types of definitions of literature, though I can think of no others. At least, however, it seems reasonable to attempt a definition of "literature" as a disjunctive category. This means that works called "literature" do not have any immanent and defining attribute in common. It follows that discourses are categorized as "literature" as a consequence of some socio-cultural judgment. This is best understood by considering what has been mentioned before, the instability of the boundaries of the literature field. Certain works, such as Carlyle's *French Revolution*, are no longer read as history but rather as literature. Yet certainly it was first published as history, and as recently as 30 years ago was included in one historian's bibliography as one of the best English histories of that event. Buffon and any number of originally philosophical works are read now as literature. Some time ago a psychologist recommended to me the works of Jung, not because of their scientific or psychological value, which he discounted, but for their splendid imaginative and literary qualities. Schopenhauer and Nietzsche are not infrequently labeled bad philosophy but good literature. Richard Hooker and Sir Thomas Browne are categorized as literature but not as anything now significant in terms of the non-literary genres in which their works were originally written. A work of literature, then, is such because someone has judged it to be a work of literature.

If we modify the first type of definition (literature as an expression or product of the imagination) to the definition of literature as a fictive discourse as well as a disjunctive category, what has happened to such works becomes obvious. It is asserted that their non-fictiveness is no longer of importance or significance or value but that they can be profitably read as fictive discourses. The definition of whether a discourse is fictive or non-fictive is then a matter of someone's judgment. And indeed the history of science itself is filled with statements originally judged to be non-fictive but now judged to be fictive. This can best be explained by the judgment that all discourse is fictive, that all utterance, all linguistic behavior, is fictive.[2] Discourse is a construct of that which lies outside of language. Culture, in the full, anthropological, sense, consists of directions for a performance, and language is subsumed by culture. Even "descriptive" statements—such as, "There is a mouse in the corner over there"—are in their full form instructions for a performance: "If you look in the corner over there, you will see a mouse—if he's still there." All words which are referential—an inadequate term but one which will have to serve here—are categorial, even proper names, because a proper name categorizes separately perceived configurations. Hence the disagreement on the attributes of bearers of proper names.[3] Moreover, categorial words are not under genetic or perceptual control. Verbalization makes the human construction of the world free or, more precisely, indeterminable. What makes it possible to recategorize a non-literary work as a literary work is that its fictiveness continues, no matter how it is categorized.

What makes a discourse a work of literature, then, is that it is identified as fictive. Such identifications may be internal: "Once upon a time." They may appear in the title: *Jim James: A Novel.* They may be prefatory: "I heard a good joke the other day." The conventions of fictive identifications are innumerable, but can be uncertain. Is *The Tale of Genji* a novel or a memoir? They may be situational; they may be typographical; they may be tones of voice. Whatever they are and however the announcement of fictiveness is made, that announcement is a cultural convention.[4] Furthermore, since behavior is indeterminable, those conventions can be played with, can be modified. Thus the script of a theater piece can be read apart from the theatrical situation, and theater pieces may or may not have scripts. In the same way an *exemplum* can be extracted from a sermon and presented as literature.

But if this disjunctive definition of literature as a discourse identified as fictive is accepted, we are bound to ask why such identifications should be made. That is, what are the consequences of such announcements? It is a sentimentality to conceive of language as "communication." Rather language organizes, directs, controls, and modifies behavior. If, because of language, human behavior is indeterminable, then humans are not social animals in the same sense that bees and ants are, or even the higher mammals, much of whose behavior is certainly cultured, or learned, but is still under perceptual if not full genetic control. And if humans are not social, then interaction,

which is economically necessary and ineluctable, must be controlled. The accomplishment, language, which makes human
behavior indeterminable is also the instrument which for the
most part makes it determinable. Ultimately, however, the
sanction for the control language exercises is force. But if force
fails, there is no recourse. Consequently the burden of interactional control falls upon language.

Two attributes of human behavior need to be explained, and
explained in the same way: deviance from established norms
and channeling of behavior within those norms. To the degree
any behavior is badly transmitted, to that degree there will be a
spread of deviance. But how is behavior maintained? Why is
there not far greater deviance than there is? In any society there
is, statistically speaking, only very little. (Wealthy societies can
tolerate far more than can poor societies.) The answer, I believe,
lies in the phenomenon of redundancy, the endless repetition of
the same verbal (and non-verbal, under the control of verbal)
instructions in various verbal and non-verbal semiotic modes.[5]
Without such redundancy, including instructions that individuals give to themselves, behavioral patterns deteriorate, as a
language learned in adolescence will deterioriate if it is not continually used. Even frequent but irregular use is not enough to
maintain competence. One forgets the dates in a literary field
one has ceased to teach and study. Now the literatus is part of
this redundancy system, simply because he is a human. Any
individual is a precipitate of the indescribably complex control
system which is language; with infinitely rare exceptions, his
presence or absence, his existence or nonexistence, makes no
difference. His behavior is controlled by that system, but
because of the brain's capacity for random response, deviance
(innovation, creativity, the imagination) is constantly being introduced in, on the whole, minute and statistically insignificant
amounts. The decisions the literatus makes, then, are under the
control of the linguistic behavior of his culture, and his fictive

discourse exemplifies the verbal redundancies of his culture. At the higher cultural level those redundancies are organized into and justified by ideologies. A work of literature is a discourse, the fictiveness of which is announced, and which exemplifies the redundancies and ideologies of the culture in which it originates. From this point of view literature (even orally repeated jokes) is of the highest importance in maintaining behavior by constantly exemplifying verbalizations of a level higher than the work itself, "higher" here meaning "subsuming." The characteristic of the literary situation for the receiver is that he is not required to do anything immediately in response to the instructions received. Literature, then, maintains the redundancies of a society in those situations in which performance, other than attentiveness, is not required. Literature (and the other arts) maintains redundancies during periods of economic disengagement, or periods of disengagement from control by hierarchical institutions such as religious, schooling, and governmental institutions which, however, maintain economic competence. (This is true of other activities as well, such as participation sports or stamp-collecting. Spectator sports, however, fall within the boundaries of art.) The literary conventions of fictiveness are announcements of the suitability of such discourse for periods of economic and institutional disengagement.

But there is a joker here. I have already implied the identification of randomness, deviance, innovation, creativity, imagination. Periods of economic disengagement, obviously, are periods of the greatest tolerance for randomness of behavior, that randomness which is the most striking product of the human brain. The games of children are economically preparatory; they are abstractions of adult interactional patterns. The play of children, in which they discover their own interests, is marked by randomness. Because of this tolerance for randomness, literature is, first of all, a disjunctive category; and, second, one that not only maintains behavior but also modifies

it. The justification for the teaching of literature is that, by providing exemplifications of a variety of ideologies, it modifies the
overall behavior of the student in the direction of flexibility. As
situations change, patterns of economically engaged behavior
must change. A certain portion of the society, gradually sifted
for decisions at a higher socio-economic level, is trained by the
literature of high culture in perceiving the possibilities of alternative modes of behavior and alternative ideologies, and in
randomization and innovation. (This does not deny that high-
culture literature can be and frequently has been used only for
exemplificatory redundancy.) Furthermore, literature, because
of its disjunctive character, and because of its potentiality for
incoherence, can be used to undermine regnant ideologies. To
Pope ("What oft was thought . . ."), literature is properly employed in the modification of the exemplification of ideological
redundancies in the direction of clarity and effectiveness. To
writers at a high cultural level for nearly the past 200 years—a
time of extraordinarily rapid culture change at all levels of social
organization, from the fundamental economic modes of interaction to the construction of the most exacting ideologies—not
merely the modification but the undermining of ideological redundancies has been the most valued objective—even, in some
instances, to the point of undermining ideological behavior itself.

What is literature? It is a discourse which exploits in periods of
economic and institutional disengagement the fictiveness of utterance by announcing that fictiveness, and thus has the
capacity to maintain the redundancies of its culture, to modify
those redundancies, and to undermine them. Thus it has the
capacity to support the economic interactional patterns of its
culture, to modify them, and to destroy them.

## NOTES

1. See Jerome S. Bruner, *A Study of Thinking* (New York, 1956), p. 159. Bruner takes the category of disjunction from Bertrand Russell's *Introduction to Mathematical Thinking*, 1919.

2. In J. L. Austin's terminology, all utterances are "performative," i.e., instructions for behavior. Utterances of which such words as "truth," "real," "descriptive," etc. are predicated are utterances for which the predication is a "performative" instruction that such utterances should control our behavior, or must control our behavior, if the predicator has sufficient power to enforce his predication; cf. the Inquisition and General Amin.

3. The problem of proper names is one of the more notorious of the many failures of philosophy. John R. Searle does a considerably better job than most in his essay "Proper Names and Descriptions," *Encyclopedia of Philosophy*. "We learn to use proper names and we teach others to use proper names only by ostension or description, and both methods connect the name to the object only in virtue of specifying enough characteristics of the object to distinguish it from other objects." (VI, 490) He appears to ignore, however, the fact that we encounter what he calls bearers of proper names in a series of situations spread over as much as a lifetime. The characteristics (or attributes) change. John Jones, a gentle man, may become savage, but it is still convenient to call him John Jones. Cobbs Creek may have its course changed and straightened, but it is still Cobbs Creek. The consequence of the institution of proper names is a stabilization of behavior by stabilizing response. Searle is at least aware of the imprecision of proper names, and sees something of its advantages. Were it not for the instability of the attributes, one of the most powerful devices of fiction would be impossible: the establishment of the attributes of a proper name, the deascription of some attributes and the ascription of others. This is known, inaccurately, as "character development."

4. This is something children have to learn. Initially, the socialization of children, i.e., bringing them under linguistic control, requires that all statements be accepted by the child as "true," an acceptance traditionally backed up by the force of the parent. The child must subsequently learn that some utterances are "not true," are "made up," are "a story," and that the utterer of a "story" is not "telling a lie" when it is announced that the "story" is indeed "made up," that is, does not require obedience or acceptance as "true." Children very often have a great

deal of trouble in learning this distinction and are inclined to believe *Star Trek* to be history.

5. There is no adequate theory of signs available at present. Peirce's distinctions among "icon," "index," and "symbol" are untenable, since one may respond to an "icon" as if it were a "symbol" or an "index." He is in fact talking about modes of response. Morris' notion of "disposition to respond" does not depend upon phenomenal observants. My own position corresponds with G. H. Mead's position that the meaning of a sign is the response to that sign. Unfortunately Mead did little with this idea. But at least, depending upon Hegel, he broke with the tradition that the meaning of a sign is immanent, and also with the very confusing and inadequate notion of "reference." A sign, then, is a configuration for which a response has been conventionalized, but this use of "convention" does not exclude conventionalization within the behavior of a single individual, nor does it exclude the notion that such conventionalization may occur only once. Nor does it exclude error, or what is judged by someone to be an inappropriate response. Irony depends upon the possibility of judgments of inappropriateness. My own discussion of signs in *Man's Rage for Chaos* is highly unsatisfactory, dependent as it is upon Morris. In *Art and Pornography* the theory of signs is vastly improved, but still inadequate. In a forthcoming book, *Explanation and Power: An Inquiry into the Control of Human Behavior*, the theory of signs is, I believe at the moment, in a reasonably satisfactory condition.

# Toward a Semiotics of Literature

## *Robert Scholes*

*Literature* of course is a word, not a thing. In casual conversation the word is used in many ways, some of them in conflict with one another. *Literature* may be thought of as true writing vs. false, as beautiful writing vs. useful, as non-true writing vs. true/false writing, and so on. It can be thought of as consisting of a few established generic forms, such as poem, play, and story, with such debatable genres as the essay and the film lurking on the borders. Most departments of literature function with no better concepts than these, and, as F. E. Sparshott has ironically pointed out (in *Centrum* III, 1), they proceed with all the confidence in the world.

To some extent I sympathize with the traditional muddle here. Often what begins as clarification ends as nonsense, producing categories so exclusive or inclusive that they bring all attempts at systematic thinking about literature into disrepute. And yet, we who study what we call "literature" cannot help but desire to understand better what we are doing. My attempt

This is a version, abridged by the editor, of a public lecture delivered at the University of Iowa in 1976. A fuller text appears in *Critical Inquiry* 4 (1977), 105-20.

to deal with the problem here is based on the formalist, structuralist, and semiotic tradition of critical thought, but at certain crucial points I shall bend that tradition in what I take to be a necessary direction. Some might even say that I have bent it beyond the breaking point.

The word *literature*, I wish to argue, should be used to designate a certain body of repeatable or recoverable acts of communication. Later on I shall elaborate on the "certain" part of the definition, which requires the exclusion of some repeatable or recoverable communicative acts from the literary category. But first I must define the other terms in this definition. *Repeatable or recoverable* requires that something called literature have a certain durability. This may take the form of a written text, a recorded utterance, a reel of film, or something transmitted orally, like a saying, joke, myth, or epic poem. In the oral forms, what is recovered is not usually an identical text but a recognizable structure—the "same" joke or epic poem in different words—but this "sameness" brings such works within the limits of this definition of literature. A saying or performance which is not recoverable or repeatable, whether a forgotten joke or a lost manuscript, may well have been literary, but it is no longer a part of literature, since literature consists of the body of available performances only.

The word *act* in the definition of literature being proposed here requires that our repeatable or recoverable utterance be a deliberate action on the part of some sentient being. A mistake is not literature. But it can be made literature by someone else's performance of it. Any utterance or human gesture can be made literary by its being deliberately incorporated into another utterance. Any trivial or vulgar bit of speech or gesture may function in a literary way in a story or play, for instance, or even in a Joycean "epiphany," just as a piece of driftwood or trash may be incorporated in a work of sculpture, or any found object be turned into visual art by an act of selection and display.

Finally, the word *communication* in the definition must be considered. It has been used here because it includes some non-verbal systems of signification as well as the expected verbal forms. A category termed *literature* which excluded theater and film would be embarrassing and awkward for many reasons, among which is the fact that what is recognizably the same work (Henry James's *Washington Square*, for instance) may exist effectively as a printed text, a stage performance, and a film. The word "communication" may seem to open the way too far to non-verbal forms like mime and dance, which are clearly communicative, and even to all the visual and musical forms of expression. Most music "communicates" something, as does most visual art, though clearly there is a broad range from representational forms to "pure" or abstract forms. Here it may be useful to limit the meaning of communication in this definition to utterances that are reasonably susceptible to verbal restatement or paraphrase. Even so, this will be an untidy border—partly because highly iconological and iconographic works of visual art as well as vocal and programmatic music are to some extent literary.

More important at the moment is that part of the definition originally masked by the word *certain*. What quality, you will wish to know, makes any given communicative act a work of literature? I, like any good Prague School structuralist, will answer, in a word, "literariness." This response, of course, is logically splendid but entirely meaningless until the new term is given a less tautological semantic coding—which will be our business here. The major contribution of Roman Jakobson to literary study was his deliverance of us all from "literature" as an absolute category. "Literariness," he has taught us, is found in all sorts of utterances, some of which are not especially literary. And a "literary work" is simply one in which literariness is dominant. Obviously, this allows for borderline cases and disputation, but this is undoubtedly an advantage, since "literature" as an absolute category always provokes disputation anyway, and by making the argument turn on "literariness," we should at least know what kind of evidence ought to decide such disputes—if (and it is a large "if") we can define "literariness" in a satisfactory way.

It may be, of course, that we need not define literariness as an aspect of utterance at all. One might, in fact, overturn the whole problem by doing as Jonathan Culler suggests in *Structuralist Poetics*, regarding literature not as a function of the work itself but as a special way of reading. Culler suggests that the issue ought not to be the literariness of the text but the "literary competence" of the reader, and that competence is primarily a mastery of generic conventions—a position with which I am in sympathy. But are all conventions literary? Are all texts potential fictions? The problem of literariness will not go away, whether we locate it in the text, the reader, or the system. The solution, I am about to argue, lies in seeing the "literary" as a quality that transforms all the major functions of an act of communication, including the role of the reader—which brings us back to Roman Jakobson, especially to his "Closing Statement: Linguistics and Poetics" (in *Style in Language*, ed. Thomas A. Sebeok).

The six features of a communicative act as popularized by Jakobson's analysis are sender, receiver, contact, message, code, and context. In Jakobson's view, a literary utterance may be distinguished from a non-literary utterance by its emphasis on its own formal structure. This emphasis forces us to consider the utterance as a structured object with a certain density or opacity. It is not a transparent vehicle through which our thoughts are directed to some context or action. It is an entity to be contemplated in its own right. This formulation is closely related to many other views, such as those of I. A. Richards and the New Critics. It rests ultimately on a Kantian assumption about the purposelessness of esthetic objects.

It is in part a useful formulation, but I find it objectionable for a number of reasons. For one, it applies much better to verse, especially to highly formulaic verse, than to prose fiction or drama. For another, it abandons much that has been gained by seeing literariness as a feature of communication rather than as a mode of a purposeless activity called "art." For once this notion of art is allowed into the picture, all those aspects of literature which are cognitive or instructive are found to be impurities. Rather than accept the notion that much (if not all) literature is a kind of failed art, we who have made literary study a central concern in our lives must seek a definition which accounts for this centrality. Seeing literature as a refinement or elaboration of the elements of communication rather than as a vulgarization of the elements of art is the necessary first step in this direction. Jakobson's neat formulation pays too great a price for its neatness. It turns back toward esthetics just when it should continue on with semiotics, and the result is a definition of literariness that excludes many of the most important qualities of all literature, including much poetry. It is time now to move toward a formulation that will yield us a more satisfactory notion of literariness.

Stated as simply as I can put it, we sense literariness in an utterance when any one of the six features of communication loses its simplicity and becomes multiple or duplicitous. Let me illustrate this first with some minimal cases. We are all familiar with what happens when we sense a difference between the maker of an utterance and the speaker of it. We say then that the words are those of a "persona" of the author, meaning, as the word implies, that the author has donned a mask. Whenever a communicative act encourages us to sense a difference between maker and speaker, our literary competence has been activated. This is true not only in such obvious situations as when we encounter the words of characters in plays or stories, but in essays also, whenever the essayist adopts a tone or role that seems to be a deviation from some anticipated norm. Even in casual conversation, when a speaker adopts a particular tone, register, or dialect for a given occasion, we notice this as a kind of literary behavior. In written prose a device like the ironic presentation of argument in Swift's "Modest Proposal" is simply an extreme case of this duplicity of the "sender" of a communication.

Similarly, if the words of an utterance seem not to be aimed directly at us but at someone else, this duplicitous situation is essentially literary. John Stuart Mill emphasized this when he said that poetry is not heard but overheard. It is perhaps unfortunate, but situations of eavesdropping and voyeurism are in part literary—which is no doubt why they figure so prominently in avowed literary texts. The literary competence of readers with respect to this feature of communicative acts is often a matter of imagining the person to whom the utterance is addressed or of perceiving meanings which are not intended for, or not understood by, the ostensible auditor. Every communicative subtlety requires a corresponding subtlety of interpretation.

We are placed in a literary situation also when the contact is not simple. If spoken words are presented to us in writing, for instance, either the writer or the reader must supply the features of oral communication lost in this translation—as Laurence Sterne reminds us when he takes such pains to record Corporal Trim's posture, gesture, and emphasis as the Corporal reads a document aloud in *Tristram Shandy*. Sterne, of course, by recording in writing the reading aloud of a written document makes the situation doubly literary with respect to the contact. Similarly, all descriptions of things normally perceived visually tend toward the literary because they seek to "translate" what would be a visual contact into a verbal one. The notion that all written documents are "literature" is based on this process. In fact, the more difference we sense between the verbal contact of print and our normal means of perception of the objects named in any printed text, the more literary the utterance is likely to be. It is therefore probable that all writing contains at least traces of literariness, but we must remember that literariness does not equal literature until it dominates any given utterance.

Duplicity in the form of the message itself, though immensely complicated, is the aspect of literariness which we presently understand best because it has been most carefully studied. Jakobson and Richards and all the Formalists and New Critics have alerted us to the various sound effects and syntactic patternings of verse as well as to the ironies, ambiguities, paradoxes and other duplicitous features of poetic messages. I do not wish to dwell on these features here except to point out that they function not to cut the work off from the world by making it a self-contained object—as so many theoreticians have argued—rather, they function to create a literary tension between the utterance as communicative and externally referential on the one hand—and as incommunicative and self-referential, on the other. A poem usually tantalizes us by being a mirror and a window at the same time, as Murray Krieger, among others, has argued.

I have saved the most complicated for last: code and context. We can postpone code even further, since all the features we have been considering as literary may be described in terms of conventions or devices that transform ordinary discourse into literary discourse. As for the problem of context, Jakobson himself removes it from the literary sphere, simply saying that an utterance which emphasizes its context is referential, not poetic, and many theoreticans, like Richards, oppose referential to non-referential discourse as a way of describing the difference between utilitarian and aesthetic texts. My intention here is to argue for a contrary assumption. And in doing so I must break with a powerful tradition in semiotic studies that runs from Saussure to Barthes and Eco.

The most powerful assumption in French semiotic thought since Saussure has been the notion that a sign does not connect a name and the object it refers to, but consists of a sound-image and a concept, a signifier and a signified. Saussure, as amplified by Foucault, Barthes, and Eco, has taught us to recognize an unbridgeable gap between words and things, signs and referents. The whole notion of "sign and referent" has been rejected by the French structuralists and their followers as too materialistic and simple-minded. Signs do not refer to things; they signify concepts, and concepts are aspects of thought, not of reality. This elegant and persuasive formulation has certainly provided a useful critique of naïve realism, vulgar materialism, and various other -isms which can be qualified with crippling adjectives. But it hasn't exactly caused the world to turn into a concept. Even semioticians eat and perform their other bodily functions just as if the world existed solidly around them. That language would generate words like "orgasm" or "tonsil" without any assistance from non-verbal experience seems to me highly unlikely. In my view, if language really were a closed system, it would be subject, like any other closed system, to increase in entropy. In fact, it is new input into language from non-verbal experience that keeps it from decaying.

To isolate literariness in the context of an utterance we need a terminology that will enable us to recognize different aspects of contextual reference. The terminology I wish to offer is based on three related binary oppositions, or three aspects of a single, ultimate opposition: absent vs. present, semiotic vs. phenomenal, and abstract vs. concrete. A neutral, unliterary context is present, phenomenal, and concrete. That is, the context is present to both sender and receiver of a given message. It is *there*, perceptually available to both of them, as free of semiotic coding as possible, and it is more like a thing than like an idea. For instance, if two people are together in a room, looking through a window, and one says, "It is raining," the context is concrete, phenomenal, and present. If, however, they open a book and read the words, "It is raining," the context is still concrete, still potentially phenomenal, and yet, because it is absent, the meaning of the phrase is totally different. The meaning can no longer be directly referred to the rain outside the window, nor to sunshine outside the window if it were sunny. It is raining not in present reality but in a space we have learned to call fictional. To enter fictional space through the medium of words, we must reverse the processes of perception, generating the images, sounds and other perceptual data that would be available through our senses if we were in the presence of the named phenomena.

If the same phrase were to occur in a letter, since the sender and receiver are not present to one another, and therefore not both in the presence of the phenomenon referred to, the phrase would again generate a fictional space, and the more the writer tried to turn the phenomenon of the rain, which only he had perceptual access to, into words, the more concretely that space would be filled and extended. Any elaborate description of the rain would perforce become more literary. (It is worth noting that a "description" that substituted analytical or "scientific" categories for the perceptual categories of human observation would be less literary because less concrete. What we mean by "concrete" is "description according to our normal modes of perception." The codes of fiction are tied to our perceptual system as well as to our language.)

If the letter-writer were to begin by describing the rain outside his window and to end his letter by saying, "When I said it was raining before, and described all that stuff, it wasn't really raining. I made all that up"—and if we were to receive that letter and read it, how would we react? And if he added a postscript in which he asserted that when he said he had "made up" the rain he was lying. . . ? And so on? The message contradicts itself, aggressively reminding us that we have no access to the context. We can never know whether the writer was looking out a real window at a real rain or not. The fictional status of the "rain" does not depend on the fact or unfact of rain but on the absence of the "real" context from the reader. Any description we read is a fiction. On the relation of such fictions to our "real" context, more later.

A context that is present and phenomenally available does not invite the literary the way an absent context does. In fact, literariness based on a present context is likely to result from some semiotic violation of that context. If one of our rain-watchers should say to the other. "Nice weather we're having," this would instantly be perceived by the other as a simple irony. In fact this transaction would be so instantaneous that the complex process involved might be lost. What happens in such a situation is this: "A" says, "Nice weather." "B" is aware that the context denies the statement—the phenomenal denies the semiotic. But knowing that "A" is aware of the actual situation, and that "A" is aware that "B" is aware of it, he knows finally that "A" is referring to a fictional context—where the weather is indeed nice—as a way of signaling his disapproval of the actual phenomenon of this particular rain. It is this complex process of comparing two contexts that allows us to say that the apparent meaning of the phrase is not the real meaning. What we might regard as the "figure" or trope, irony, is in fact a function of context and cannot be determined from the form of the message alone. Upon examination, other figures that seem to be more purely verbal, like puns and metaphors, will be seen to function by juxtaposition of contrasting contexts rather than at some purely verbal level. Irony, of course, is only the most extreme semiotic violation of present context. Any recoding of the phenomenal will contain some measure of literariness because it changes the contact (as was observed above), and the more such recoding may be recognized as a distortion, the more literary it will seem.

Having seen how fiction results from the semiotic generation of an absent context or the distortion of a present one, we should perhaps pause to consider how such fictions differ from two near relatives, the lie and the mistake. Assume that only one of our characters can actually see out the window, and for reasons of his own he decides to deceive the other person. (Note that the more concrete I make those reasons the more fictional this scene becomes.) He says it is raining when actually it is not, and he deceives the other into accepting this view. By creating two contexts he has indeed generated a fiction, but his companion, accepting his statement, is aware of a single context only. For this reason there is no fiction. Because she (note how the more specific feminine pronoun further fictionalizes the scene) accepts his translation of the phenomenal into the verbal as purely transparent and referential she perceives neither fiction nor lie in his statement. For him, of course, it is both a fiction and a lie, that is, a fiction presenting itself as fact with the intent to deceive. For us, eavesdropping on the scene, recognizing the whole thing as an artificial, illustrative context, the scene is entirely fictional, despite its function in this non-fictional discourse. Similarly, if the person who glances out the window misperceives the phenomenon outside it, reporting rain falling but not deceiving intentionally, this utterance is not a fiction to the speaker but may appear to be one to an auditor who happens to check up on the statement. The natural impulse for such an auditor would be to wonder whether the textual discrepancy should be attributed to a lie or a mistake—and such wondering would require him to fictionalize in order to reach a decision. This is so because all specification or concretization of human motives is presentation of a context that is unavailable, absent, beyond direct perception.

Up to now we have been concerned with the minimally literary. Obviously, things like a single ironic comment about the weather are not likely to be preserved in the annals of literature—but such things look toward more elaborate literary structures. The doubling of contexts is the beginning of the kind of literariness characteristic of fiction. Such doubling also opens the way to other literary effects that depend on the contrasting qualities of the contexts invoked by a particular message. We can find such multi-contextuality operating, often with surprising sophistication, at a level of discourse not very far removed from conversations about the weather. I propose to demonstrate this briefly by considering the literary elements of a few bumper stickers that were prominent in our automotive dialogue several years ago.

Take for instance a bumper sticker that says, simply, "Peace." The conventions of bumper sticking enable us to interpret this as a proposition: "The driver of this car is in favor of peace." If the driver happens to drive in a particularly hostile and violent manner, the contrast between the intended verbal message and the behavioral signs may well amuse us. We, as spectators to this scene, may put the intended context of the sticker message (some political situation of war or violence) and the unintended revelation of the behavior into a new context of our own. We may mentally fictionalize this situation, inventing a character who says one thing and does another, and so on. But it is our own performance that is literary here, not the performance of the sticker-owner or the sticker-maker.

Take another instance, in which the behavior of the car to which the sticker is attached will be ignored. Imagine a sticker that says "Peace" and bears a picture of a dove. The dove symbolizes peace here mainly by cultural reference to biblical and other texts. It strengthens the word by adding these biblical contexts to the text, perhaps reminding us of who the Prince of Peace was and so on. As we bring these cultural contexts to bear on the phenomenal context, some act of war or violence, we perform, again, a minimally literary act. Here, the realities of the political situation against which the sign must be perceived have a powerful effect on our interpretation. A "Peace" sticker had a more concrete and specific context for Americans during the Vietnam war than it does in December 1976 as these words are written.

Suppose now a bumper sticker that says, "Make Love Not War." This requires us to bring something very concrete, the physical act of love, into opposition with something also phenomenal but less concrete. To make love is to do a very specific thing. To make war is to do any number of possible things, not named specifically in this message. But the private context of love-making and the public context of armed combat come together somehow in our minds, reinforced by the form of the message, in which the same verb governs two disparate nouns. This is a figure of speech, which the rhetoricians can name for us, but the point is that the figure unites two disparate contexts. Furthermore, the whole thing makes concrete that original abstraction, "Peace," by turning it into the specific form of physical love.

I have seen a version of this sticker that adds a visual sign: two rhinoceroses copulating. This addition of another context compounds the wit, the literariness of the message. To show such obviously martial beasts performing their thunderous analogue to the love-making of human couples reminds us in a very complex way of our connection to and difference from other animals; it may remind us of the warrior Mars, in his armor, courting Venus; or it may cause us to wonder whether we humans have advanced as much over the other beasts in our capacity for love as we have in our military capability. All these reflections are an aspect of our literary competence as interpreters, to be sure, but they are encouraged by the text, which unites words and picture to point to so many relevant contexts in our semiotically coded cultural world. We might observe further here that the purely semiotic play of context makes the sticker more interesting in itself and less dependent on any particular socio-political context than a simple "Peace" sign, which needs a war as context to fulfill its semiotic function.

Take another sticker that says, "Make Love Not Babies." This is perhaps the most literary of all the stickers we have considered. It replaces some direct mono-contextual sign such as

"Zero Population Growth" or "Fight Overpopulation," and it makes these general and rather abstract notions concrete. But it also alludes in a purely semiotic way to the chronologically earlier sign, "Make Love Not War." That is, one context here is essentially semiotic—in this case verbal, while the other is essentially phenomenal, addressing the question of overpopulation. Once again, the sign-maker has taken advantage of our English-speaking propensity to "make" everything under the sun, in order to let that verb govern two different subjects. But for those readers who know the earlier "Make Love Not War" sign, he has done something special; he has prepared a trap, a surprise of the sort Stanley Fish made famous in *Surprised by Sin* and *Self-Consuming Artifacts*. The anti-war reader and the pro-birth-control reader may not be the same person. And even if a person holds both these attitudes, the shift in the last word of the second sign from "War" to "Babies" comes as a shock. Where the first sign took love and war, those natural, almost binary, opposites and juxtaposed them, this sign brings together eroticism and conception, which are, after all, intimately connected. The overpopulation problem, phenomenal to be sure, but generalized and almost abstract, is brought home to our very beds. And the statement invokes yet another context, the theological, which in our tradition has habitually insisted that procreation is the only justification for the act of love.

It is perhaps fair to question whether I have been too competent an interpreter here, gone to too many contexts in reading this particular message. There are two answers to this. One is that the message itself certainly started me going, and the things I brought back as interpretants certainly enrich the literariness of the message in an appropriate way. The problem may simply be whether one wishes to credit the sign-maker, the message, or the reader with the literariness that emerged from the whole communication act. Frankly, I doubt if it is either possible or desirable to settle these matters entirely, either with respect to bumper stickers or more ambitious acts of communication. That is one answer. The other is that the point of the illustration is simply to show how multiplication of contexts is an important feature of literary communication, wherever the act of multiplication originates. Finally, it should be observed that even this sign, which makes so much of semiotic multiplication of contexts, would lose something vital if the phenomenon of overpopulation did not exist as a reality or a real threat in the social context of this utterance.

Up to now, we have been considering the dynamics of literariness in minimal situations, just one level removed from ordinary discourse—acts of communication not usually regarded as literature. At this point it will be necessary to shift to the other end of the verbal spectrum—to codify briefly the major elements of literariness and to correlate them, if possible, with what are traditionally recognized as the major forms of literature. The following table should help tidy things up:

1. Duplicity of sender—role-playing, acting
2. Duplicity of receiver—eavesdropping, voyeurism
3. Duplicity of message—opacity, ambiguity
4. Duplicity of context—allusion, fiction
5. Duplicity of contact—translation, fiction
6. Duplicity of code—involved in all the above

The forms of discourse that we regularly recognize as literature—play, poem and story—are dominated by the four conventions listed here. The theater is an arena specifically structured to facilitate role-playing by actors and eavesdropping/voyeurism by spectators. The poem is dominated by sound effects and verbal strategies that stimulate our awareness of the message as a specific, unique thing. And the story is a description of situations and a narration of actions which are not present to us but are totally created by the discourse, requiring us to visualize and respond emotionally to events we cannot enter as persons, though we may well connect them to our personal experiences.

The last statement can stand some elaboration, since it touches again on the key question of how semiotic systems may or may not be connected to the phenomenal or experiential world. The argument being presented here is that one context, made out of perceptual and experiential data held in common by author and audience, is always invoked by any fictional or mimetic context, whether "realistic" or "fantastic." This "real" context provides a background against which we perceive and measure any pseudo-experiential or fictional context presented to us. At this point we must consider the view that the "real" context is also a fiction, since it is based on past experience, no longer directly available. This view is partly true. Our memories of experience must be differentiated from the experience itself. But so must our memories of actual experience be differentiated from any ideas we may acquire about things we have never experienced through our own perceptions. As memory grows fainter the events remembered lose their reality. But it is not until we try to reconstruct these fading events that fiction is generated. The passage of real experience into the past is not itself fictional, but all attempts to reconstruct are precisely that: fictions. Fiction is not what is lost but what is constructed. Our memories are of events to which we once had access as persons, with power to influence them by our presence at the time when they occured. But in the pseudo-experiential context of constructed events we are not present as persons—ever.

Many fictions insist that their context is not fictional at all, that they speak directly to us of the things around us. Others insist that their context is of imagination all compact, that in their fictional worlds is no contamination from our own. Both, of course, are wrong. Our world, our life, the knowledge we have of what our senses have allowed us to perceive, is with us always, and we know analogues in our own experience for the fairest damsels, the cruelest ogres, and the bravest heroes of all fairyland. Much of literary competence is based upon our ability to connect the worlds of fiction and experience. And much of our literature quite rightly insists upon that very connection.

When a writer allows his book to be called *Winesburg, Ohio,* for instance, his title names both a fictional town and a real state, telling us that this is fiction, yes, but that it has a real context as well. When a writer calls his book *Dubliners,* and situates the fictional names of his characters among the real names of his city, he is asking us to use the fiction not as some pure artifact but as information about the way real people behave in a real place. And we must *not* see this as a regrettable impurity in otherwise beautiful art; we must see it as a strong assertion of the cognitive function of literature, which is an essential part of it. The real context is always present; the fictional one does not efface it but brings some aspects of it into a particular focus for our scrutiny. All fairy tales tell us something about reality.

Both plays and stories generate fictional contexts, as I have been suggesting, but a performance or enactment (whether of a play proper or of a story dramatized for the occasion) alters the way in which a fictional context is generated. (So too, of course, does cinema, but the coding of fictional films would require separate treatment.) Dramatization by actors of fictional situations reduces the need for fictionalizing by a single interpreter or reader, since it transfers some of the interpretive burden to director and actors, while it allows each spectator to submerge his or her individual interpretive identity in the collective reaction of an audience. The burden of literariness in live theater is divided among a number of aspects of communication, but it is dominated by the situation of enactment itself.

Poems, too, can be enacted, and they certainly generate fictional contexts, but the dominant feature of poetical composition is surely to be found at the level of the message itself, where verification, figuration, and other linguistic strategies make themselves felt. And just as poems are frequently fictional, plays and stories regularly use the linguistic resources of poetry. And all three of these forms regularly enrich their contextual reference by pointing toward other communicative acts, by quoting, alluding, parodying, and otherwise generating a context that is entirely semiotic and intertextual. Major literary works are all comments on their own form, on the generic tradition or traditions from which they take their being. The study of literature, then, must involve the study of communicative process in general—or semiotics—and in particular the development of the codes that govern the production and interpretation of the major kinds of literature, and the sub-codes that inform the various genres that have developed in the course of literary history. After all, each "form" is only a codification of certain communicative procedures that have proved effective through time. Conversely, forms less obviously literary often turn to the codes of literature for their own purposes. Essays, for instance, are not necessarily literary but become so to the extent that they adopt the dominant qualities of any of the three major forms of literature. The more an essay alludes or fictionalizes, the more the author adopts a role or suggests one for the reader, the more the language becomes sonorous or figured, the more literary the essay (or the letter, the prayer, the speech, etc.) becomes.

Finally, I wish to make clear that literariness in itself ought not to be confused with value. All plays are literary but not all are equally valuable. And our reasons for valuing a play may have as much to do with its non-literary function as with its literary form. To the extent that a work of literature points toward our experience as living human beings, we may value it for what we call its "truth" or "rightness"—which is not a specifically formal quality but a matter of the fit between a message and its existential context. This opens up an area for discussion too large to be considered here. Suffice it to note that literary coding of discourse is a formal strategy, a means of structuring that enables the maker of the discourse to communicate certain kinds of meaning. We may, of course, value some literary utterances mainly for their formal elegance, but we also may value literary utterances for the insight they provide about aspects of existence, and it would be foolish to pretend this is not so simply because such insight does not lend itself to formal codification.

This means, of course, that the student and teacher of literary texts will have to be something of a historian and something of a philosopher if he or she wishes to approach full understanding of the texts—and even something of a person. Many literary works assume experience of life as an aspect of their context shared by writer and reader. Some works refuse to open to us until we are sufficiently mature. Others close as we lose access to some contexts through growing or forgetting. No study of literature can be purely formal, and all attempts to reduce literary study to this level are misguided if not pernicious. To the extent that semiotic studies insist that communication is a matter of purely formal systems, they too may be misguided if not pernicious. Many semioticians would argue that the meaning of any sign or word is purely a function of its place in a paradigmatic system and its use in a syntagmatic situation. But I wish to suggest that meaning is also a function of human experience. For those who have experienced such things as marriage or bereavement the words themselves will signify something different than they will for those who have had no experience of these things—and much of literature is based on attempts to generate semiotic equivalents for experiences that seem to defy duplication in mere signs.

Having uttered this necessary corrective to extreme versions of formalist and structuralist theory, I must conclude by re-affirming my own position as a student of literary semiotics. My whole argument here has been an attempt to show how the formal qualities of literature are the result of a process that multiplies or complicates the normal features of human communication. This activity must be based upon the pleasure inherent in the semiotic processes themselves—in their ability to generate and communicate meaning—which is an indispensable aspect of human existence. The skills involved in making and interpreting the most complex literary structures presently being produced in our culture are of a high order, and they require training beyond mere linguistic competence for their development. The value of such training to our whole culture lies in the ways that people trained in the semiotic subtleties of literary study may themselves use our communicative media to generate the ideas we need to keep that culture alive and functioning in a time which is certain to bring us to the point of crisis.

# Index

Aagaard-Mogensen, Lars, 176n4
Abrams, Meyer H., 76n3, 77n11, 139n7, 139n12, 142
Altieri, Charles, xv
Amin, Idi, 229n2
Anscombe, Gertrude Elizabeth Margaret, 77n8, 157n2
Apollinaire, Guillaume, 59
Argyle, Duke of, 23n17
Aristotle, 7, 27, 30, 40, 41, 42, 43, 44, 46, 127, 128, 183, 187, 192, 213
Arnold, Matthew, 25, 53
Artaud, Antonin, 58, 59
Auerbach, Erich, 85, 88n6, 88n9, 127, 128, 129
Augustine, Saint, 85, 137
Austen, Jane, 25
Austin, John Langshaw, xv, xxiin3, 100n1, 111, 143, 168, 169, 177n12, 208, 229n2

Bachelard, Gaston, 122, 125n22
Balzac, Honoré de, 223
Baran, Paul A., 100n17
Baretti, Giuseppe, 18
Bar-Hillel, Yehoshua, 192-93, 202n5, 202n6
Barthes, Roland, 17, 21, 22n2, 52, 116, 125n3, 207, 211, 214, 216, 237, 238
Bateson, Frederick W., 109, 117, 119, 125n14

Baudelaire, Charles, 134
Baumgarten, Alexander Gottlieb, 21
Beardsley, Monroe C., xv, 77n7, 158n6, 177n17
Beauvais, Vincent of, 131
Beck, Lewis White, 200n1, 202n5
du Bellay, Joachim, 17
Bellow, Saul, 91, 96, 100n5
Berkeley, George, 21
Berkenhout, John, 19
Beserman, Simone, 91, 94, 100n4, 100n8, 100n9
Bierwisch, Manfred, 147
Black, Max, 77n9, 158n9
Blair, Hugh, 18
Blanchot, Maurice, 17, 22n2
Bloomfield, Morton W., 76n3, 158n5
Bohr, Niels, 32
Boltzmann, Ludwig, 119
Borges, Jorge Luis, 43, 87
Bossuat, Robert, 139n13
Boswell, James, 18, 22n11, 25
Brady, Frank, 76n4, 177n9
Bragdon, Claude, 154
Brion, Friederike, 204n11
Brooks, Cleanth, xxiiin8, 109, 147
Brown, Robert L., Jr., xv, 158n12, 159n23, 159n25, 160n32, 177n11, 204n11
Browne, Sir Thomas, 224

Browning, Elizabeth Barrett, 147, 153
Browning, Robert, 151
Bruner, Jerome S., 229n1
Bruss, Elizabeth, 159n29
Buffon, Georges Louis Leclerc, 223, 224
Burckhardt, Sigurd, 184
Burger, Warren, 25
Burke, Edmund, 21, 25, 199
Burke, Kenneth, 77n11
Burroughs, Edgar Rice, 220
Burton, Robert, 132
Butler, Christopher, 176

Caesar, Gaius Julius, 17
Capote, Truman, 73, 132
Cardozo, Benjamin Nathan, 25
Carlyle, Jane, 25
Carlyle, Thomas, 223
Cavell, Stanley, 77n9
Cervantes Saavedra, Miguel de, 87
Chambers, Robert, 19
Champollion, Jean François, 80
Chandler, Raymond, 45
Chatman, Seymour, 217n5
Chaucer, Geoffrey, 131, 133
Chomsky, Noam, 157n1, 211
Cicero, Marcus Tullius, 17, 22n3, 83, 131, 139n9
Clarke, John Henrik, 100n2
Cohen, Marcel Samuel Raphaël, 87n1
Colbert, Jean Baptiste, 17
Cole, Peter, 159n27, 159n28
Coleridge, Samuel Taylor, 27, 30, 31, 109, 142, 187
Colie, Rosalie, 185

Collingwood, Robin George, 8, 15n3
Colman, George, 19
Cooper, Lane, 18, 138n1
Crispin, Claude, 18
Croce, Benedetto, 119
Crowley, Ruth Ann, 60n1
Culler, Jonathan, 76n2, 77n7, 158n6, 158n15, 159n19, 234

Dante Alighieri, 21, 44, 128, 131
Darwin, Charles, 25, 31, 32
Davenport, Edward, xiv
Davidson, Donald, 112n2
Defoe, Daniel, 21, 100n6
Denina, Carlo, 20, 23n17
DeQuincey, Thomas, 31
Derrida, Jacques, 78n11, 195, 200, 201n3
Descartes, René, 192, 197, 200
Dickens, Charles, 36
Dickie, James, 76n2
Dijk, Tuen A. van, 158n15, 201n4
Doctorow, E. L., 96
Donagan, Alan, 158n6
Donato, Eugenio, 201n3
Donne, John, 43
Dowden, Edward, 33
Dryden, John, 17

Eaton, Marcia, 169
Eco, Umberto, 194, 203n8, 237, 238
Edwards, Jonathan, 22n10
Elder, Marjorie, 140n18
Eliot, Thomas Stearns, 37, 43, 72, 198
Ellis, John M., 32, 162, 163, 164, 203n11
Ellman, Richard, 139n4

Enders, Horst, 125n7
Ennis, Philip, 91
Epstein, Barbara, 97
Epstein, Jason, 97, 100n5
Erasmus, Desiderius, 17
Euclid, 119, 190

Ferber, Edna, 220
Ferguson, Adam, 19
Ferguson, Charles, 84, 88n7
Fish, Stanley E., 100n1, 163, 169,
   204n11, 207, 209, 217n8, 244
Fleming, Walther, 14
Foucault, Michel, 203n7, 238
Le Franc de Pompignan, Jean-
   Georges, 20
Freeman, Donald C., 159n17,
   159n18
Freud, Sigmund, xxiiin7, 172,
   177n16
Friedrich, Hugo, 117, 125n7
Froissart, Jean, 137
Frost, Robert, 134, 173
Frye, Northrop, xx, xxiiin13, 35,
   41, 46n1, 46n3, 121, 125n19,
   188n1, 271n6

Galbraith, John Kenneth, 100n17
Garbo, Greta, 207, 211
Gelb, I. J., 87n1
Gellius, Aulus, 17
Genovese, Eugene, 25
Gibbon, Edward, 21
Gilbert, Allan H., 76n6
Ginsberg, Allen, 63, 64, 66
Giorgi-Bertòlá, Aurelio de, 20
Goethe, Johann Wolfgang von,
   21, 123, 204n11
Golden, Leon, xxiiin10
Goldin, Frederick, 140n17

Goldman, Alvin, 169
Gombrich, Ernest Hans Josef, 182,
   189n3
Goodman, Nelson, 15n4, 15n7
Goody, Jack, 87n2
Gower, John, 131
Grabes, Herbert, 128, 139n11,
   140n21
Grabowicz, George, 61n7
Gramsci, Antonio, 99
Granet, François, 19
Green, Allan, 100n8
Greenlaw, Edwin, 16
Greimas, Algirdas Julien, 201n4
Grice, H. Paul, 153, 158n12,
   159n27, 160n31
Guest, Edgar, 146

Habermas, Jürgen, xxiiin7
Hajda, Jan, 100n3
Hamburger, Käte, 118, 122,
   125n10, 126n24
Hancher, Michael, 177n14
Hardison, O. B., xxiiin10
Harman, Gilbert, 112n2
Harris, Stuart, 100n8
Hart, Thomas R., 88n10
Hartmann, Nicolai, 121, 125n18
Havelock, Eric A., 82, 88n3
Hawthorne, Nathaniel, 135
Hegel, Georg Wilhelm Friedrich,
   74, 77n11, 192, 197, 230n5
Heisenberg, Werner, 25
Herbert, George, 66, 147
Herder, Johann Gottfried, 19
Hirsch, Eric Donald, Jr., xiv, 53,
   61n5, 61n10, 65, 66, 67, 68, 69,
   76n4
Hölderlin, Friedrich, 119
Holland, Norman, xvi

Homer, 21, 33, 43, 44, 72, 82, 85, 127

Hook, Sidney, 202n5

Hooker, Richard, 224

Hoover, Julie, 96, 100n11, 100n12, 100n13, 100n14

Hopkins, Gerard Manley, 162, 173

Horace (Horatius Flaccus), xix, xxiiin11, xxiiin12, 83

Householder, Fred W., 84

Howe, Irving, 96

Hume, David, 25

Hurd, Richard, 139n12

Husserl, Edmund, 51

Ingarden, Roman, xv, xxiin2, 15n5, 49, 50, 54, 57, 59, 60n1, 61n7, 61n11, 120, 121, 123, 125n17, 125n20, 126n29

Ívanov, Vjačeslav, 122, 125n21

Jacobs, Roderick, 218n13

Jakobson, Roman, xvi, xxiin4, 233, 234, 235, 237

James, Henry, 36, 200, 233

Jarvie, Ian C., 44, 45

Jaucourt, Louis, chevalier de, 18

Jensen, Hans, 87n1

Jerome, Saint, 85

Johnson, Samuel, 19, 30, 130

Joyce, James, 36, 127, 131, 232

Jung, Carl Gustav, 224

Kadushin, Charles, 96, 97

Kant, Immanuel, xxiin6, xxiiin14, 21, 28, 74, 116, 190, 192, 200n1, 202n5, 234

Katičič, Radoslav, 117, 125n9

Katz, Jerrold J., 112n2

Kavanagh, James Francis, 88n8

Kayser, Wolfgang, 116, 120, 124, 124n1, 126n31

Kazin, Alfred, 96

Keats, John, 25, 151, 155, 174

Kellogg, Robert, 88n4

Kernan, Alvin B., 53, 61n5, 61n6, 166, 176n1

Kierkegaard, Søren, 31

Koestler, Arthur, xxiiin12

Kostelanetz, Richard, 94, 98, 100n8, 100n10, 100n15, 100n16

Krieger, Murray, xvi, 237

Labov, William, 153

Langlois, Ernest, 140n20

Lathem, Edward C., 140n15

Lawrence, David Herbert, 36

Leavis, Frank Raymond, 208

Leech, Geoffrey, 201n4

Lessing, Gotthold Ephraim, 19

Levin, Martin, 96

Levine, George, 218n10

Lewis, David, 112n2

Lichtenstein, Heinz, 212, 218n11

Loewenberg, Ina, 176n8

Lord, Albert, 88n3

Lotman, Jurij, 177n19

Louis XIV, 17

Lucretius, 33

Lyas, Colin A., xxiin1

McCanles, Michael, xvi

Macaulay, Thomas Babington, 25

McElroy, Elizabeth Warner, 100n3

McFadden, George, xv, xxiin2

McFarland, Thomas, 66, 76n5

McGuinness, Bernard Francis, 201n1

MacKay, Alfred F., 112n4

Mackenzie, Lady Elizabeth, 23n17

McKeon, Richard, 139n12

Macksey, Richard, 88n10, 201n3
Macmillan, Harold, 25
Madden, William, 218n10
Maier, Rudolf N., 124, 126n24, 126n28, 126n33
Malamud, Bernard, 96
Mandelbaum, Maurice, 64, 76n3, 77n11
Margolis, Joseph, 112n1
Maritain, Jacques, 126n34
Marvell, Andrew, 189n5
Marx, Karl, xxiiin7, 197, 221
Matthews, Robert, xv
Mattingly, Ignatius G., 88n8
Mead, George Herbert, 230n5
Menestrier, Claude François, 18
Merrill, Daniel D., 112n4
Michaud, Guy, 135, 140n16
Michener, James A., 95
Mill, John Stuart, 34, 146, 147, 236
Milton, John, 19, 30, 45, 66, 76n6
Montaigne, Michel, 17, 21, 54
Moorman, Mary, 25
Morgan, Jerry, 159n27, 159n28
Morris, Charles W., 230n5
Mukařovský, Jan, xxi, xxiiin15, 147
Müller, Günther, 120, 125n16
Murasaki, Shikibu, 39, 40, 41, 42, 46, 46n2
Muschg, Walter, 124, 126n34

Navasky, Victor, 92, 100n7
Nichols, Stephen G., Jr., 139n8
Nietzsche, Friedrich, xxiiin7, 31, 224
Nin, Anaïs, 154

O'Brien, Gordon W., 139n13

Ohmann, Richard, xv, 67, 68, 69, 74, 76n7, 77n7, 99n1, 159n21, 169, 208, 217n5
Olson, Charles, 71
Olson, Kenneth R., 60n1
Oppel, Horst, 122, 126n26

Palmer, John, 76n4, 177n9
Palmer, Leonard Robert, 88n5, 88n6
Parry, Milman, 88n3
Pascal, Blaise, 21
Patchen, Kenneth, 59
Pater, Walter, 31
Paul, Saint, 85, 134
Paulhan, Jean, 117, 125n5
Pears, David Francis, 201n1
Peckham, Morse, xvi, 207, 209, 217n3, 217n9
Peirce, Charles Sanders, 194, 230n5
Pepys, Samuel, 206, 207, 214, 216
Perkins, Moreland, 202n5, 202n6
Perrault, Charles, 17, 20, 23n7
Petherham, John, 18
Petronius, 83
Pindar, 119
Plato, 21, 30, 82, 86, 139n12, 139n13, 199
Pliny, 33
Plotinus, 139n13
Pollmann, Leo, 119, 125n13
Pope, Alexander, 132, 197, 228
Pound, Ezra, 59
Pratt, Mary, 100n1
Price, Martin, 76n4, 177n9

Quine, Willard Van Orman, 202n5
Quintilian, 16

Rabelais, François, 17

Rand, Ayn, 199, 200
Ranke, Leopold von, 119
Reichert, John, 173
Richards, Ivor Armstrong, xxiiin12, 105, 167, 234, 237
Richardson, Samuel, 100n6
Riffaterre, Michael, 117, 125n8
Rimbaud, Arthur, 58
Rivers, Elias, xv
Robbe-Grillet, Alain, 71, 72
Robbins, Harold, 95
Roberts, Thomas J., 60n2, 217n1
Rosenbaum, Peter S., 218n13
Roth, Philip, 96
Rothstein, Eric, 203n10
Rousseau, Jean Jacques, 182
Russell, Bertrand, 229n1
Rymer, Thomas, 18

Sabatier de Castres, Abbé, 19
Sartre, Jean Paul, 74
Saussure, Ferdinand de, 117, 211, 237, 238
Schafer, Roy, 208
Scholes, Robert, xvi, 88n4
Schopenhauer, Arthur, 224
Searle, John R., xv, xxiin3, 99n1, 143, 148, 158n10, 158n11, 158n13,158n14, 159n21, 159n22, 159n28, 160n33, 167, 177n12, 204n11, 229n3
Sebeok, Thomas A., 234
Segal, Erich, 94
Selden, John, 18
Sengle, Friedrich, 120, 125n15
Shakespeare, William, 19, 21, 25, 54, 72, 153, 157, 174, 209
Sharifi, Hassan, 158n6
Shaw, George Bernard, 199
Shelley, Percy Bysshe, 30, 31, 32, 198

Sidney, Sir Philip, 66, 76n6, 198
Singer, Irving, 202n5
Smith, A. M. Sheridan, 203n7
Smith, Barbara Herrnstein, 169, 173, 174, 175
Smith, Harry, 100n10
Smith, Ralph, 77n7
Solzhenitsyn, Alexander, 132, 134
Sontag, Susan, 210
Sparshott, Francis E., xiv, xvii, 76n2, 231
Spenser, Edmund, 71
Spillane, Mickey, 146
Spinoza, Baruch, 190, 192
Staiger, Emil, 124, 126n32
Stalnaker, Robert C., 112n4
Starobinski, Jean, 124, 126n30
Steinmann, Martin, Jr., xv, 158n6, 158n12, 169, 204n11
Stendhal (Marie Henri Beyle), 133, 139n12
Sterne, Laurence, 44, 236
Stevenson, Charles L., xxiin1, 142
Strelka, Joseph, xv, 126n24, 126n33, 126n34
Stroup, Thomas B., 177n16
Styron, William, 90
Susann, Jacqueline, 95
Sweezy, Paul M., 100n17
Swift, Jonathan, 236

Tacitus, 31, 33
Tennyson, Alfred, Lord, 174
Tertullian, 17
Thorpe, James, 217n6
Thucydides, 82
Tichy, Monique, 100n12, 100n13, 100n14
Tilghman, Benjamin R., 76n2, 77n9
Tiraboschi, Girolamo, 19

Tober, Karl, 123, 126n28
Todorov, Tzvetan, 172
Trask, Willard R., 139n2

Updike, John, 96
Urban, Wilbur Marshall, 122, 126n25
Uris, Leon, 95

Vergil, 33, 44, 72, 83
Verlaine, Paul, 58, 59
Voltaire François-Marie Arouet), 19

Waith, Eugene, 139n9
Waley, Arthur, 46n2
Wallace, Irving, 95
Wallerstein, Immanuel, 221
Walpole, Horace, 137
Walters, Barbara, 94
Warren, Austin, 124n2, 137, 140n22
Wehrli, Max, 117, 119, 125n4, 125n12
Weidlé, Wladimir, 118, 119, 122, 125n11, 126n27

Weitz, Morris, xxiin5, 62, 63, 65, 76n1, 76n3, 142, 157n3
Wellek, René, xiv, 54, 116, 124n2, 125n21, 137, 139n8, 140n22, 161
Wheelwright, Philip, 122, 125n23
White, Hayden, 21, 78n11
White, Morton G., 202n5
Wilcox, Ella Wheeler, 220
Williams, Raymond, 55, 60n3, 61n9
Williams, William Carlos, 59, 148, 149, 155, 159n20
Wimsatt, James I., xv, xxiiin8
Wimsatt, William K. 31, 61n5, 129, 139n8
Winkler, Emil, 126n28
Wittgenstein, Ludwig, xii, xxiin1, 26, 69, 73, 77n9, 142, 191
Wolff, Robert Paul, 201n1
Wölfflin, Heinrich, 119
Wolterstorff, Nicholas, 112n5
Wordsworth, Dorothy, 109
Wordsworth, William, xxiin6, 30, 40, 109, 173, 198
Wouk, Herman, 95
Wyatt, Sir Thomas, 178, 189